ESSENTIALS OF

# INFORMATION PROCESSING

# E S S E N T I A L S   O F
# INFORMATION PROCESSING

THIRD EDITION

## NANCY A. FLOYD

Homewood, IL 60430
Boston, MA 02116

Cover illustration: Tracy Rea

Sponsoring editor: Lawrence E. Alexander
Project editor: Ethel Shiell
Production manager: Irene H. Sotiroff
Designer: Robyn B. Loughran
Artist: Progressive Typographers Inc.
Compositor: Arcata Graphics, Kingsport
Typeface: 10/12 Cheltenham Book
Printer: R. R. Donnelley & Sons Company

**Library of Congress Cataloging-in-Publication Data**

Floyd, Nancy A. (Nancy Arthur)
    Essentials of information processing / Nancy A. Floyd.—3rd ed.
      p.    cm.
    Includes index.
    ISBN 0-256-09131-5
    1. Electronic data processing.   I. Title.
    QA76.F57  1991
    004—dc20                            90–43942

*To John William*

# Preface

## The Intended Audience for This Book

The growth and development of computers has affected almost every aspect of our lives. Consequently, the student taking an introductory information processing course today may be majoring in computer studies, may be in a related field such as business, or may use computers only in support of his or her area of expertise. This diverse group of students—enrolled in two- or four-year colleges, computer information systems (CIS) majors or nonmajors—has one important, unifying goal: the need to learn both how to use a computer and the fundamental computer concepts. By providing in-depth coverage of essential concepts, *Essentials of Information Processing* is intended to support a practical first course in computer information processing for nonmajors, as well as for majors who are enrolled in an introductory course combining the teaching of factual information about computers with the opportunity for hands-on computer use. This would include introductory information processing courses alone, with a programming language such as BASIC, or with microcomputer applications: word processing, spreadsheets, and/or database.

## Why This Book Was Written

Students today are interested in gaining the practical information they need to deal with computers in the workplace. They need to learn key concepts and important terminologies without being burdened with unnecessary detail. They need to learn to *use* computers but they also need to learn *about* computers. This book was written because the available textbooks did not satisfy students' needs. Specifically:

1. The big, four-color introductory texts are too big for many courses. They contain too much material to cover in the time available. Because of this,

many professors must attempt to make the big books "fit" their courses by eliminating chapters, thereby also eliminating coverage of valuable concepts. Other professors attempt to solve this problem by assigning selected readings from within each chapter, thereby creating gaps that can cause problems in student comprehension.

**2.** Even more elaborate "surgery" is necessary if the professor wants to include coverage of a computer language such as BASIC or of microcomputer applications.

**3.** Material may be deleted but the price remains the same. Professors pay a price in time spent tailoring the text to meet their course requirements; students pay the price of an expensive four-color book of which they use only a portion.

**4.** The smaller introductory information processing books also may miss the mark in satisfying course needs. Some texts have shallow coverage of too few concepts. These texts, in attempting to be shorter, end up with a coverage that lacks depth and fails to include important topics.

**5.** Many texts do not have a practical orientation. Some texts contain material that is too technical for nonmajors—for example, focusing primarily on programming. Others focus on the societal implications of the computer without covering enough technical material. Still other texts look only at microcomputers. For many reasons, these texts fail to address what the average person needs to know about dealing with computers in his or her career and family activities.

## Why You Should Consider This Book

I really believe *Essentials of Information Processing* will better suit your course needs than any other book because:

**1.** This book is designed so that all the material can be covered in one term, with or without a lab. This permits maximum flexibility for those professors who want to cover BASIC programming or microcomputer applications as well as essential information processing concepts. The decision to include topics was based on whether that information was essential to both majors and nonmajors.

**2.** This book is responsive to trends in the way information processing is being taught today. For example, more courses are including segments on microcomputer applications. The professor using this book is given the flexibility to accompany the text with any software of his or her choice rather than building specific software into the text. In response to requests, this third edition has rearranged the sequence of topics to that preferred by a majority of users. Additional material on cache memory, OS/2 and Macintosh OS, CD-ROM, CAD/CAM, desktop publishing, graphics, and computer viruses is included. In addition, since many of the test bank questions appeared with both the first and second edition, the entire text bank has been rewritten.

**3.**   This book offers a practical, microcomputer-oriented approach to information processing concepts. Content is presented so that students can identify with it and immediately use it in their own lives. Students are taught what they need to know to interact with computers and the persons who program those computers. Also, this book covers practical information about the type of computer that students are most likely to encounter—the microcomputer. This microcomputer orientation throughout the text is bolstered by two chapters that are microcomputer specific. Chapter 6, "Microcomputer Applications," is now illustrated using Microsoft® Works rather than Symphony®. In addition, other chapters contain sections on how to store and handle diskettes, how to select and purchase software, how to read computer advertisements, and a checklist for purchasing hardware.

**4.**   This book is up to date. Topics include robotics, decision support systems, fifth-generation computers, expert systems, and artificial intelligence.

**5.**   This book was written for students. It presents essential concepts in a concise, clear, easy-to-understand manner so that students will be interested and encouraged rather than intimidated. Discussions are not overly technical. Concepts are explained through the use of objects and events with which students can relate. For example, in the explanation of how matrix construction creates letters, the matrix pins of a printer are compared to the individual bulbs that light up to show the score on a basketball scoreboard (Chapter 3). The functional use of a second color also enhances student interest. Carefully developed in-text learning aids ensure student comprehension. These include:

**Chapter Objectives.**   After studying the chapter, students can use the list of objectives to test their understanding of the chapter contents.

**Overview.**   Following the Chapter Objectives is a brief introduction that previews chapter content.

**On-the-Job boxes.**   Each chapter contains this feature, which highlights how computers are used in the business world and reinforces chapter concepts.

**Summary.**   All chapters end with a brief section summarizing the topics covered. Students can use this feature for review and study purposes.

**Definitions.**   Terms are boldfaced and defined on first mention within chapters. All boldfaced terms appear in the end-of-text glossary.

**Exercises.**   Each chapter ends with discussion questions that test student comprehension of chapter contents.

**Projects.**   Following the Exercises are Projects to expand students' learning experience beyond the text.

**6.**   The Study Guide is now included at the rear of the text. Pages are perforated so that professors wishing to see assignments may have them removed from the text. In addition, the Study Guide contains case studies for all chapters except the first.

### How to Use This Book

*Essentials of Information Processing,* third edition, is designed so that all material may be completed in one term. Specific suggestions on how to use the book in the various course configurations can be found in the Instructor's Manual. The conciseness of the text offers the professor the flexibility to decide to:

### Use the Text by Itself

This book is self-contained; it covers all essential computer concepts. For the class taught without a lab, the Projects at the end of each chapter offer students some exposure to computer use. If there is a programming lab, and a brief introduction to BASIC is desired, the BASIC appendix can be used. If the section is made up of majors who need to understand data representation, Appendix B, which covers binary, octal, and hexadecimal numbering systems as well as EBCDIC and ASCII, may be added. The Study Guide is available to all students; they don't need to purchase a separate text.

### Use This Text with a Language Supplement

Irwin's Cohen, Alger, and Boyd, *Business BASIC for the IBM PC with Cases,* might be suitable for a machine-specific business approach. Other language supplements may also be used.

### Use This Book with a Microcomputer Supplement

This text may be used with several of Irwin's texts. Dravillas, Stilwell, and Williams, *Power Pack for the IBM PC,* offers generic explanation of packages and comes with software. Spence and Windsor, *Using Microcomputers: Applications for Business,* offers generic concepts and hands-on coverage of 15 popular business packages and hands-on software. Spence and Windsor, *Microcomputers in Business: WordStar, dBase II and III, and Lotus 1-2-3,* or Chao C. Chien, *Introduction to the Microcomputer and Its Applications: PC–DOS, WordStar, Lotus 1-2-3, and dBase,* would also be appropriate choices.

### Supplements

Because of the large number of adjunct faculty, part-time faculty, and teaching assistants who often teach an introductory course, a solid package of instructional supplements has been created. These include:

1. Instructor's Manual. This supplement, written by Nancy A. Floyd, contains:

   Answers to all exercises in the book.
   Chapter outlines to use as lecture guides.
   Transparency masters of key figures in the text, modifications of text figures, and totally new illustrations.

2. Additional lab exercises and lecture material to supplement the text.

3. Accompaniment notes that address how to use this book (1) with a BASIC text, (2) with a microcomputer text, and (3) with both a BASIC and a micro-computer text.

4. Teaching tips for the instructor.

5. Annotated journal references.

6. Topics for discussion relevant to chapter contents.

7. Test bank questions. The printed version of the test items includes approximately 1,300 items using the following formats:

   Multiple choice.
   Fill-in-the-blank.
   Matching.
   Short answer.
   True/false.

8. A computerized testing package is available from the publisher to all adopters.

## ACKNOWLEDGMENTS

I am indebted to the many people who contributed to the development of the third edition of this book: to my husband and family who supported my decision to write it and to the following reviewers whose feedback and suggestions were invaluable.

### Reviewers

Lana Barrett
*University of Kentucky and Owensboro Community College*
*Owensboro, KY*

Renee A. Fecteau
*San Jose City College*
*San Jose, CA*

Douglas Lee Hall
*St. Mary's University*
*San Antonio, TX*

Gerald R. Magliano
*Johnson County Community College*
*Overland Park, KS*

Steve Mosena
*Indian Hills Community College*
*Ottumwa, IA*

Raymond Rogers
*Mount Wachusett Community College*
*Gardner, MA*

Thanks are due my fellow faculty and staff members at Eastern Mennonite College, especially Lois Layman, Ron Stoltzfus, Spencer Cowles, and Randy Reichenbach. Thanks are also due my students who have offered many suggestions; their interest in and enthusiasm for information processing makes my teaching and continued learning joyous.

Special thanks are due the staff of Richard D. Irwin: Sponsoring Editor Larry Alexander, and Editorial Coordinator Lena Buonanno. Their guidance and support made it all possible.

I assume full responsibility for any errors or inaccuracies. Any comments, criticisms, suggestions, or improvements are welcome. Write to me in care of Richard D. Irwin, Inc., 1818 Ridge Road, Homewood, Illinois 60430.

**Nancy A. Floyd**

# Contents in Brief

# Contents

Please note that at the beginning of each chapter there are two sections: Chapter Objectives and Overview. Following the main body of each chapter there are four sections: Summary, Vocabulary, Exercises, and Projects.

# ESSENTIALS OF
# INFORMATION PROCESSING

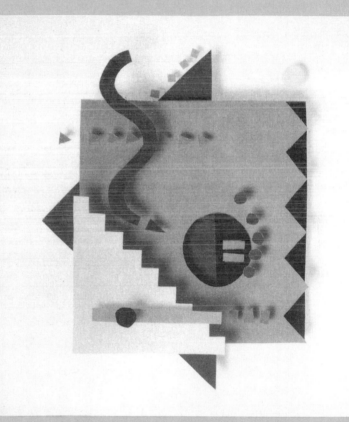

# Introduction

**CHAPTER OBJECTIVES**

*After completing this chapter, you will be able to:*

1. Define the term *computer*.
2. Recount the evolution of computers.
3. Discuss how computers affect our lives.

## OVERVIEW

Few people in the United States today are not in some way influenced by the computer. Do you run? Nike uses the computer as an aid in designing their running shoes. Do you surf? Microcomputers are used in competitions to increase scoring accuracy. Perhaps you are only an armchair athlete. Computers are used to provide the instant statistics available in most games. In business, computers keep and analyze records. They build models of future business activity and then use them to forecast the results of alternative business decisions. They locate tumors, handle airline reservations, approve credit purchases, design machinery, and authenticate the authorship of documents. Even as you were driving to class today, computers may have controlled the stoplights along the way.

Computers intimidate some of us. We even have a name for this fear: **cyberphobia.** Many sufferers have physical symptoms such as a rise in blood pressure and profuse sweating. These people forget that, although computers are used for highly sophisticated scientific research, elementary school children, who have no detailed knowledge of how a computer is built or how its circuitry works, also use them. The history and development of computers fascinate us (see On the Job).

Computers are everywhere. You cannot avoid them and have no reason to fear them. This book introduces you to computers—to how they work and what they can and cannot do for you.

## WHAT IS A COMPUTER?

Although the term **computer** properly refers only to the central processing unit—the part of the machine that actually performs calculations and comparisons—we use the term to refer to the entire machine. The computer is capable of interpreting commands, executing programmed instructions, receiving input, performing logical and computational operations, and producing output. These activities require the involvement of the entire **computer system.**

A computer system consists of hardware and software. **Hardware** comprises the physical components of the computer system that you can see and touch,

## ON THE JOB

The Computer Museum

The Computer Museum in downtown Boston is the only museum in the world that is completely devoted to the preservation and display of old and new computer technologies. Visitors may view a **chip** through a microscope, see the latest in computer animation, use a computer to design their own car, see recreated a vintage IBM 1401 unit record machine, play with a modern robot or view the world's most comprehensive collection of historic robots.

such as the printer and the central processing unit. The **central processing unit (CPU)** is the part of the system that executes the programs controlling the system's operation. These programs, also called **software,** are series of detailed instructions that tell the computer what to do and in what order to do it.

The system takes **input,** manipulates or changes it in some way, and then produces **output.** Suppose you had a list of the high temperatures for each day in July and wanted to find the average high temperature for the month. The input would be the list of daily high temperatures. The computer needs to manipulate this data to produce the desired result: the average high temperature. What if the computer calculated the average high temperature but never communicated it, printed it on a report, displayed it on a terminal, or used this information in any way? The data would be useless. Output communicates the information produced.

Thus, the computer system is made up of both hardware and software. The system takes input and manipulates or changes it into a new form, the output (Figure 1.1).

The input is called **data,** a collection of unprocessed facts. Once the data is processed and is in a useful form, it is referred to as **information.** People must supply this data and use the information produced. People also write the software, or programs, that instruct the computer how to process the data.

Computers are of two types: (1) **analog computers,** which process data from measurable flows such as voltage or resistance, and (2) **digital computers**—the more common for business applications—which process values measured in discrete digits. Computers are also identified by describing their size and power. **Microcomputers** are the smallest. Also referred to as desktop computers or personal computers (PCs), they are designed around a microprocessor chip and primarily support one user at a time. **Minicomputers** are mid-sized. Like mainframes, minicomputers support multiple users but are slower and have less memory. **Mainframe computers** are the largest and

**FIGURE 1.1**

The list of temperatures is the data input. The data is then processed to produce an average, and this average temperature is then communicated as the output.

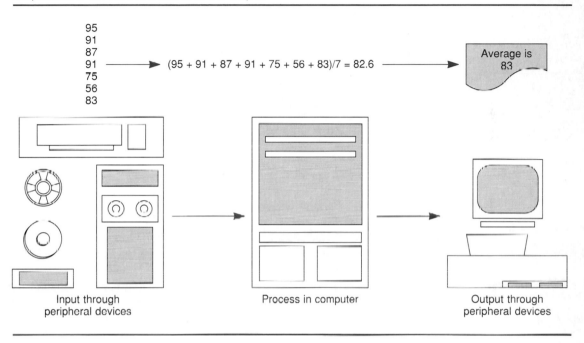

95
91
87
91 ⟶ (95 + 91 + 87 + 91 + 75 + 56 + 83)/7 = 82.6 ⟶ Average is 83
75
56
83

Input through          Process in computer          Output through
peripheral devices                                  peripheral devices

most powerful computers. They have the fastest operating speeds and the largest memories.

Let's look at an example of how a system works. Suppose that you go into a local store and want to charge a purchase on a credit card. At the service desk, the salesperson asks for your card, then runs it through a magnetic strip reader. This input device "reads" the number from your card and sends a copy to the store's computer. Here, the number read in, the input, is processed by matching it to a file of customer numbers to check if your card contains a valid number. Once the computer locates your record, it checks to see if your card has been lost, stolen, or has expired. If your card is valid, the processing continues. The computer then must decide if you have good credit or if you are behind in paying your bills. Your credit is good, so a message—the output— is sent back, allowing the cashier to charge the purchase.

## FROM CALCULATING MACHINES TO COMPUTERS

People are always looking for an easier way to perform some task. The development of the computer began with a search for a machine that could perform mathematical calculations mechanically. Earliest history might go back to the development of the arabic numbering system, with its use of the character zero. Others might say it began with the development of the Chinese **abacus** or the Japanese **soroban.**

More recent innovations include the contributions of the French mathematician **Blaise Pascal** to geometry, and the development of the **Pascaline** calculator in the mid-1600s. This machine incorporated eight movable dials. There was a window showing the current value over each dial. This calculator was capable of both addition and subtraction.

To add 28 and 132, the user would first turn all dials until zeros appeared in each window. A stylus was inserted into the slot marked 8 in the units position. The dial was rotated clockwise until it was stopped by a bar similar to the one found on rotary telephone dials. Next, the stylus was inserted in the dial at the 10s position into the slot marked 2. The dial was again rotated until it, too, was stopped by the bar.

These steps were repeated for the second and any subsequent numbers to be added. At the end of dialing in each number, the result could be read from the windows.

**Gottfried Leibniz,** a mathematician and philosopher who was born about 20 years after Pascal's birth, later developed a calculator that enabled the user to add, subtract, multiply, divide, and extract square roots.

Although these and many other calculating machines were developed, the first "computer" was designed by Charles Babbage.

### The First "Computer"

**Charles Babbage,** an English mathematician, is credited with designing the first computer, although this machine was never produced. He first invented a **difference engine** (Figure 1.2). This machine was designed to calculate mathematical tables, which people at that time had to calculate by hand, often inaccurately. His research, funded by the British government, resulted in the building of a prototype in 1822.

While working on the difference engine, Babbage conceived of a machine he called the **analytical engine.** Collaborating with him, his friend, the mathematician **Augusta Ada,** Countess of Lovelace, proposed the idea of programming the "engine" with cards. For her contributions, she is usually considered the first programmer. The proposed analytical engine would be able to receive instructions input from punched cards. These instructions would then be stored internally in the computer's memory. Once the calculations were complete, the engine would print out the results. These steps—input and processing using stored instructions, followed by output—are the actions modern computers require. Unfortunately, this machine was never produced and Babbage died without seeing significant interest in his machines.

**FIGURE 1.2**
The difference engine, designed by Charles Babbage, automated the calculation of mathematical tables. (Courtesy IBM Corporation and Neuhart-Donges-Neuhart Design)

## Punched Cards and the 1890 Census

The next major event related to computer development did not occur until the late 1800s. The U.S. census of 1880 took eight years to tabulate, making it outdated by the time the calculations were completed. Using the same tabulating method, the census of 1890 would have taken even longer; it might not even have been completed before the census of 1900.

**Herman Hollerith** developed a punched card to store statistical information for the Bureau of the Census. He also developed a machine to automatically tabulate this data (Figure 1.3). Each card contained one record; thus, the tabulating machine he developed to process the cards was referred to as **unit record equipment.** Each punched card was passed over a series of electrical contacts. When a hole was encountered in the card, contact was made. The data found within that card was tabulated and the results shown on numbered dials. This process speeded up tabulations so effectively that the 1890 census was completed by 1892.

**FIGURE 1.3**
The tabulating machine designed by Herman Hollerith used punched cards to tabulate the results of the 1890 census. (Courtesy IBM Corporation and Neuhart-Donges-Neuhart Design)

Hollerith left the Bureau of the Census and founded the Tabulating Machine Company, which marketed his machines worldwide. This company merged with several other companies during the following years and in 1924 was renamed the International Business Machine Corporation (IBM).

## The Electromechanical Computer Arrives

Hollerith's machine was primarily mechanical. During the late 1930s and early 1940s, **Howard Aiken,** a professor at Harvard, was researching the feasibility of an **electromechanical** computing machine—that is, a machine with both mechanical and electrical components. It would be capable of multiplying, as well as accumulating totals. In 1944, this IBM-sponsored research produced the Automatic Sequence Controlled Calculator, usually called the **Mark I** (Figure 1.4). The Mark I was able to multiply two 23-digit numbers in about six seconds, or add the two numbers in about one third of a second. Since it was electrome-

**FIGURE 1.4**
A group led by Howard Aiken developed the Automatic Sequence Controlled Calculator (the Mark I) at Harvard. (Courtesy IBM Corporation)

chanical, it was incapable of speeds as high as those of the electronic computers being developed during the same period; however, it remained in use at Harvard for many years.

## The Electronic Computer: Who Gets the Credit?

During the 1940s, the electronic computer was being researched at both Iowa State and the University of Pennsylvania. Between 1937 and 1942, Dr. **John Atanasoff** and a graduate assistant, **Clifford Berry,** developed an electronic computer at Iowa State. They called this machine the Atanasoff-Berry Computer, or the ABC. The university showed little interest in this invention, so it was never patented. Eventually it was stored in the basement of the physics building and almost forgotten.

Dr. **John W. Mauchly** and **J. Presper Eckert, Jr.,** completed the first fully operational electronic computer, the **Electronic Numerical Integrator And Calculator (ENIAC),** in 1946 at the University of Pennsylvania (Figure 1.5). Mauchly was familiar with Atanasoff's research, had talked to him, and had seen the ABC. The ENIAC consisted of more than 18,000 **vacuum tubes** (light-bulblike devices through which electric current can pass) and could perform 200 to 300 multiplications or 5,000 additions per minute. Its weakness was that the program was wired into the computer. To change the program, it was necessary to rewire the computer.

**FIGURE 1.5**
The Electronic Numerical Integrator And Calculator (ENIAC), weighing about 30 tons, was developed at the University of Pennsylvania by John W. Mauchly and J. Presper Eckert, Jr. (University of Pennsylvania Archives)

Initially, credit for invention of the first electronic computer was given to Mauchly and Eckert. This recognition was contested, however, with many people pointing to the influence of the ABC on ENIAC research. In 1973, a federal court ruling officially gave legal credit to Atanasoff and Berry for development of the first electronic computer.

## Separation of Computer and Program

As mentioned previously, the ENIAC had an obvious problem. Each time the user wished to run a different program, the computer had to be completely rewired. An American mathematician, **John von Neumann,** solved the problem by developing the "stored program concept." He suggested that the series of instructions, called the **program,** be entered from an external device such as a card or paper tape and then stored internally within the computer. Changing the program would then require only inputting new instructions to the computer instead of rewiring it. With von Neumann, Mauchly and Eckert developed the **Electronic Discrete Variable Automatic Computer (EDVAC),** the first computer to use the stored program concept.

## BUILDING ON THE FOUNDATION

With the development of the EDVAC, the versatility of the electronic computer became more obvious. Many people began to recognize its potential usefulness in business.

### The First Generation: Computers Reach Private Industry

The first commercially available computer was the UNIVersal Automatic Calculator (**UNIVAC I**—Figure 1.6), developed at Remington Rand Corporation by Mauchly and Eckert. It was first installed at the U.S. Bureau of the Census in 1951. The UNIVAC attained national prominence in 1952 when it was used to perform the calculations that predicted the results of the Dwight D. Eisenhower/Adlai E. Stevenson presidential election with only 5 percent of the votes in.

**FIGURE 1.6**

The first commercially available electronic computer, the UNIVAC I (UNIVersal Automatic Calculator), was first marketed in 1951. (The Charles Babbage Institute/University of Minnesota)

The commercial success of the UNIVAC brought several other manufacturers into the growing market: Honeywell, Burroughs, RCA, and IBM. Input media were still primarily punched cards and paper tape. Vacuum tubes were used for memory in these computers. Perhaps you have seen an old radio that used vacuum tubes and remember how large it was and how much heat was generated when it was turned on. These early computers also were huge and generated much heat.

The language in which these **first-generation computers** were programmed was unique to the machine using it; thus, the term **machine language** (machine language is also the lowest level of computer language). A person able to program in one computer's machine language was not necessarily able to program in another computer's language without extensive retraining. Each operation, such as to add or to move, was represented by **binary digits (bits)** (see Appendix B for more information on binary digits). Each instruction was detailed and precise. These characteristics made machine language extremely difficult to learn and slow to write. An early improvement was the introduction of **assembly languages,** which used letters instead of numbers to represent the operation to be performed. **Fields**—items of data such as addresses or pay rates—might be referred to by name rather than by location. Since the machine could no longer understand these instructions, the program was translated back into machine language by a program called an **assembler.** Once translated, the program could be run.

## Transistors: The Second Generation Begins

The **transistor** was developed by Bell Labs in 1947 and soon found its way into computer technology, replacing the vacuum tube. The development of the transistor made possible the small radios we use today. Computers that used transistors also became smaller, more reliable, and faster. Because the smaller computer generated much less heat, computer rooms required less cooling. Transistors marked the beginning of what are referred to as **second-generation computers,** which were most popular between the mid-1950s and mid-1960s.

The advent of assembly languages during the first generation meant that all programs had to be translated before they were run. If one had to translate the language anyway, it seemed only logical to develop a language that was more meaningful to humans than the assembly languages. Assembly languages were still widely used, but FORTRAN (FORmula TRANslator), the first of the high-level languages, was developed in 1955 by IBM. COBOL (COmmon Business Oriented Language), a high-level language created for business applications, was developed by representatives of government and various industries in 1959 and is still widely used.

Because the computer was now capable of running faster, paper tape and punched cards were too slow. More data could be processed than could be read in. It was necessary to develop input materials that could be processed more rapidly to avoid an input bottleneck. **Magnetic tape** (plastic tape that stores data as small magnetized spots) and **magnetic disks** (specially coated platters that store data as magnetized spots) were developed and grew in popularity. These magnetic devices provided more rapid input and also served as secondary storage devices.

## The Third Generation: Computers and Their Families

The problems arising during the second generation of computers were caused mainly by their success. As more companies purchased and used computers, the usefulness of the computer became increasingly obvious. Companies found new tasks for their computers; they eventually found uses exceeding the computer power they had. They had to upgrade and purchase larger and more powerful computers.

Unfortunately, second-generation computers were often not compatible, even when made by the same manufacturer. This meant that upgrading often required rewriting existing programs because they would not run on the new, larger computer. The **peripheral devices** (devices attached to the computer) such as tape drives might also have to be replaced, since they might also be incompatible with the new computer.

In 1964, IBM announced the 360 family of computers. The concept of a **family** of computers was new. The intention was to market computers that were upwardly compatible. The smallest computers could have programs written for them that would run on the largest computers in the family. Suddenly, upgrading no longer meant extensive revising of programs. Almost all manufacturers today use the family concept. **Third-generation computers** had arrived.

Computer size was further reduced as **integrated circuits (ICs)** replaced transistors (Figure 1.7). These ICs consist of thousands of minute circuits that have been etched into a small chip of silicon. With the development of ICs, reliability and processing speed continued to improve. Because of the increased processing speeds, new hardware was developed to store much larger quantities of data. Devices were developed that permitted more efficient accessing of the data. **Visual display terminals** also came into use (Figure 1.8).

The increased processing speeds and new types of input and output devices necessitated some changes in the way computers processed data. Computers were now able to run more than one program at a time. This ability, called **multiprogramming,** permitted computers to service several users simultaneously. The computer might be printing an inventory listing, calculating the week's payroll, and making a copy of the accounts receivable file at essentially

**FIGURE 1.7**
The trend toward miniaturization continued as integrated circuits (ICs) replaced transistors.
(*a.* Dan McCoy/Rainbow, *b.* Gary Cralle/The Image Bank)

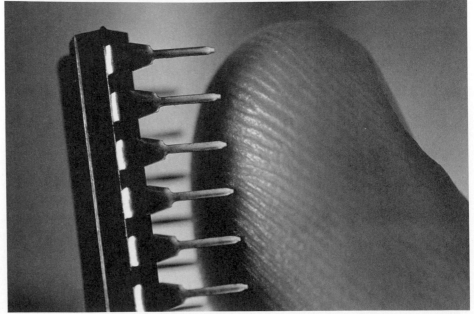

**FIGURE 1.8**
Visual display terminals provide rapid access to data by displaying it on a televisionlike screen. If a permanent copy is needed, a printer can be attached. (Mark Weidman)

the same time. A version of multiprogramming, called **time-sharing,** permitted more than one user to use the computer concurrently, often from more than one remote location. Although there were several users, each seemingly had exclusive use of the machine.

## The Fourth Generation: A Population Explosion

The **microprocessor,** a processing unit completely contained on a single chip of silicon, was developed during the early 1970s. This inexpensive chip, capable of performing logical and arithmetic functions, soon appeared in many other devices: microwave ovens, automobiles, watches. The IC of the third generation was replaced by **large scale integration (LSI),** with 100 or more ICs on a single chip. Soon, LSI was replaced by **very large scale integration (VLSI),** with over 1,000 ICs per chip. The decreasing size and cost of microprocessors ushered in the age of the microcomputer, the desktop-sized computer.

Computer languages were also evolving. In the third generation, languages had been designed for the programmer's understanding. In the fourth generation, languages could be understood by everyone—programmer and nonprogrammer alike.

**FIGURE 1.9**

Across time, memory size and speed have increased while cost has decreased.

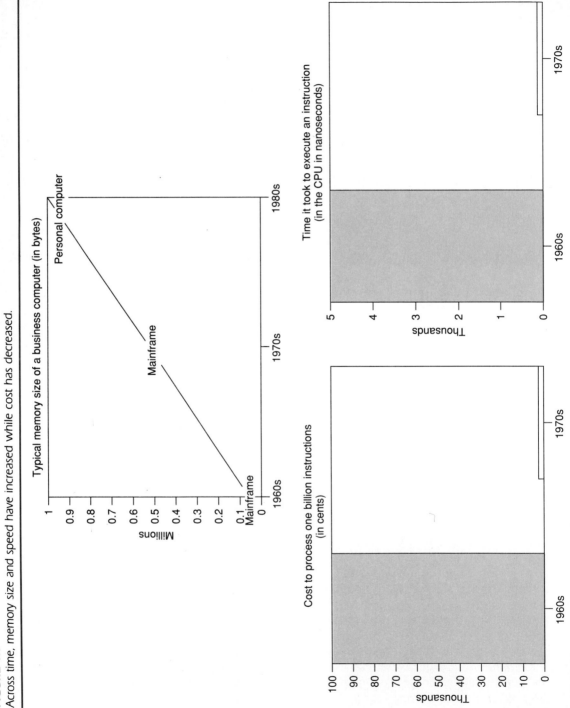

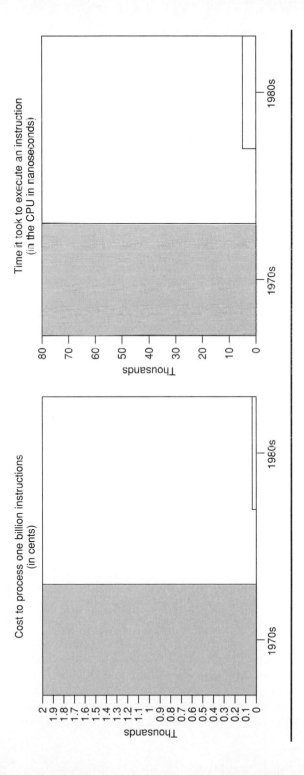

### Learning from Experience: The Fifth Generation

**Fourth-generation computers** were programmed by people who provided detailed instructions describing what the computer was to do. In 1981, a computer conference was held in Japan as part of a 10-year plan. This conference, sponsored by the Japanese government and the computer industry, considered the next steps in computing technology—**fifth-generation computers.** These steps included producing computer programs that would solve problems using deductive reasoning. A program would no longer spell out the choices to be made but would instead permit the machine to reason through a problem, much as a person would. It would involve developing a computer with very sophisticated software capable of understanding our natural, spoken languages. This field is referred to as **artificial intelligence (AI).** Areas of research in artificial intelligence include, among others, robotics, speech and image recognition, natural language processing, and expert systems. These topics will be discussed in more detail in Chapter 12.

### Where Are Computers Today?

Computers are everywhere today. They keep track of our telephone bills, store our medical and insurance records, process our tax returns, and give us our bank balances. They automate our traffic lights, validate our credit cards, produce our paychecks, notify us when our inventory is low, and check our licenses after a traffic violation. Family farms and multinational corporations purchase them. First-graders and Ph.D. candidates use them.

Employment opportunities abound in the computer field. Industry needs programmers, systems analysts, operators, and data entry personnel. Support personnel are also needed in such areas as marketing and education. The number of programmers in the United States increased 16 percent between 1983 and 1985; systems analysts increased 28 percent. Although many people fear that increased computer usage will eliminate jobs, it will actually create new jobs. Existing jobs will change as many more professionals in fields other than data processing begin to use computers routinely in their work.

### SUMMARY

Computer use is becoming increasingly widespread. Computer systems, made up of hardware, including the central processing unit, and software also require data and people, just as the preelectronic data processing systems did.

Early attempts to design calculating machines led to the development of the Pascaline and Leibniz calculators in the 17th century. During the 1800s, Charles Babbage designed his differential engine with the aid of Augusta Ada, Countess of Lovelace.

The early designs of Babbage have evolved into the computers of today. The vacuum tubes of the first generation were replaced by the transistors of the second generation, followed in turn by the ICs of the third generation. LSI and VLSI heralded the trend toward microminiaturization in the fourth generation. Across time, computing speeds, reliability, and primary storage capacity increased while cost per character stored decreased (see Figure 1.9). The evolution continues with the artificial intelligence research and other software development being carried on today.

## VOCABULARY

## EXERCISES

1.  Match the following terms with their meanings:

    1.  Hardware.
    2.  Unit record.
    3.  IC.
    4.  Software.
    5.  Time-sharing.
    6.  CPU.
    7.  Multiprogramming.
    8.  Data.
    9.  Electromechanical.
    10. Microprocessor.

    a.  Circuits etched in a silicon chip.
    b.  A collection of unprocessed facts.
    c.  A historical type of computing equipment, such as punched card equipment.
    d.  A machine having both mechanical and electrical components.
    e.  The programs used by a computer system.
    f.  The physical components of the computer system.
    g.  The part of the computer that actually performs calculations and comparisons.
    h.  A processor with all processing circuits contained on one chip.
    i.  The execution of two or more programs concurrently on the same computer.
    j.  Use of the computer by more than one user at a time but with each appearing to have exclusive use of it.

2. Match the following inventors with their inventions:
   1. Babbage.             a.  Stored program concept.
   2. Hollerith.           b.  Punched card.
   3. Aiken.               c.  ABC.
   4. Atanasoff.           d.  Analytical engine.
   5. Mauchly/Eckert.      e.  ENIAC.
   6. Von Neumann.         f.  Mark I.

3. Match the following generations with one of their characteristics:
   1. First generation.    a.  Family of computers.
   2. Second generation.   b.  Vacuum tubes.
   3. Third generation.    c.  Artificial intelligence.
   4. Fourth generation.   d.  Transistors.
   5. Fifth generation.    e.  Microprocessor.

## PROJECTS

1. Keep a log for 24 hours. This log should contain an entry for each time you do something that involves the use of a computer—for example, making a purchase that involves a credit card check by a point-of-sales terminal, making a withdrawal from an automatic teller machine, or receiving a computer-generated bill.

2. Analyze the transactions in the log. Indicate whether the computer was of primary benefit to a person, to the activity itself, or to both. Also decide if the computer made the activity easier or harder, for you and for the business. What were your reactions to the use of the computer?

3. Do additional research on the Atanasoff/Berry versus Mauchly/Eckert debate. Paired with someone else, debate who should receive credit for developing the first electronic digital computer.

4. Do some research on Japan's 10-year plan for developing artificial intelligence. Report on what you find.

5. Visit your computer lab. Find out what equipment (hardware, software, operating system) is available.

6. The chips that are the basis for microprocessors are changing, and microcomputers are changing with them. Do some research on Intel's 80386. What is the impact on microprocessors and microcomputers?

# 2

# The Central Processing Unit and the Operating System

**CHAPTER OBJECTIVES**

*After completing this chapter, you will be able to:*

1. Identify the components of the central processing unit.
2. Describe what occurs during a machine cycle.
3. Explain how main storage differs from secondary storage and the purpose of each.
4. Differentiate between multiprogramming and multiprocessing.
5. Describe the purpose of an operating system and compare several current ones.

## OVERVIEW

Imagine that you own a small retail store. Your inventory is now kept manually but you are considering keeping the inventory on a computer. When a truck arrives at your store, the driver takes a list of receipts to the inventory clerk, who begins to read the list.

Once the clerk reads the data, he processes it by matching the receipts to a current inventory list. The clerk compares the item number of an entry on the receipt list to the item number of an entry on the current inventory. If the inventory's item number is not the same as the receipt's item number, the clerk does not update it but continues to look for the matching inventory item. When the item numbers match, he adds the number received to the current inventory balance.

Your clerk performs the two functions expected of a computer's processing unit: logical decisions and mathematical calculations. How the computer performs these two functions is the subject of this chapter.

---

## I. CENTRAL PROCESSING UNIT

*— performs all processing functions*
*① ALU*
*② control.*

The central processing unit, also called the CPU, is the hardware that performs the processing functions. It has two primary parts, the arithmetic/logic unit and the control unit. Housed within the same physical device is the internal storage unit, also called **main memory** or **primary storage.** This is where the programs and data are stored while in use.

*CPU - hardware that performs the processing function*
*① ALU*
*② Control*

### Arithmetic/Logic Unit

The **arithmetic/logic unit (ALU),** as the name implies, contains all the circuitry necessary to perform the computer's arithmetic and comparison operations. It can calculate or round off numbers, compare algebraically or logically, and so on. For example, if you write the instruction ADD A to B, the ALU performs the addition.

*ALU - performs all arithmetic + comparison operations*

### Control Unit

*[handwritten margin note: Control unit - directs all the activities of the computer]*

The **control unit** directs the activities of the computer. It also controls the activities of the **input/output devices** as instructed by the programs. The control unit transfers data and instructions between the ALU and main memory. In general, it controls the flow of data within the system.

### Internal Storage

*[handwritten margin note: Int. storage - data + instructions being processed]*

**Internal storage,** also called *main memory* or *primary storage,* contains the data and instructions being processed after they have been received from the input units. Data and instructions must be stored within internal storage before being processed, since this is where the control unit will look for them.

In Chapter 1, you read that various materials have been used to form the memory of a computer: vacuum tubes, transistors, and integrated circuits. Actually, the only requirements are that the material used to form the memory be capable of having two different states (off/on, positive/negative, polarized/nonpolarized) and that it is also possible to read which of the two states exists without changing it.

*[handwritten margin note: bit - memory cell]*

As suggested above, each physical memory cell, called a *bi*nary digi*t* or **bit,** is capable of maintaining one of these two states. By grouping bits together in units called **bytes,** elaborate codes are possible. These codes make it possible to represent all of our letters, numbers, and special symbols. Some of these codes are discussed in more detail in Appendix B.

Memory size is described in terms of how many bytes it contains. You may think each byte as holding one character. Memory size is measured in **kilobytes (K), megabytes (MB),** or **gigabytes (G).** A kilobyte is approximately 1,000 bytes (1,024 bytes); a megabyte is approximately 1 million bytes (1,048,576 bytes); and a gigabyte is approximately 1 billion bytes.

The second requirement is that it is possible to read or recognize which of these states exist without altering it. This ability to read without destroying the information read is called **nondestructive read-out.**

Several types of internal storage are available. The two most common are random access memory (RAM) and read-only memory (ROM).

### *Random Access Memory*

*[handwritten margin note: 2- RAM - memory which can be altered]*

One of the great advantages of computers over most machines is that they can be used for different purposes at different times. This is done by changing the program or programs being run. The part of storage that holds programs and the data they use is called **random access memory (RAM).**

RAM's contents are easily changed; in fact, they change constantly during the execution of a program as new data is read and processed. As new programs are loaded into RAM memory, they overlay what was there before, altering the contents. This is sometimes referred to as a **destructive write-to.** However, the reading of the programs or of the data used by those programs does not alter the contents of memory—the nondestructive read-out mentioned in the previous section.

### Read-Only Memory

A second type of internal storage is called **read-only memory (ROM)** because its contents can only be read, not altered. These contents are loaded once, usually by the computer's manufacturer.

ROM is used to hold those instructions meant to remain in memory (storage) permanently. These instructions include parts of the operating system such as those programs that control computer operations regardless of which user program is running. They might also include a **compiler,** a program that translates a user-written program into the computer's language so that it can be executed (more on languages later).

*[handwritten margin note: ROM—memory which can only be read.]*

### Cache Memory

Programs and/or data are loaded into RAM from secondary storage prior to use. Once in RAM, they can quickly be accessed. RAM serves as a high-speed storage area. For some computers, even faster access time is required. These are designed with **cache memory.** Cache memory is even faster than RAM but is significantly more expensive. It is, therefore, much smaller and is used to hold only those instructions and data that are likely to be needed by the CPU in the immediate future.

*[handwritten: 3.]*
### Registers  *[handwritten: — holds memory temporarily, during programs execution]*

Linking the CPU and internal memory are several storage locations called **registers.** They are used to hold data and instructions temporarily during a program's execution. Since the contents of registers can be quickly located and retrieved, data and instructions are normally moved from main memory to a register just before they are processed.

### Bus Lines  *[handwritten: — physically links main memory, registers + CPU.]*

**Bus lines,** special electrical cables, are the physical connection linking main memory, the registers, and the CPU (Figure 2.1). The CPU, registers, and main storage work together to enable a program to be run. The easiest way to see how these various components work together is to walk through one machine cycle in detail.

**FIGURE 2.1**
Data and instructions must be located in internal storage before they can be processed.
Registers serve as high-speed access areas between internal storage and the CPU, where
the instructions are processed. The data and the instructions are transferred within the computer
via channels that carry electrical signals. These channels are called *bus lines*.

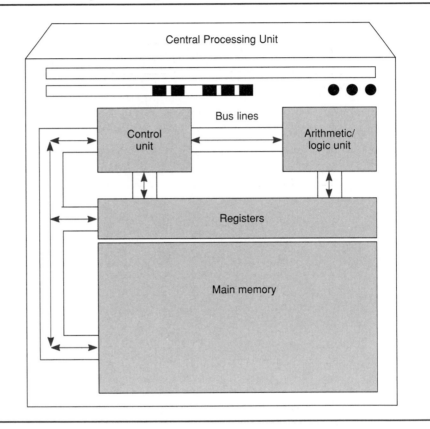

_(handwritten: 4.)_

## THE MACHINE CYCLE

_(handwritten margin notes:_
_Cycle-operations necessary to execute a language instruction_
_I-time - time required to pull an instruction + prepare it for processing_
_E-time - time needed to locate data, execute instruction + store results)_

A **machine cycle** (Figure 2.2) consists of the series of operations necessary
to execute a single machine language instruction. This cycle is divided into
two parts, **instruction time (I-time)** and **execution time (E-time)**. I-time is
the time necessary for the control unit to pull an instruction from main memory
and prepare it for processing. E-time is the period required to locate the data
needed, execute the instruction, and store the results in main memory.

**FIGURE 2.2**
Outline of a machine cycle.

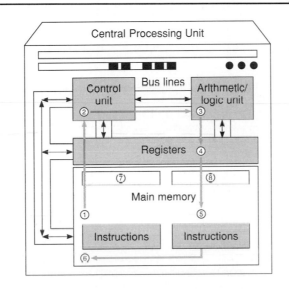

In I-time, (1) the control unit fetches the next instruction to be executed from the CPU; (2) it interprets what this instruction is to do and where the needed data is located; and (3) it passes control to the arithmetic/logic unit.

In E-time, (4) the ALU executes the instruction and returns control to the control unit; (5) the control unit stores the data in main memory, if necessary; and (6) it now returns to step 1 to locate the next instruction.

As data is read in, it is stored in input buffers (7). Before it is written out, the record is created in an output buffer (8). The rest of main memory is available for work areas.

The time required to complete one of these machine cycles is so brief that it cannot be described in terms of the minutes or seconds with which we usually describe elapsed time. New terms must be used. Cycle times are described in **milliseconds** (thousandths of a second), **microseconds** (millionths of a second), **nanoseconds** (billionths of a second), and **picoseconds** (trillionths of a second). Processing speed is also described in **megahertz (MHz),** which stands for 1 million cycles per second or **MIPS** (million instructions per second). Cycle times will vary with the particular computer being used.

## PROCESSING TECHNIQUES

As Figure 2.2 shows, to execute a single machine language instruction, the computer must fetch, translate, pass control, execute, and store. How does the computer know which of these activities to perform? How does it start? What makes it work?

A computer with all the necessary hardware still needs something else to make it work: software, the programs that direct the activities of the computer. Software is of two types: application programs and systems software.

**Application programs** perform specific functions such as accounting, spreadsheet processing, and inventory control. These programs determine how the payroll or inventory is to be run, but they do not provide all the detail necessary to run it. Another group of programs serve as go-betweens for application programs and hardware. These programs, referred to as **systems software,** control the operation of the computer system. They include the operating system, utility programs, compilers, and performance measurement systems.

For example, consider a simple request to read a record. The programmer asks that a record be read. If the record is to be read from a tape, the tape must be started, the record copied into memory, and the tape stopped. If it is to be read from disk, the access arm mechanism must be moved, the correct read/write head switched on, and the record copied into memory. The programmer does not give these detailed instructions on *how* to read the record. These instructions are a part of the programs that make up the operating system. Regardless of which operating system is used, it must be **booted** (or loaded into) the computer before the computer can be used.

The **operating system** is a series of programs designed to manage resources: hardware, other software programs, and data. Its purpose is twofold: to make it easier to use the hardware and to allocate the computer's resources efficiently among the various users. Peripheral devices such as tapes and disks must be managed. A program requests information from a disk; multiple users all send data to a central printer; an operator requests that a program be canceled; several programs are being processed during the same time period in a multiprogramming environment—these and other tasks are managed by the programs making up the operating system.

Operating systems vary from simple to extremely complex. Those designed for single-user, nonmultiprogramming microcomputer systems are less complex. They manage only a limited number of resources under the control of one user. Other operating systems are designed to support the activities of hundreds of users, many peripheral devices, and the concurrent execution of multiple programs. These systems are much more complex. They must allocate the use of memory among all the users, must manage conflicting demands for the use of peripheral devices, and must support the queuing of jobs. A queue is a structure in which an element can be added only at the end; you might prefer to think of it as a line. In a multiprogramming environment, many programs are being run concurrently. Although jobs may be submitted one after the other, the most efficient way to run them may not be in the same order as that in which they were submitted. By use of multiple queues, jobs awaiting execution may wait in one of several lines or queues.

For example, two very large, long jobs might be submitted one after the other. If they were run together, nothing else could run until they were done. When part of the operating system, queue management programs permit the operator to determine the characteristics of jobs sent to each queue. As jobs are submitted, they are sent to the appropriate queue. Selection of the next job to be loaded is then dependent both on the time and priority with which it as submitted and the queue to which it was assigned—all managed by the programs of the operating system.

There are two measures of how efficiently the resources are used. The first, **throughput,** is the amount of processing that occurs in a given period. The second measure is called **turnaround;** this is the elapsed time between job submission and output receipt.

The speeds at which data is processed have increased dramatically during the past few years. However, improvements of the speeds of peripheral devices have been much less dramatic. This has led to a significant speed disparity between the CPU and the peripheral devices. For example, calculating the amounts on a paycheck is much quicker than printing those amounts on the check itself. Buffers, spooling, multiprogramming, and multiprocessing are all used to improve efficiency.

## Buffers

**Buffers** are storage areas used to collect data as it is transferred into or out of memory from the peripheral devices. However, if the computer had only one buffer, it would have to wait for the data to be moved into the buffer from the peripheral device before it could process the record. The use of multiple buffers improves efficiency.

For example, suppose a program is designed to read records from tape, and now two buffers are present instead of one. As the program begins, it waits for the first buffer to be filled before beginning processing. While the record in the first buffer is being processed, however, the second buffer is being filled. When a second READ instruction is issued, the record in the second buffer is processed at the same time the first buffer is being refilled (Figure 2.3).

As the record is being processed, other buffers are refilled in preparation for use. Since a record is usually waiting in the buffer to be processed, time wasted waiting for a record to be brought in from a peripheral device is significantly reduced.

**FIGURE 2.3**
The introduction of multiple buffers significantly decreased idle computer time, here represented by the white areas. With only one buffer, while a record is being loaded, no processing can occur. With multiple buffering, one buffer can be refilled while the records in another buffer are being processed. Each record shown here represents a physical record or block consisting of three logical records.

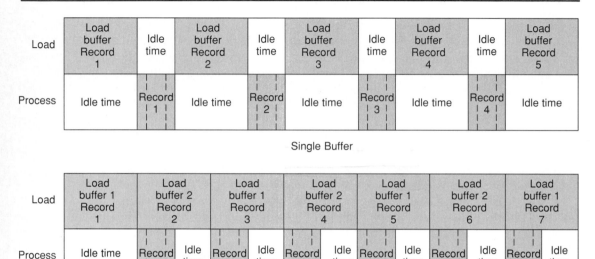

Single Buffer

Double Buffer

## Spooling

Punched cards and printers are the slowest of all peripheral devices. Since data can be processed more rapidly than it is written out, time is wasted waiting for the peripheral device to become available. Even buffering does not always result in efficient computer use. For example, several programs running concurrently may all need to use the printer.

One technique that increases efficiency still further is called **spooling.** In spooling, the records are written to a high-speed **direct access storage device (DASD),** a type of secondary storage device, usually a desk. Later, they are read into the computer or, in the case of printed output, are written to the printer (Figure 2.4).

Documents held on a spool for printing can be restarted easily in case of paper jams, can be redirected to another printer if desired, and can print multiple copies. Spooling also enables the operator to group printed reports so that all those using like forms are printed at the same time. Finally, documents can be printed by priority rather than in chronological order.

**FIGURE 2.4**

Spooling of print files means the files are stored for printing later. One program can produce many printed reports, even if the shop has only one printer, because the reports can be printed individually at different times.

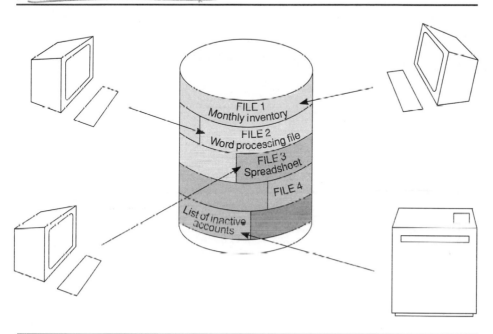

## Multiprogramming

*execution of 2 or more programs.*

Buffering and spooling have increased machine efficiency, but idle time is still a problem. One program may not use all the peripheral devices, so some devices sit idle while that program is running. A program may also waste time waiting for data to be transferred into main memory.

To reduce this idle time, operating systems have been developed to utilize the CPU and the peripheral devices more fully. These operating systems permit multiprogramming, also known as **multitasking,** the concurrent execution of two or more programs.

In multiprogramming, the time wasted waiting for the completion of an input/output operation is now spent processing another progam's data. When that program needs more data, no idle time occurs; another program uses the available processing resources of the CPU (Figure 2.5). In other words, the CPU switches back and forth between (or among) jobs.

**FIGURE 2.5**

Multiprogramming permits several programs to share internal storage and CPU services at one time. Program 1 may be writing to tape, program 2 using the CPU, program 3 printing a report, and program 4 reading data in from a disk, all apparently simultaneously.

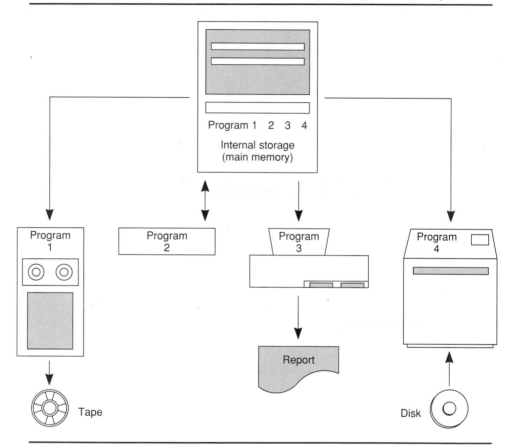

## Multiprocessing

*program execution by more than one processor.*

Whereas multiprogramming or multitasking is the concurrent execution of more than one program by the same processor, **multiprocessing** is program execution by more than one processor; that is, two or more instructions can be executed simultaneously. Each processor may function independently, permitting the farming out of input/output functions or other computer activities.

# OTHER SYSTEMS SOFTWARE FEATURES

In addition to the operating systems (some popular operating systems are discussed at the end of the chapter), other programs make using a computer easier and more efficient. These systems software programs include utility programs, interpreters, compilers, and performance measurement programs.

## Utility Programs *— data processing*
*Conditions.*

**Utility programs** perform functions that almost every data processing installation needs, such as sorting records and backup files and initializing disks (preparing disks to receive data).

## Interpreters *— translates source language into machine language; one instruction at a time.*

The programmer writes a program in a computer language such as BASIC, COBOL, or Pascal. This version of the program is called a **source module** or **source code.** Since the computer can execute a program only when that program is in the computer's machine language, the source module must be translated before the program can be run.

An **interpreter** is a program that reads one of these source language instructions and translates it into machine language. Once this instruction is translated, it is executed. The next instruction is then translated and the cycle repeated.

Interpreting a program saves space on the program library because the program is translated each time it is run. The program takes longer to run, however, since it must be interpreted each time it is executed. Interpreters are most effective when the program is not to be run regularly.

## Compilers *— translates an entire program.*

A compiler is also a program. It takes the entire source language module and translates it into a machine language version called an **object module** (Figure 2.6).

Whereas the interpreter translates only one instruction before the computer attempts to execute it, the compiler translates the entire program before execution is attempted. Compilers are most useful when a program is to be run regularly; since the compiler has created a machine language version of the whole program—the object module—no time is wasted in retranslating the program each time it is run. Additional library space is used, however, since the object module must be saved. (Languages are discussed more extensively in Chapter 4.)

**FIGURE 2.6**
During the compile process, the source language program is translated and an object module in machine language is generated.

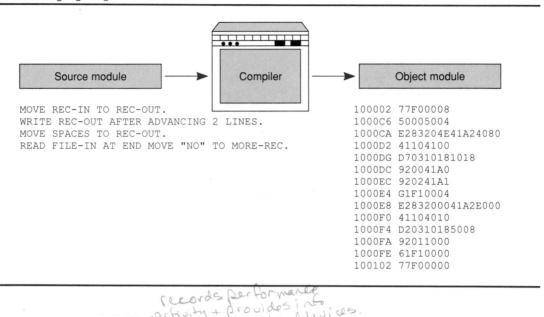

| Source module | Compiler | Object module |

```
MOVE REC-IN TO REC-OUT.                          100002  77F00008
WRITE REC-OUT AFTER ADVANCING 2 LINES.           1000C6  50005004
MOVE SPACES TO REC-OUT.                          1000CA  E283204E41A24080
READ FILE-IN AT END MOVE "NO" TO MORE-REC.       1000D2  41104100
                                                 1000DG  D70310181018
                                                 1000DC  920041A0
                                                 1000EC  920241A1
                                                 1000E4  G1F10004
                                                 1000E8  E283200041A2E000
                                                 1000F0  41104010
                                                 1000F4  D20310185008
                                                 1000FA  92011000
                                                 1000FE  61F10000
                                                 100102  77F00000
```

*records performance*
*activity + provides info*
*on system + peripheral devices.*

## 6. Performance Measurement Programs

A student's performance may be measured by grades, a car's performance by miles per gallon. The computer system's performance is reported and analyzed by **performance measurement programs.** For example, a computer operations manager might want to know what percentage of time the CPU was used, how many times a printer was written to or a disk read, or how many errors occurred as a disk was written to. These questions are all answered by the performance measurement software. This software records performance activity and provide information on system and peripheral device use.

## 10. SOME POPULAR OPERATING SYSTEMS

There are many operating systems in use today. Some of the popular ones include **OS–MVS, MS–DOS,** and **UNIX.** A new one is **OS/2.** OS–MVS was designed to run on mainframe computers, **Macintosh OS** and MS–DOS on microcomputers. UNIX is run on all sizes of computers except for the smallest microcomputers. OS/2 and Macintosh OS support multitasking.

Each operating system is described in terms of the word size of its microprocessor: usually 8 bits (binary digits), 16 bits, or 32 bits (see On the Job). Typically, a word is the amount of data that is contained in one register and that is

## ON THE JOB

### The Connection Machine

Many microcomputer changes have involved increasing from 8- to 16- to 32-bit processors. However, one recent change has been radically different. In 1986, Thinking Machines Corporation introduced its Connection Machine.

The Connection Machine, developed in a project sponsored by the Defense Advanced Research Projects Agency, is a massive parallel processing computer. It links 16,000 to 64,000 processors and is capable of processing data at up to 1 billion instructions per second. The front end is a conventional computer that contains the program. Single data-element instructions are executed here while instructions that operate on the entire data set at once are passed to the Connection Machine. Each data element is there assigned to an individual processor, allowing simultaneous execution by thousands of processors.

moved across the bus lines at one time; the bigger the word, the more data that can be moved in parallel across the bus line and thus, the faster the machine. A bigger word also accommodates larger addressable memory locations, more machine language instructions, and greater accuracy and efficiency in manipulating numbers in the registers.

## OS–MVS

OS–MVS (Operating System–Multiple Virtual Storage) was designed by IBM for its 370 series mainframes (mainframes are the largest, fastest class of business computers supporting large numbers of users). It handles multiprogramming in a virtual memory environment.

In **virtual memory,** a program to be executed is stored on a DASD, usually a disk, and divided into segments called **pages.** These pages are moved into main memory as they are needed. Since all parts of a program are not needed at the same time, this permits more programs to reside in main memory simultaneously and improves throughput.

## MS–DOS

MS–DOS, or MicroSoft Disk Operating System, was developed by Microsoft, Inc. It is a leading operating system in the microcomputer market. The most popular 16-bit system, it is designed for computers that support only one user at a time. MS–DOS can be used on many small computers and is the operating system used with the IBM PC compatible clones. The version used on the IBM PCs themselves is called **PC–DOS.**

Many versions of MS–DOS have appeared since it was first introduced, each more powerful than its predecessor. MS–DOS can now support many high-level languages and handles disk input/output very efficiently.

### Macintosh OS

Macintosh OS is the operating system used on the Macintosh computers. It is graphics and mouse oriented. It also features pull-down menus, its own file management system, easy customization, and will support multitasking. On many models, it permits easy sharing of files with DOS systems.

### UNIX

UNIX, developed at Bell Laboratories in 1969, is a general-purpose system that supports several terminals. Since it is portable—able to be moved from one machine to another—application programs written for one machine using UNIX can be moved to another with minimal effort.

Because it was designed to handle multiusers handling many tasks, UNIX resources can be shared among several users. UNIX began as a programmer tool; many of its commands resemble programming instructions. Thus, it has a reputation for being difficult to understand for users who are not data processing personnel.

UNIX is widely available. Although it requires a relatively large system by microcomputer standards, more versions are being developed for small systems. It is currently available for microcomputers, minicomputers, mainframes, and even supercomputers.

### OS/2

OS/2 was a joint development of IBM and Microsoft. It requires a large memory, since it is a multitasking system designed to use the 80286 or 80386 Intel chip-based machine. (The 80286, 80386, and 80486 will be discussed further in Chapter 5.) OS/2 also provides a DOS-compatible window. Another version, OS/2 Extended, is available for IBM PC ATs and PS/2 machines.

Because OS/2 is a new addition to the family of operating systems, improvements are still being made to it. The original release did not support communications and network products, but subsequent releases are expected to do this.

## CRITERIA FOR EVALUATING THE OPERATING SYSTEM

All operating systems cannot run on all computers, but many computers can use one of several operating systems. Several factors must be considered when choosing an operating system.

Operating systems are evaluated first in terms of what they do. Does the operating system do what you need to have done? If several operating systems can perform at the level you need, other considerations include the following:

1.  How much memory does the computer have, and of this memory, how much will the operating system use?
2.  How easy is the system to use?
3.  Is the system well documented? That is, are the accompanying instructions or user's manual easy to understand?
4   How secure is the system? Is one user safe from another's activities?
5.  In what language is the operating system written? If it is written in a high-level rather than a machine-level language, it is probably portable.
6.  How easy will it be to upgrade and install a larger, more powerful system?

## SUMMARY

The central processing unit runs the computer. It consists of the control unit and the arithmetic/logic unit. The control unit directs the activities of the computer system, whereas the ALU performs all the necessary arithmetic and logical functions. Other parts of the computer hardware include registers and bus lines.

Operating systems provide an interface between the application programs and the hardware. They free the programmer from coding many detailed instructions. Operating systems also provide more efficient use of computer resources through such techniques as multiprogramming, multiprocessing, and spooling.

Various operating systems such as MS–DOS, Macintosh OS, UNIX, OS–MVS, and OS/2 are available. In addition, many computers are using their own proprietary operating systems or their own version of one of the systems mentioned above. One important proprietary system is the Macintosh OS, which uses pull-down menus (they appear as needed), icons, and a mouse. Many types of programs are available to make the operation of a computer easier and more efficient. They include utility programs, compilers, interpreters, and performance measurement programs.

## VOCABULARY

Application programs    *28*

Arithmetic logic unit
(ALU)    *23*

Bit    *24*

Boot    *28*

Buffers    *29*

Bus lines    *25*

Byte    *24*

Cache memory    *25*

Compiler    *25*

Control unit    *24*

Destructive write-to    *25*

## EXERCISES

1. What are the two main parts of the CPU? What is the purpose of each?
2. Explain the difference between ROM and RAM. What is the purpose of each?
3. What is the purpose of a register? Of a bus line?
4. Describe the steps required to execute a machine instruction.
5. Why is an operating system so useful?
6. What programs measure machine efficiency?
7. Define spooling, multiprogramming, and multiprocessing.
8. Why are utility programs provided?
9. What is the difference between an interpreter and a compiler?

10. Describe some characteristics of the operating systems discussed: UNIX, MS–DOS, Macintosh OS, OS/MVS, and OS/2.

## PROJECTS

1. You are purchasing a microcomputer. It will be used for a variety of applications. Several operating systems are available, including MS–DOS and UNIX. What questions might you want answered before you decide which operating system to use?
2. Read this month's issue of several computer magazines. What operating systems are advertised? Which of their features are emphasized as selling points?

# 3

# Hardware: The Peripheral Devices

## CHAPTER OBJECTIVES

*After completing this chapter you will be able to:*

1. Describe the characteristics of the various input and output devices.
2. Explain the differences between sequential and random access and the advantages of each.
3. Explain the purpose of secondary storage.
4. List several devices that must be accessed sequentially and several that may be accessed randomly.
5. Explain how data is stored on disk and on tape.

## OVERVIEW

In Chapter 2, we considered how an inventory control clerk processed inventory receipts, using them to create a new, updated inventory. The clerk processed them by using his brain to add the receipts to the existing inventory. We expanded the explanation to show how similar this was to the way the computer would process the same information.

Before the clerk was able to process the data, however, it was first necessary to read the data. As humans, we use our senses to receive data; our eyes, ears, and sense of touch constantly provide information for us to process. Our brains store data and our mouths and hands provide a way for us to disseminate the information we have produced. We even have secondary storage units such as our address books and file folders.

A computer system, too, requires more than just the CPU to process information. It requires **input devices** that can read data and translate it into a form that is understandable to the computer, **machine-readable format.** It needs **secondary storage devices** to hold data where it can be quickly retrieved for processing. It also needs **output devices** to translate the information from its storage as bits within the computer to forms that we can understand.

This chapter describes some of the common input devices: terminals, optical recognition, MICR and other magnetic strips, and voice. Secondary storage devices including magnetic tape, magnetic disk, and optical disk are described, as are output devices including printers, plotters, microfilm, microfiche, and voice.

## INPUT DEVICES AND MEDIA

The earliest method of providing computer input was to accumulate data in batches where the activity occurred and then to take these batches to a central location where the data would be put into a form the computer could read. This method had two disadvantages: it was not timely and was often inaccurate.

New devices were developed in response to these disadvantages. Timeliness was improved by changing from batching to transaction-oriented processing, which is the processing of each transaction as it occurs. Accuracy was improved by decreasing the number of times the data was handled. The earliest input devices, such as punched card reading devices have largely been replaced by terminals, optical recognition devices, and other methods of directly inputting data from the source itself, such as bar code readers, magnetic ink character recognition (MICR), and voice.

## Terminals —peripheral devices

**Terminals** are peripheral devices through which data is entered into or output from the computer. Many terminals are portable; they can be moved from place to place to facilitate data handling. Two of the most common types of terminals are the visual display terminal (VDT) and the point-of-sale terminal (POS). Although microcomputers are frequently used in networks or as intelligent terminals, their hardware characteristics will be discussed in Chapter 5.

### Visual Display Terminal

The visual display terminal enables us to easily interact with a computer. A VDT consists of a TV-like picture tube (the **cathode ray tube** or **CRT**) and a keyboard. The display unit may also be a matrix display made up of **LEDs (light-emitting diodes),** such as seen on cash register terminals (Figure 3.1). Terminals using an **LCD (liquid crystal display),** a substance that glows when electrically charged, have recently been introduced. These terminals are more compact and have a longer life expectancy. LCDs also use less power than LEDs.

LED
LCD

 Since the output is displayed on the CRT and cannot be moved without moving the entire terminal, the terminal is usually located where the information is needed. If the user requires a copy of the transaction, a printer may be attached to the terminal to produce **hard copy** (results printed on paper or stored on microfilm/fiche).

 VDTs display either alphanumeric information (letters and numbers) or graphics (charts, graphs, and so on). Other features include color and the ability to *highlight* (to increase the brightness of certain fields), to *split* the screen (to display more than one screen of information on the same screen), and to *scroll* (to roll the information across the screen line by line, either forward or backward).

 The keyboard may be either a part of the device itself or a detachable, self-contained unit. The layout often resembles that of the typical typewriter keyboard (QWERTY), although many other formats are available. One notable difference from the typewriter keyboard is the presence of many more keys. In addition to the letters, numbers, and special characters of the typewriter, the terminal keyboard will also contain function keys, special keys, and often a numeric keypad. Function keys let you perform an activity with one keystroke. For example, pressing F1 (function key 1) might enable you to save a file on disk. The special keys include the cursor keys that enable you to move the cursor around

**FIGURE 3.1**

LEDs are used to display information on many items, including cash registers, clocks, and microwave ovens. (Superstock)

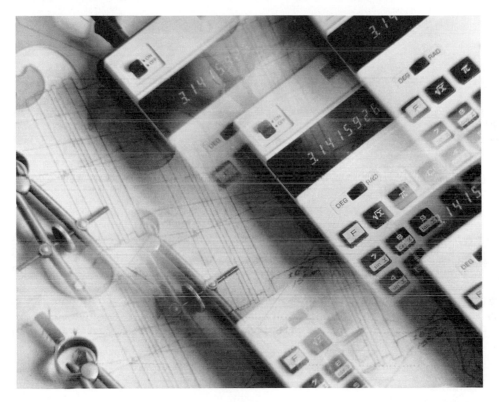

the screen, as well as the CTRL, DEL, RETURN/ENTER, and ESC keys. Which control and function keys appear is dependent on the manufacturer.

Some keyboards are specially adapted to harsh environments. You may have noticed the keyboards on the terminals in fast-food restaurants: They often have a sealed surface to protect them from damage due to spilled food and drinks as well as from possible moisture from grease in the atmosphere. One difficulty in using these keyboards is that users may not sense when a key is pressed. Most people prefer some sensation, either audible (the slight click) or tactile (the feel of a key giving under their finger), when a key is pressed.

### Point-of-Sale Terminal

Today, the **point-of-sale terminal (POS)** is frequently used in grocery and department stores (Figure 3.2). In addition to functioning as a cash register, the POS may also send sales data to a central computer. Some POS terminals have their own storage device, such as a tape, which holds the data for later

**FIGURE 3.2**

POS terminals often use a wand reader to identify data on price tags. The sales information is used not only to charge the customer but also to update inventory and to produce other sales statistics.

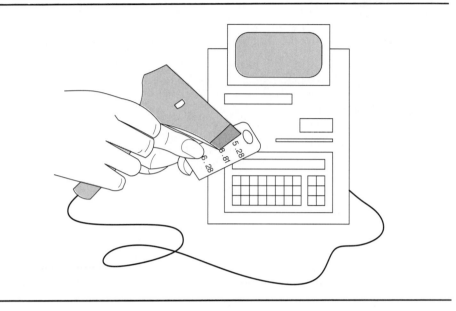

transmission to the computer. Although many of these POS terminals have data entered through a keyboard, others use **wand readers** to "read" tags attached to the products being sold. A wand reader is held in the hand and waved over the line of code to be read. It is used to read various printed fonts as well as OCR fonts and bar code. After the data is entered, the terminal can display information back to the customer on a display screen. Often, the terminal is attached to a printer, which makes a copy of the transaction for the customer.

Point-of-sale terminals are a type of, and could be referred to as, point-of-activity terminals since they have applications other than in sales.

*S.* Terminals may be "dumb" or "intelligent." A **dumb terminal** lacks the necessary logic and memory to process data. Although data may be entered or received through it, the computer with which it communicates does all the processing. An **intelligent terminal** has built-in processing capacity. It has memory and a processor but lacks the secondary storage devices (disk or tape) of a microcomputer.

*1.* ## Optical Recognition  *— computer reads information*

**Optical recognition** permits greater accuracy than other input devices in that the computer reads information from the source itself; keying of the data is

**FIGURE 3.3**

*Erase carefully—your grade depends on it. Mark sensing cards are frequently used to automate test grading. The student records her answers on the card by making a dark pencil mark in the correct slot. The answers are then automatically compared to the correct ones by the scanning device.*

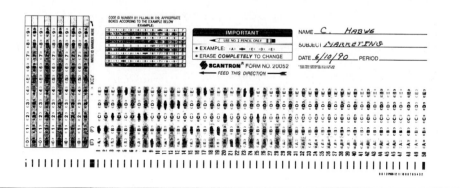

not required. Optical mark sensing, optical character recognition (OCR), and bar codes all use optical recognition.

## Mark Sensing

You probably have taken a test in which you were given a preprinted form consisting of questions followed by a series of columns marked a, b, c, d, and e. You may have been asked to make a heavy pencil mark in the boxes representing the correct answers. If you changed your mind about a response, you had to erase the incorrect answer carefully because the answer sheets would be machine-graded (Figure 3.3). This is a form of optical **mark sensing** in which the document is scanned with a light beam, which identifies the location of the marks.

## Optical Character Recognition

**Optical character recognition (OCR)** reads not only marks but also letters and numbers printed with normal ink, as long as the characters are printed in a standard print **font** (typeface style or design—Figure 3.4). Occasionally, handwritten characters can also be read if highly stylized printing is used. However, many problems are involved in reading handwritten characters, because styles are so individualized.

## Bar Code

Another type of optical character is called a **bar code.** A bar code called the **universal product code (UPC)** is used most often in grocery stores (Figure 3.5). A bar code reader identifies a series of marks representing the item code.

**FIGURE 3.4**
The OCR-A print font is used on most source documents read by optical character readers. OCR-A characters on a document usually indicate that a computer will process the document.

To obtain the price to be charged, the computer matches this code to a file of item numbers and their current prices.

This automation makes pricing an item rapid and accurate: rapid because stamping the price on each item is unnecessary, and the cashier does not have to key in as much information; accurate because it is consistent—the same price will be charged each time the item is purchased. This eliminates the possibility of the cashier hitting a wrong key and price. Although supermarkets most often use it, bar coding is also employed in such diverse locations as libraries (to identify books) and railways (to facilitate tracking of freight cars).

## Magnetic Ink Character Recognition

**Magnetic ink character recognition (MICR)** encoding is most often used in the banking industry. For example, look at a check from your checkbook (Figure 3.6). You will notice that several groups of highly stylized characters are printed at the bottom. These characters are imprinted in magnetic ink, which can be read by special-purpose **reader/sorters.** When your check is returned to your

**FIGURE 3.5**
Many people think that the bar code found on grocery items contains the price. It does not; the bar code contains the *product code,* which is used to locate the product's price from a file.

bank for processing, the check amount is also MICR encoded. The reader/sorter then reads the entire check, and the amount of the transaction is deducted from your account. The reader/sorter also can sort the checks in customer account number sequence. This simplifies the task of returning your canceled checks each month.

Each of these input methods—terminal usage, OCR, and MICR—improved accuracy by bringing data entry closer to the original source.

**FIGURE 3.6**
Your checks are returned each month after the MICR-encoded account number sorts them.

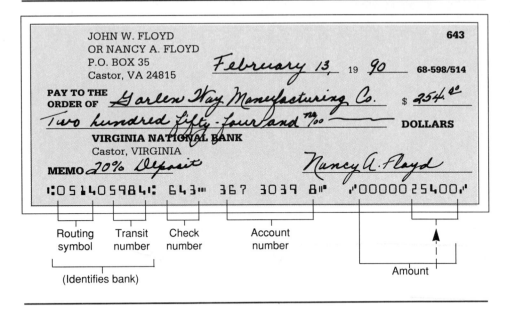

## Light Pen

The **light pen** (Figure 3.7) is used to modify pictures or data on the CRT screen. It is a wand with a light-sensitive cell at the tip. As the tip of the light pen touches the CRT screen, it closes a photoelectric circuit, and the computer system recognizes this spot's location.

Some screens can also sense touch. Operating much as an electric eye does, these CRTs can sense an object the size of a human finger because the presence of that finger interrupts the light beams around the screen's surface. This interruption allows the system to recognize this spot.

## Mouse

The **mouse** is a small box with a ball built into the bottom. Whenever the mouse is moved across a surface, the **cursor,** a light, bar, or arrow on the CRT that indicates current screen location, is moved across the screen. The movements of the cursor correspond to those of the mouse. The mouse may also be used to activate choices on the **menu,** a list of activities from which the user may choose (Figure 3.8). Mouse usage is steadily increasing. The mouse is a required piece of hardware on many microcomputers.

**FIGURE 3.7**
Light pens use a light-sensitive stylus that is connected by a wire to the terminal. When the user brings the pen to the desired point on the CRT screen and presses a button, the terminal recognizes the location. Light pens are used to draw images in graphics systems and to select options from the menu. (Gabe Palmer/The Stock Market)

**FIGURE 3.8**
When the mouse is moved across a surface, the cursor is moved correspondingly across the screen. (Dan Esgro/The Image Bank)

As microcomputer hardware and software become more complex, they also become easier to use. Users select from menus on which activities are represented by **icons** (pictures representing an activity). When the cursor is positioned next to the icon desired, the operator can press a button on the mouse causing that activity or menu option to be carried out. As windowing becomes more common, a mouse is often used to move between windows.

## Voice Recognition

To be able to speak to the computer and have it carry out verbal instructions would be the most convenient input method of all. It would be rapid because no keying would be required, and convenient because those with no computer knowledge could use it. Since no physical motions would be required, it also would make computer power more available to many physically disabled persons.

To recognize speech, the input device must convert the speech to a digital code that the computer can accept. When **voice recognition** is used today, the computer is usually "trained" to recognize the voice of one user. The user repeats words, phrases, or letters to the computer, which stores them in their digital patterns (Figure 3.9). Later, the phrase, word, or letter spoken to the

**FIGURE 3.9**
A voice recognition system takes spoken input and converts it to digital symbols.

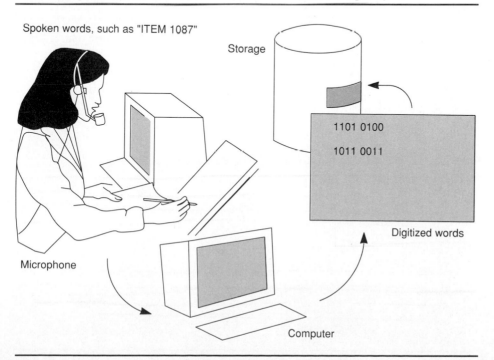

Spoken words, such as "ITEM 1087"

Storage

1101 0100
1011 0011

Digitized words

Microphone

Computer

computer is matched to the digital patterns formed and stored when the computer was trained. Many limitations exist, however: the computer must be trained to the user; the computer has a vocabulary limited to those words, phrases, and sounds for which it was trained; and background noises may become part of the sounds being digitized. Anything interfering with the user's normal voice may also cause misunderstandings. A cold or even normal hoarseness may distort the sound pattern of the voice.

Some voice systems can recognize multiple voices, but these generally have an even more limited vocabulary than a system trained to a single voice.

## SECONDARY STORAGE DEVICES AND MEDIA

Main storage, that part of the computer that holds data and instructions for processing, cannot store all the programs and data an organization needs. Secondary or **auxiliary storage** is used to expand the capacity of main storage or memory.

**FIGURE 3.10**

Reels of tape have the data recorded across the tape surface. A tape cassette records data serially.

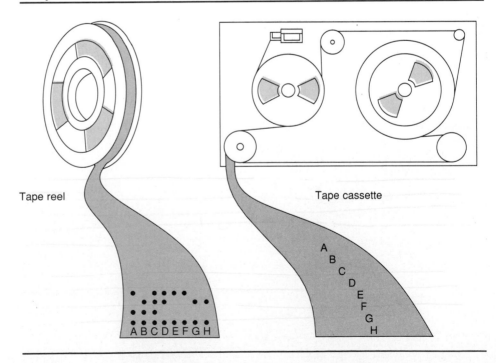

Tape reel

Tape cassette

A B C D E F G H

A
 B
  C
   D
    E
     F
      G
       H

Data storage technology accounts for 20 to 30 percent of computer hardware sales today. The United States now has several university research centers devoted to data storage technology. Secondary storage requires a material that is fast to read, reasonable in cost, and capable of holding a large amount of data. Media used as secondary storage include magnetic tape and magnetic disks. Mass storage devices are also used.

## Magnetic Tape

Magnetic tape is similar to the tape used with tape recorders. Data is recorded as a series of magnetic dots on the tape. In reels of tape, usually ½-inch wide and 2,400-feet long, the characters are recorded *across* the tracks on the tape. On tape cassettes, characters are stored serially down the *length* of the tape, one at a time (Figure 3.10).

Tape is also stored on cartridges (Figure 3.11). These cartridges, resembling

**FIGURE 3.11**
Irwin tape backup systems slide easily into one of the floppy disk slots of microcomputers based on MS–DOS and PC–DOS. Capable of backing up 20 to 120 MB hard disks in either 3½-inch or 5¼-inch sizes, Irwin internal drives use the microcomputer's existing floppy controller and power supply, thus eliminating expense, saving valuable space, and conserving power. Powerful, flexible, menu-driven EzTape™ software can save or restore a single file, groups of files, or an entire hard disk on shirt pocket–sized minicartridges. (Courtesy Irwin Magnetic Systems Inc.)

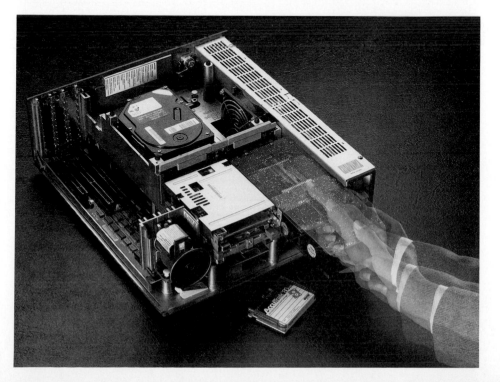

**FIGURE 3.12**

A tape drive has only one read/write head. All tape must pass this head in sequence to find and read the information the user wants.

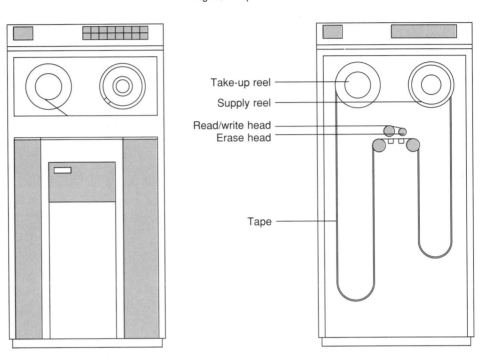

Magnetic Tape Unit

Take-up reel

Supply reel

Read/write head
Erase head

Tape

videocassettes, are not designed to replace tape reels. Instead, they are intended to store backups of disk files for later retrieval, usually in case current data is destroyed and must be recreated.

Tapes have a high density; that is, many characters can be stored in a small space. Usually 1,600 to 6,400 characters can be stored in an inch of tape. Since it usually takes one **byte** (a string of usually six or eight adjacent binary digits) to record one character, the density is referred to as the **bpi** (bytes per inch) of the tape. A tape that stored 6,400 characters per inch would be 6,400 bpi.

Reels of tape are processed at a fairly high speed, but the serial recording slows down tape cassettes. The time required to copy a character from the tape surface to main storage is called the **transfer time.** The number of characters copied per unit of time is referred to as the **transfer rate.** In cassettes, this is about 100 characters per second, whereas reels have a transfer rate of approximately 10,000 to 1 million characters per second.

**FIGURE 3.13**

Interrecord gaps permit a tape to reach the proper speed before the data is read from or written to (recorded on) the tape.

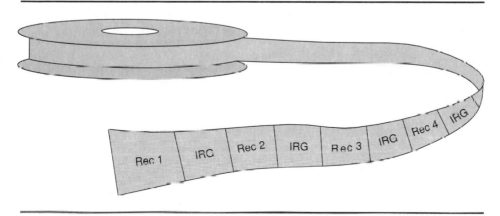

The biggest disadvantage to the use of tape as a secondary storage medium is that it must be read sequentially, one record after another. All previous records must pass under the **read/write head** to reach the record the operator is searching for (Figure 3.12). (The read/write head is an electromagnet that reads the magnetized spots on the tape and translates them into electrical signals; more on this later.) Another disadvantage is that tapes do not fully use their recording surface, as the rest of this section will explain. Once a record is read, the program must process it: comparing, moving, and calculating the data. If the tape continued to move, the next record might pass the read/write head before the program was ready to process it. Therefore, the tape drive comes to a stop once a record has been read and starts again when the computer is ready for the next record.

Have you ever stopped and then restarted a tape player while a music tape was playing? If you have, you will remember that the music was distorted when the tape was restarted. This resulted because the music was recorded at one speed and is played back at another. If it weren't corrected, the same distortion would occur in reading magnetic storage tape as the tape starts to move again and the tape drive reads it. The distortion is prevented by something called an **interrecord gap (IRG)** or **interblock gap (IBG)** (Figure 3.13). This is a space on the tape between records, or the distance the tape must move before it again reaches recording speed. Since an inch of tape may hold 1,600 to 6,400 characters and the IRG may be ½ inch or more of unused space, much space can be wasted.

To help cut the waste, records on tape are often grouped together into **blocks** called **physical records.** An entire block is read at one time, which eliminates the need for an IRG between each logical record (Figure 3.14). The

**FIGURE 3.14**
Blocking data decreases wasted space on a tape.

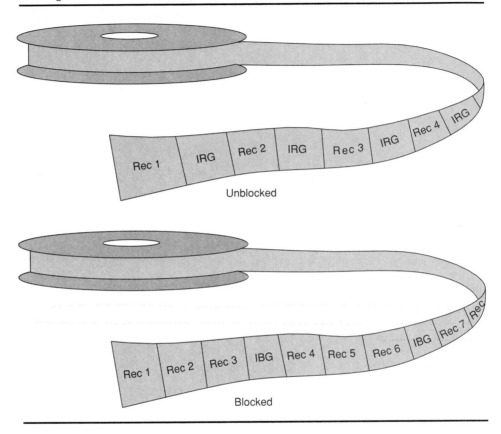

Unblocked

Blocked

block being read is stored within the main memory of the computer. As the records are processed, one logical record from the block is made available to the program each time a new record is needed.

Tape is very effective when used to hold sequential files for batch applications. It is also used to hold backup copies of files.

## Magnetic Strips — credit card strips.

**Magnetic strips** are short strips of magnetic tape affixed to items such as credit cards and badges. The magnetic strip can be read only by specialized readers. It is frequently encoded with identifying information such as your account number. Since a large amount of information may be encoded in a small space, some also contain historical information. Recently, **smart cards** have been developed. These smart cards resemble the magnetic strip cards but they also contain a microprocessor and memory. They are much more difficult to tamper with than the strip card and may even be programmed to self-destruct if the wrong password is entered several times.

## Magnetic Disk

Magnetic disks are platters whose surface is coated with a material that can record magnetic spots. The read/write head on a disk drive moves much as does the arm on a record player; therefore, disks can be **accessed** (moved from secondary storage to main memory) randomly, a great advantage over magnetic tape (which, as you just learned, must be accessed sequentially). Disk storage is the most common secondary storage media (Figure 3.15)

**Hard disks** are made of metal. Several hard disks can be grouped together and mounted on a spindle to form what is called a **disk pack.** The access arm of the disk drive has one read/write head per recording surface. The arm can be moved in and out across the surfaces of the disks, stopping a fixed number of times on its way. The recording pattern is a series of concentric circles on each platter's surface. Each circle is referred to as a **track** (Figure 3.16).

Since the access arm contains one read/write head for the surface of each disk in a pack, the user can read from or write information to several tracks without repositioning the access arm. These read/write heads ride just above the disk's surface, never actually touching it but, instead, riding over it on a thin cushion of air. Tracks that can be accessed by one positioning of the access arm are called a **cylinder** (Figure 3.17). Data is located by its **address**— that is, by the cylinder and the track carrying the data (both cylinder and track are identified by number). Once the address is known, the access arm can be moved to the proper cylinder and the read/write head serving this track switched on.

Some disks use **sectors** rather than tracks and cylinders. Each sector has a unique address. The operator locates information by moving the read/write head to the sector with the desired data. Hard disks are becoming cheaper and smaller than ever. Today, 765 million bytes can be stored on a 5¼-inch unformatted disk. Since smaller disks are less expensive to purchase and also less expensive to use, 14-inch disks are being replaced by 10½-inch, 5¼-inch, and even 3½-inch disks. Disk arrays are often used. An array consists of several hard disks operating in parallel as a unit. This unit or subsystem appears to the computer as being one larger device. Disk and tape drives are also now sometimes manufactured in one combined unit.

A 5¼-inch **floppy disk,** a platter made of a flexible plastic material, is stored within a cover or jacket to protect it. It is read through a slot in the cover. A second slot, when uncovered, permits the user to send output to (write on) the disk; when covered, it inhibits writing. Floppy disks are used on all types of computers but most frequently on microcomputers. Because floppies are

**FIGURE 3.15**
Large banks of disk drives are frequently seen at mainframe sites. (Courtesy UNISYS Corp.)

**FIGURE 3.16**

A track is the circle of information that can be read by one read/write head with one positioning of the access arm.

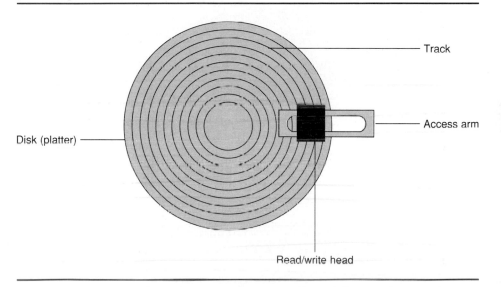

**FIGURE 3.17**

The access arm stops one time for each cylinder on a disk.

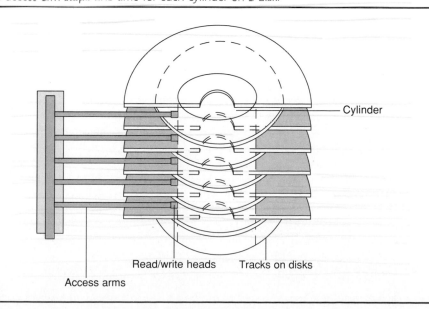

**FIGURE 3.18**
The disk drive reads a floppy disk through the slot in its protective cover.

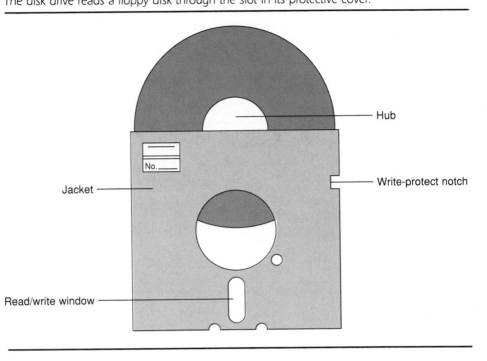

Hub

No.____

Write-protect notch

Jacket

Read/write window

easily removed, carried, and stored, careful handling is required to avoid damage (see Using Floppy Disks box and Figure 3.18). It should also be noted that, although the read/write head does not touch the surface of a hard disk while reading it, the head does actually ride on the surface of a floppy disk.

The 3½-inch floppy is becoming common. These smaller, more dense disks are encased in a rigid plastic container. The read/write window is covered by a metal curtain that slides back when the disk is within the drive. This improved disk housing makes the 3½-inch disks more rigid and less susceptible to damage than the 5¼-inch floppy disks.

The time involved in obtaining a record from a disk depends on three factors: (1) the time necessary to position the access arm at the right cylinder **(seek time)**, (2) the time necessary for the disk to revolve until the correct record is located under the read/write head **(rotational delay)**, and (3) the time necessary to read the record and place a copy in memory (transfer time).

## 3. Mass Storage Devices

**Mass storage devices** are designed to facilitate the storage of and direct access to very large volumes of information. A mass storage device is made up of

## Using Floppy Disks

1. Floppy disks, or **diskettes,** should be handled carefully, as you would handle a record or a tape cassette. A small scratch or dent can render part or all of the diskette useless.

2. Floppy disks should not be placed into or removed from the disk drive while the system is being turned on or off. They also should not be placed into or removed from the drive while read or write operations are actually taking place (usually indicated by a red light on the drive).

3. Keep diskettes away from magnetic fields because strong magnetic fields can erase stored data. Sources of magnetic fields include AC motors, magnets, TVs, radios, transformers, some telephone ringers, and library book detectors.

4. Handle the diskette by the jacket only. Do not touch any of the exposed surfaces, especially the read/write window. The surface is easily scratched. Trying to clean a diskette by wiping may also scratch the surface of the diskette.

5. Avoid contaminating the diskette. Food, grease, fingerprints, cigarette ashes, dust, and other particles may damage it.

6. Also avoid exposing the diskette to excessive heat. For example, do not leave diskettes in your car on warm days, or in direct sunlight.

7. To ensure that the diskette is kept as clean as possible, keep it in its protective jacket when it is not in use.

8. Do not write on the diskette jacket with anything that can cause a dent, such as a hard-tipped pen or a pencil. Use a felt-tipped pen, or write on a label first and then affix the label to the jacket.

9. Store your floppy disks in a vertical file, as you would store records. This protects their sides from pressure.

10. Back up your disks frequently. Back up disks while you are working, and make backup copies to store at another location of anything you want to save. Remember, disks can be damaged and data can be lost. Backing up provides a copy in case you lose the original.

data cells resembling a honeycomb (Figure 3.19). Within each data cell is a cartridge containing a long strip of magnetic recording material. When data is required, the cartridge containing the desired information is withdrawn by a mechanical arm.

The strip of recording material is removed from the cell and wrapped around a drumlike device, where it is read. This provides a combination of direct and

**FIGURE 3.19**
In this mass storage device, each data cell contains a cartridge with magnetic recording material. (Courtesy IBM Corporation)

sequential access: removing the data cell is direct, and reading the tapelike recording material is sequential. Because of the mechanical movements involved and the sequential steps in reading the data, the reading process is relatively slow.

## Optical Disks

**Optical disks** are a recent development in data storage technology (Figure 3.20). There are three types for computers. **CD–ROM** stands for compact disk-read only memory. They can be read but not changed. **WORM** stands for write once, read many. They can be written to once, read repeatedly, but not rewritten. Erasable CDs are the newest type. They can be rewritten repeatedly.

Lasers are used to burn the data into the disk, making a permanent storage record. The data is later read by shining a laser beam through the bottom of the disk and monitoring the amount of light reflected back.

The biggest disadvantage of CD–ROM technology is that the optical disks have not been reusable, so they could not be updated. Once the information was burned into the CD–ROM disk, it remained there. However, this same disadvantage makes them an excellent medium for archival (historical) storage, since

**FIGURE 3.20**
Durability and density characterize optical disks. (William Whitehurst/The Stock Market)

they have excellent durability. CD–ROM disks are frequently used in **interactive video systems,** systems that use a CD–ROM or videodisc under the control of a computer to create an interactive education program (see On the Job 1).

Write-once, read-many devices (affectionately known as WORMs) are very useful in those applications when data must not be erased and extensive data must be stored. For example, Pfizer stores graphs of the spectra of chemicals on their WORM disks. This enables them to write the information and store it on a shelf where it will remain available for several years. (To demonstrate their durability, one vendor served pastries on one 12-inch platter, wiped it clean, inserted it into the reader, and then read it.)

## ON THE JOB 1

Interactive Video at Harvard

The Harvard Law School Interactive Video Project, like other projects at several other law schools, produces video disks on the law. Not only can students learn what the law is, but the disks also illustrate other people practicing the necessary skills.

The action, whether a trial, arrest, and so on, is viewed on the video. The student than may insert him- or herself into the action by pressing a key on the computer keyboard. Once involved in the action, the student may interact with the action, such as by selecting one of a choice of actions. The action is then evaluated and the correct response indicated. The writing, designing, producing, programming, and distribution of the disks involve students, faculty, and staff from across the law school. Current topics and those in progress include negotiation skills, search and seizure law, legal ethics, and so on.

One of the newest developments in optical disk technology is an optical disk capable of being reused. Erasable optical disks will be used like the traditional floppy disks but with a much larger capacity. Where the floppy may store 1.4 MB, the optical disk can store in the hundreds of megabytes.

Laser technology is also being used to create cards that can hold a large volume of data (see On the Job 2).

## OUTPUT DEVICES

The tapes and disks discussed earlier are also used for output and to hold information until the computer reads it again. This section, however, discusses those devices that produce output intended for use by people: printers, plotters, visual display units, microfilm or microfiche, and voice output.

### Printers

**Printers** are probably the first machines that come to mind when one considers output devices. Retail sales of impact printers exceeded 1.4 million in 1987.

Printers are attached through a port, a physical connector through which a computer and an external device exchange information.

Printers are categorized by: (1) how much information can be written at a time, (2) how the characters are formed, or (3) how the image is transferred to the paper.

## ON THE JOB 2

### Medical History on a "Credit Card"

Imagine 2 million bytes of storage in your wallet or credit card case! Drexler Technology Corporation has recently developed a card that can hold that much data—the Drexler LaserCard. Imagine the applications. Prepaid debit purchases, medical records, electronic publishing, and access authorization are only a few. Blue Cross/Blue Shield of Maryland has developed a system, the Life Card System, to improve the quality of health care by using the laser card. With up to the equivalent of 800 typewritten pages of your medical history on a single card, admittance to emergency facilities is speeded up, diagnosis is made more accurate, and medications are prescribed more appropriately. In an emergency, when the patient is unable to respond, the card can speak for the patient, perhaps even saving a life.

The slowest and least expensive printers usually print only one character at a time, moving the print element each time a character is printed, just as a typewriter does. More often, a printer will have many print elements and print an entire line at once. Depending on the model, this line will usually consist of 80, 120, 132, or 144 characters. The highest-speed printers, such as the laser ones, may print an entire page at a time or even print front and back.

*daisy wheel - letters*
*dot matrix - dots*

The printing element either may print solid characters or produce a series of dots to form the character. The **daisy wheel** is a printing element that produces solid characters (Figure 3.21). It produces a high-quality character similar to that of a typewriter. The type of print character you have seen in many mass mailings uses a **dot matrix** construction. The matrix is a grid of pins (Figure 3.22); activating the appropriate pins forms the character.

To understand how the matrix construction works, visualize the scoreboard from the last football or basketball game you saw. The board probably consisted of a grid or matrix of lightbulbs. The score was indicated by turning on certain bulbs while leaving others off. The lighted bulbs formed the number of the score. Similarly, the activated pins of the dot matrix form the character to be printed. The quality is based on the density of the pins; the closer the pins, the more solid the character appears.

Printers also use different mechanical methods to imprint the characters. **Impact printers** use a striking motion to form characters. In this case, the printing element strikes an inked ribbon, and the ink is transferred to the paper.

Impact printers include the daisy wheel and dot matrix discussed earlier. Since the daisy wheel—like a typewriter—prints a solid character, it produces what is called **letter-quality** type. The mechanical movement of the wheel, however, causes it to print slowly, at about 55 characters per second (cps).

**FIGURE 3.21**
The daisy wheel produces a typewriter-quality print character.

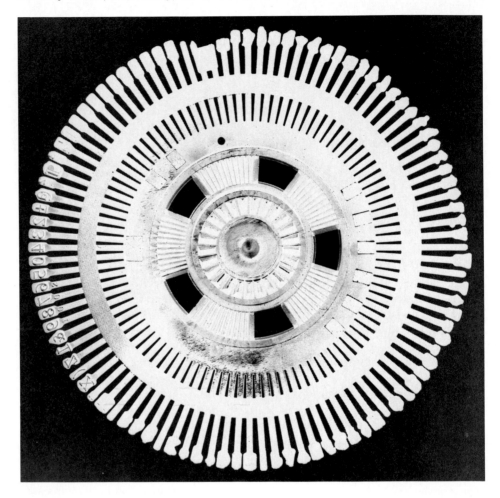

As you saw in Figure 3.22, the quality of dot matrix print depends on the density of the dots. In draft mode, dot matrix printers print about 200 to 400 cps. Slowing down for overstrikes, a **near letter quality (NLQ)** print is produced at only about 40 to 80 cps.

Nonimpact printers form characters without striking the paper. They include inkjet, electrothermal, electrostatic, and laser printers. As a class, they are quieter and faster than impact but cannot, of course, produce multiple carbon copies.

The print head of an **inkjet printer** contains tiny nozzles through which ink is sprayed onto the paper—an effect similar to dot matrix characters. Because

**FIGURE 3.22**
The quality of a dot matrix character can be varied by changing the density of the dots.

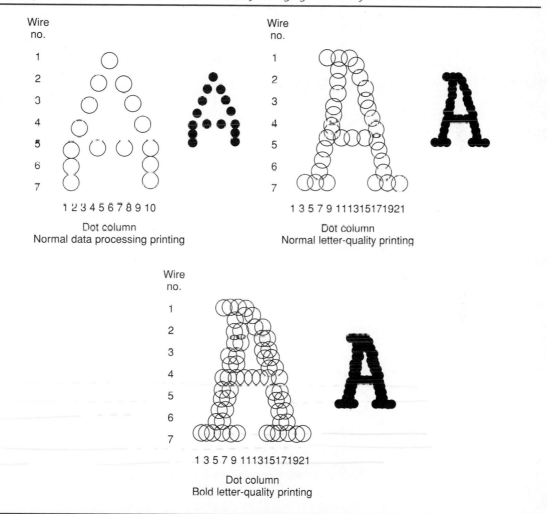

multiple colors of ink can be used at the same time and sprayed through adjacent nozzles, inkjet printers are capable of producing high-quality output in color.

**Electrothermal printers** use specially coated paper. The paper's chemical coating changes colors when heat is applied. The characters are burned into the paper.

**Electrostatic printers** use an electrical charge to form the characters. When the paper is passed through a solution of ink particles of the opposite charge, the particles are attracted to the oppositely charged portions of paper, thus forming the characters.

**Laser printers** create the print image by having a laser beam scan an electrically charged drum. Ink or toner with the opposite charge sticks to the drum and is then transferred to paper by pressure and heat.

Originally, laser printers were costly and were used only for mini and mainframe computer applications in which speed and quality were critical. The production of smaller, lower-cost laser printers has made them popular on microcomputers. They are useful for desktop publishing since they offer near-typeset quality for text and can mix type styles, sizes, and graphic images on the same page. Their high speed is possible because they contain their own built-in microprocessor and memory. As desktop publishing becomes more popular and laser printer prices continue to decrease, sales continue to rise.

## Plotters

**Plotters** are designed to produce graphic output by moving a stylus across the surface of the paper, as directed by the computer program (Figure 3.23). Each point of the surface is assigned coordinates, as in a graph, and the stylus is directed to move from point to point according to the coordinates.

**FIGURE 3.23**
Plotters produce maps, graphs, charts, and other drawings, often in multiple colors. (John Reis/The Stock Market)

Plotters are of two basic types. In the first, usually called **flatbed,** only the pen moves. In the other, usually called **drum,** both the pen and the paper move. Because of the mechanical movements involved, plotters are usually low-speed devices.

## Microfilm and Microfiche

**Microfilm** or **microfiche** may be used as an alternative to paper output (Figure 3.24). Both increase the amount of material that can be stored by decreasing the volume of the material to be stored.

Both microfilm and microfiche store reduced (in size) images on photographic film. In the case of microfilm, the film is in long rolls, whereas for microfiche, it is in small sheets, usually 4 by 6 inches. Just one of these small sheets can hold more than 250 pages of information. The images may be photographically copied from existing paper output or created from output that was first written to tape and then mounted on a unit that displays each image on a screen. The images are then reproduced on film. Because they greatly reduce storage area, microfilm and microfiche are widely used for archival storage by organizations that must store huge volumes of output.

**FIGURE 3.24**

Using microfilm and microfiche has significantly decreased the cost of storing printed material. However, a special machine is required to read microfilm and microfiche. (Fred Bodin)

## Voice Output

**Voice output** is produced by one of two methods. In the first, words, syllables, or sounds are actually spoken, digitized, stored, and then selected to form the messages needed. With this method, usually only a limited amount of output is produced, since so much storage is required to hold all the necessary sounds.

The second method uses **voice synthesis,** the computer reproduction of the human voice. A dictionary of sound is created, and then sounds are selected from this dictionary to form the message. Little storage space is required, since relatively few phonemes (basic sound units that make up our language) are used to form most words.

Voice output is also being used as a speaking aid for disabled persons. It may be used to "read" material displayed on the CRT screen to the visually limited operator or used to produce speech for those unable to speak for themselves. To make a computer talk, two things are required: (1) a program that is resident in memory, which intercepts text and sends it to the synthesizer, and (2) the synthesizer itself, which produces the sound.

Text may be entered and interpreted using the text reading program. Alternately, those who cannot speak may, instead of entering text, key in a code representing a given sound. Additional sounds may be added to form words or phrases. Finally, the entire message may be played back as a substitute for the person's speech.

## SUMMARY

Each large and diverse group of peripheral devices was developed to meet the specific needs of various data processing shops. For example, printers are used to produce the reports that business requires; optical disks can hold similar information in a form more useful for archival storage; microfiche is still another method of storing information compactly and durably.

The trend has been toward improving the accuracy and timeliness of information by gathering data as close to the source as possible. This has led to distribution of data-gathering terminals and the development of equipment that could process OCR, microfiche, MICR, and voice input.

The variety of devices meets a variety of needs. As business requirements grow and change, the devices associated with data processing will also continue to change. Sales of the traditional storage devices remain strong. In 1987, over 13 million floppy disks were sold, as well as almost 6 million rigid disks and about 1 million tape drives.

Alternative storage technologies such as optical disks seem to have the most applications where there is limited on-line access to massive quantities of information. Sales of optical disks, although still slow, are increasing.

# ▓ VOCABULARY

## EXERCISES

1.  What is optical recognition? Name and describe its subgroups.
2.  Why is secondary storage necessary? Compare and contrast tape and disk as secondary storage media.
3.  What is a mass storage device?
4.  Is the technology easier for voice input or voice output? Why?
5.  What is the difference between a dumb and an intelligent terminal?
6.  What is meant by tape density? How is it measured?
7.  What is an IBG? a track? a sector? a cylinder?
8.  What is the name of a storage media in which data is burned in by laser?
9.  Differentiate between a daisy wheel and a dot matrix printer.
10. What technologies are frequently used as an alternative to paper output to reduce storage requirements?
11. What is meant by collecting data "at the source"? What are the advantages?

## PROJECTS

1.  You have recently opened a small construction company. You have purchased a small computer for payroll, inventory control, job costing, and so on. You also need to estimate jobs at the sites where you will be working. What types of peripheral devices might you get? Why?
2.  Describe an application for each of the following devices. Why is it an appropriate choice?
    a.  Optical disk.
    b.  Bar code reader.
    c.  Tape.
    d.  Hard disk.
    e.  OCR.
    f.  Voice.

3. During the next week, keep a log of all contacts with computerized input and output (for example, you receive a mass mailing or use a VDT or an automatic teller machine). If you had a strong feeling about the encounter, either positive or negative, record it.

4. Visit your computer lab. Learn to use your computers and some of the operating system commands. Initialize a disk to use later.

5. Make a copy for later use of the software provided with this text.

# 4

# Software

## CHAPTER OBJECTIVES

*After completing this chapter, you will be able to:*

1.  Explain what software is.
2.  Discuss custom programming and why it is necessary.
3.  Describe several popular types of applications software: electronic spreadsheets, word processing programs, and integrated software.
4.  Explain what is meant by high- and low-level languages.
5.  Discuss why so many languages exist and describe several of them.
6.  Explain the purpose of query languages.
7.  Describe what is meant by natural languages.

## OVERVIEW

The operating system software makes using a computer easier. Utility programs provide such needed services as sorting and copying of files (see On the Job 1). What, then, is the purpose of other **applications software,** and how is it written?

The two basic types of applications software are purchased packages and custom-written software. Most companies perform such tasks as inventory and payroll. Thus, software houses write and sell systems that perform these functions; these are referred to as **purchased software packages.** Other programs are written to meet the highly specialized needs of a particular company. These systems of programs, for use in only one shop, are referred to as **custom software** or **custom programs.** (The implications of choosing between purchased and custom software are further discussed in Chapter 7, The Systems Approach.)

## TWO KINDS OF SOFTWARE

### Purchased Software

Purchased software is available for all types and sizes of computers: mainframes, minicomputers, and microcomputers. It can be bought ready to run from a retail store or other software vendors.

Some purchased software is designed for a very specific use (see On the Job 2). For example, a contractor who has a microcomputer in her office might purchase a package to estimate job costs and produce the related reports. This software performs only one function—in this example, cost estimates. Other purchased software is general purpose and designed for many uses. A word processing program, for example, can produce letters for a doctor, reports for a lawyer, or homework for a young child. It can be used to write contracts

## ON THE JOB 1

Caching Software

Cache memory, described in Chapter 3, has the advantage of speed; but purchasing this memory that can run at the speed of semiconductors is very expensive. For some applications, it is possible to significantly improve performance speed using software rather than hardware.

Software caches are utility programs that take advantage of the fact that the program frequently asks for code or instructions that have been used earlier.

These cache utility programs set aside a part of RAM memory to store the most recently used data and instructions. Whenever the program requests data or code, this area is checked first. If the data or code are present, whatever is needed is transferred at electronic speeds without requiring any mechanical movements from the disk or tape drives. If the information is not in this area, it is read from the disk as usual.

Software caches are most effective with programs such as sorts that perform repetitive operations requiring extensive disk access.

and commercials or sermons and scripts; this book was written using a word processing program.

Three popular types of purchased software are electronic spreadsheets, word processing programs, and database programs. Desktop publishing and graphics packages are also becoming very popular. An integrated software package combines two or more distinct applications together. The five most common applications to be combined in an integrated package are spreadsheets, word processing programs, database management, graphics, and communications programs. All but database management are discussed in this chapter; database management programs are discussed in Chapter 10.

### Electronic Spreadsheets

Have you ever tried to find the distance between two cities by reading the distance chart on a map? For example, to find how far New York City is from Boston, you might first look down the row of city names until you found "New York." You would probably keep your finger there to mark the place while you moved your other hand across the columns to "Boston." You would then look for the distance between them at the intersection of the row and column.

## ON THE JOB 2

*Electronic Design*

Fieldcrest Mills, Inc., in Eden, North Carolina, has cut the design cycle on their oriental-patterned Karastan rugs from months to days by using an electronic imaging system.

In the past, one-of-a-kind samples of new designs were made by hand—a slow and costly process. Designers would trace the rugs, superimpose a grid to correlate with the tufts of yarn, and handpaint the design. Changing color or design was often cost-prohibitive. Developing and introducing a rug collection might take three to four years.

The new system uses a digital imaging camera to scan soft goods such as a one-of-a-kind, handmade oriental rug. The pattern is translated into data that can be displayed at CAD (computer-aided design) workstations. At the workstation, artists may choose to alter the design—to change pattern or color or to mix several designs to create a new pattern. Design changes are easily made; changes in color require only writing new color codes on the magnetic tape and rerunning them. A high-speed, color inkjet plotter can then reproduce hard-copy samples in minutes. Additionally, the system can calculate the complexity of "setting" the design to determine an appropriate pay rate. It can also automatically calculate the yarn requirements, aiding in inventory control.

The problem of long concept-to-production time periods has been largely eliminated; it is now possible to introduce an entire collection within a season.

**Electronic spreadsheet** programs, sometimes just referred to as **spreadsheets,** divide the computer screen into a series of rows and columns much as the distance chart does. The user can manipulate the data within these rows and columns in any way desired by creating formulas. Since computer memory is so much larger than the CRT screen, the amount of data stored is much greater than can be seen at any one time. The operator can scroll up and down the data or shift from side to side to review all of it. The screen is considered a window through which to view the data.

Suppose a vendor is trying to decide whether to purchase several items for resale. He or she must know the cost of each item, as well as the anticipated selling price. Figure 4.1 shows a spreadsheet the vendor created. A column represents each item, and each row represents a part of the cost: shipping,

**FIGURE 4.1**

A spreadsheet can hold much more data than is shown here on the screen. To see all the data, the user has only to scroll up or down the screen, shift from side to side, or convert the report to hard copy via the printer.

```
 H7:                                                                    SHEET
       ┌────A────────B────────C────────D────────E────────F────────G────────H────┐
   1                      ITEM 1   ITEM 2   ITEM 3   ITEM 4   ITEM 5
   2
   3    RAW MATERIAL        153      175      243      197      113
   4    SHIPPING             10       10       10       10       10
   5    OVERHEAD          84.15    96.25   133.65   108.35    62.15
   6
   7    TOTAL COST       247.15   281.25   386.65   315.35   185.15
   8
   9
  10
  11
  12
  13
  14
  15
  16
  17
  18
  19
  20
       └──────────────────────────────────────────────────────────── MAIN ─┘
  01-Jan-90   12:13 AM                                          Cap
```

overhead, and so on. In this example the shipping charge for each item is $10.00; the overhead, 55 percent of the cost.

The data is stored electronically. A formula that will calculate the total cost is created and stored. The spreadsheet program then calculates the total cost from the stored data using this formula. If overhead is changed to 70 percent of the cost or the shipping charge is decreased to $7.85, the revised total cost can be rapidly recalculated.

### Word Processing Programs

Have you ever had to turn in a report with no spelling or typographical errors? Have you ever finished typing, only to find that you had left out a paragraph or that you should have double-spaced rather than single-spaced? Did you ever need to write almost identical letters to several people? **Word processing** programs make these tasks easy, even for those of us who do not type well.

A word processing program is designed to let the user enter text, store it electronically, change the text easily, print it in the form of letters and reports, and then file it away for future use. In addition, most word processing packages include a spelling checker, a grammar checker, and a thesaurus. Word processing programs are some of the most popular and productive software available.

For example, a clerk might create a letter, making the errors found in Figure 4.2(a). After writing the letter, the clerk uses a spelling checker program and finds the mistakes that are shaded in Figure 4.2(b). Using a word processing program makes correction easy, as shown in Figure 4.2(c). The clerk then decides that the letter would look better if the margins were changed. This is also done quickly using word processing. All changes were made and viewed without putting the letter on paper. When it appeared correct, it was printed and the text stored electronically. If the letter or a similar one were needed again, it would be recalled, modified, printed, and mailed.

### Integrated Software

Electronic spreadsheet programs and word processing programs each perform one function. Spreadsheets manipulate grids of data; word processing programs manipulate text.

However, suppose you need to create a spreadsheet, manipulate data to produce a result, graph that result, and then provide textual information about the graph. **Integrated software** such as Symphony, AppleWorks, and Microsoft Works can do all this.

In Figure 4.3, a store manager has created a spreadsheet showing his costs by product *(a)*. He then uses the spreadsheet feature to calculate total costs *(b)*. Since he wishes to present the figures at a department managers' meeting, he prints a copy of the spreadsheet. Then, because he is using an integrated package, he passes the data from the spreadsheet to the graphics portion of the package. He then uses the graphics portion to convert the numerical information found in the total column of the spreadsheet into a line chart *(c)*.

### Desktop Publishing

A rapidly growing integrated application is **desktop publishing** (Figure 4.4). Desktop publishing software couples a computer with a graphics monitor to enable the user to create text, produce graphics, and assemble the text and illustrations into page formats. Once assembled, the pages are printed on a laser printer and are camera ready for the printer.

The user begins by creating text in a word processing format. This text is formatted in one of a wide variety of typefaces or fonts. The document is then assembled using page makeup software that lets the user position text and illustrations. This format may be reviewed and revised as necessary on the screen before printing. Once the final version of the document is assembled, it is printed on a laser printer, producing a professional-quality publication.

**FIGURE 4.2**

Example of a spelling checker to create a letter: *(a)* first drafts of letters often contain errors; *(b)* and *(c)* with a spelling checker, finding and correcting the errors is easy.

December 31, 1990

Ms. A. E. Johnson
Customer Relations Manager
XYZ Corporation
175 Oakdale Drive
Tightsqueeze, VA 24567

Dear Ms. Johnson:

The package of hazamashabbles arrived late
yesterday. Not only were they two weeks late,
the bax arrived damaged. When I opened it, I
found that only half of the order had been
shipped, and those items were both defective
and the wrong color.

Please cancel all future shipments against our
outstanding order effectively immediately. We
will discuss future shipments when this fiscoe
is settled.

Sincerely,

(a)

December 31, 1990

Ms. A. E. Johnson
Customer Relations Manager
XYZ Corporation
175 Oakdale Drive
Tightsqueeze, VA 24567

Dear Ms. Johnson:

The package of hazamashabbles arrived late
yesterday. Not only were they two weeks late,
the bax arrived damaged. When I opened it, I
found that only half of the order had been
shipped, and those items were both defective
and the wrong color.

Please cancel all future shipments against our
outstanding order effectively immediately. We
will discuss future shipments when this fiscoe
is settled.

Sincerely,

(b)

December 31, 1990

Ms. A. E. Johnson
Customer Relations Manager
XYZ Corporation
175 Oakdale Drive
Tightsqueeze, VA 24567

Dear Ms. Johnson:

The package of hazamashabbles arrived late
yesterday. Not only were they two weeks late,
the box arrived damaged. When I opened it, I
found that only half of the order had been
shipped, and those items were both defective
and the wrong color.

Please cancel all future shipments against our
outstanding order effectively immediately. We
will discuss future shipments when this fiasco
is settled.

Sincerely,

(c)

**FIGURE 4.3**

Example of integrated software: *(a)* individual costs are entered into the spreadsheet; *(b)* after formulas are entered, values are calculated using a spreadsheet program;

```
G6:  3789                                                      LABEL
     ┌───A────────B────────C────────D────────E────────F────────G────────H──┐
  1  │        JANUARY FEBRUARY MARCH   APRIL     MAY    JUNE                 │
  2  │ PRODUCT 1   5000    8403    7338    1564    8932    7322              │
  3  │ PRODUCT 2   2389    7895    3467    2978    3064    4222              │
  4  │ PRODUCT 3   3986    1906    4097    2980    1987    3976              │
  5  │ PRODUCT 4   2908    3895    2906    3089    2347    2096              │
  6  │ PRODUCT 5   1976    2047    3056    5067    4568    3789              │
  7  │                                                                      │
  8  │                                                                      │
  9  │                                                                      │
 10  │                                                                      │
 11  │                                                                      │
 12  │                                                                      │
 13  │                                                                      │
 14  │                                                                      │
 15  │                                                                      │
 16  │                                                                      │
 17  │                                                                      │
 18  │                                                                      │
 19  │                                                                      │
 20  │                                                              MAIN ─┘
     └
  30-Jun-90   12:17 AM                                  Cap
```

(a)

```
A7:                                                           SHEET
     ┌───A────────B────────C────────D────────E────────F────────G────────H──┐
  1  │        JANUARY FEBRUARY MARCH   APRIL     MAY    JUNE                 │
  2  │ PRODUCT 1   5000    8403    7338    1564    8932    7322    38559     │
  3  │ PRODUCT 2   2389    7895    3467    2978    3064    4222    24015     │
  4  │ PRODUCT 3   3986    1906    4097    2980    1987    3976    18932     │
  5  │ PRODUCT 4   2908    3895    2906    3089    2347    2096    17241     │
  6  │ PRODUCT 5   1976    2047    3056    5067    4568    3789    20503     │
  7  │            16259   24146   20864   15678   20898   21405   119250    │
  8  │                                                                      │
  9  │                                                                      │
 10  │                                                                      │
 11  │                                                                      │
 12  │                                                                      │
 13  │                                                                      │
 14  │                                                                      │
 15  │                                                                      │
 16  │                                                                      │
 17  │                                                                      │
 18  │                                                                      │
 19  │                                                                      │
 20  │                                                              MAIN ─┘
     └
  30-Jun-90   12:26 AM                                  Cap
```

(b)

*(continued on next page)*

**FIGURE 4.3** *(concluded)*

*(c)* with an integrated package, values can be passed from one portion of the package to another. In this instance, the values found in the spreadsheet are converted to a graph by the graphics portion.

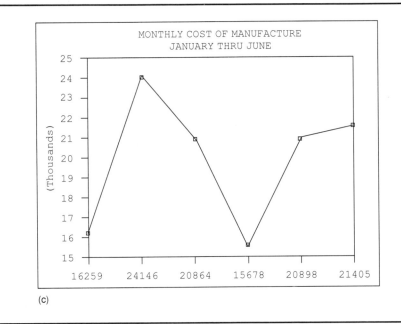

(c)

Laser printers produce excellent quality print but desktop laser printers do not produce high-quality shaded drawings or photographs. Therefore, many typesetters can now accept the formatted output from the more popular desktop publishing programs for use on their typesetting systems.

## Custom Software

Purchased software provides many necessary services, but often a user has needs so specialized that no software exists to meet them. Other users have needs that are partly met by purchased software but, to meet their needs fully, the software must undergo extensive modifications. These requirements necessitate custom programming.

Custom programs are written to meet the user's specific needs. They may be written by the user, by programmers working for the user's company, or by outside **consultants** who provide custom programming services.

**FIGURE 4.4**
With desktop publishing software and the right microcomputer and laser printer, the user can combine text and graphics in a professional-looking document. (Fred Bodin)

## Advantages and Disadvantages of Purchased Software and Custom Software

The choice is up to the user: to write or to purchase the needed software. Several factors should be considered before deciding.

Purchased software has several advantages. Since the programs and documentation are already written, the buyer knows exactly what she is getting before the purchase is made. The development costs are spread over many purchasers, making it significantly less expensive to buy. Since there are many users, the prospective purchaser may be able to talk to others now using the software. These users may be willing to describe their success or lack of it in using the purchased package. Once purchased, the software can be used immediately or be installed in a minimal amount of time. Any problems with an early version of the software are usually quickly discovered and corrected by the vendor.

Improvements to the software are also produced by the vendor and are often made available to original purchasers at a reduced cost.

The primary disadvantage of purchased software is that it may not exactly meet the needs of the buyer. Even if one package meets most of the needs, the buyer may not legally be able to modify it; if he or she can modify it, what will happen when the vendor issues a new release of the software? The modifications will require that the buyer either not use the new release or that it be modified also. If problems are found in the version originally purchased, modifications will make it more difficult to correct them.

The primary advantage of custom software is that the user can have exactly what he or she wants; no compromises must be made. There are times when an application is unique or when a process is so secret that the user cannot use any existing software or is unwilling to share information on what the software must do with those outside the organization. These times (which are much more rare than many users believe) make writing custom software essential.

The disadvantages of writing custom software are numerous. It takes time to write. Once written, it may not do the job. The cost of developing it is difficult to estimate but always higher than that of purchased software.

## LEVELS OF LANGUAGE

Programs may be written in any one of many languages. These languages may closely resemble the machine's language or be more similar to the programmer's language. Languages are classified by their level (how similar to the machine's language are they?) and by their purpose (are they designed for business or for engineering applications? do they create reports easily or allow a nonprogrammer to obtain information easily from a file?). Within the various levels and types of languages, many individual languages exist.

Regardless of the language used, the programmer converts the solution developed in the design phase to a computer program.

### Low-Level Languages

People frequently refer to computer languages as belonging to some level. They say that 4GLs are very-high-level languages, that COBOL and Pascal are high-level languages, whereas assembly languages are low level. Just what is meant by level? **Low-level languages** are either at the machine's level or close to it. Machine language is the language understood by the computer, whereas assembly languages, also low level, are more Englishlike but still similar to the machine's language.

## Machine

A computer understands machine language without any translation. Since machine language programs are written in the machine's language, they are unique to the machine for which they are written. This means that a machine language program written for the IBM PC will not run on a Wang or an Apple; nor will one written for the Apple run on a Commodore or on any computer other than the Apple.

Machine language programs are written in **binary code,** with each instruction at a detailed level. Programmers rarely use it today, since writing in binary code is so slow, awkward, and prone to error. Programmers who wrote in machine language soon developed a shorthand way of representing binary code. They began to code in either **octal code** or **hexadecimal code** (see Figure 4.5 and Appendix B, Data Representation), later translating it back into binary code.

## Assembly

Programmers writing in machine language soon realized that it would be easier to let the computer perform the conversion to binary code. This meant that

**FIGURE 4.5**

Machine language is actually written in binary (top), but hexadecimal representation (bottom) makes the machine language program easier to read. Even so, these instructions to perform an addition are not easily understood.

```
                 In Binary

1100  0100  0010  0010  1111  0000  0011  0000  0100  0001  1000  0011
1111  1010  0010  0000  1111  0000  0011  0000  1110  0000  0001  0110
1111  0100  0010  0001  0100  0001  1011  0011  1111  0000  0011  0001
```

```
          Hex Representation

    C422F0304183
    FA20F030E016
    F42141B3F031
```

the computer had to translate the program before running it. For example, if MOVE was represented by 0011 0111 in binary code, the programmer codes 37 in hexadecimal code. The translator program than interprets it as 0011 0111 in binary code. A second development was the addition of mnemonic instructions or **symbolic code,** a set of easily remembered abbreviations resembling the words they represent. This level of language is referred to as *assembly language*. It is still unique to the machine and detailed, but with mnemonics it is much more understandable to the programmer (Figure 4.6).

**FIGURE 4.6**
This assembly language program simply moves two fields that were described as constants to the print line. Because it is not very similar to English, you might not have realized what a simple program it is.

```
WANG VS INTEGRATED EDITOR - VERSION  6.09.16        11:00 06/30/90      PAGE       1
INPUT FILE IS S23ASMB1 IN LIBRARY STDSOURC ON VOLUME CCPACK

MENU       CODE                             BEGINNING OF NON-MODIFIABLE SECT.       000100
           BALR      13,0                   ESTABLISHES 13 AS THE BASE REGISTER     000200
           USING     *,13                   PLACES THE ADDRESS OF THE FIRST      C  000300
                                            INSTRUCTION IN REGISTER 13              000400
           LR        3,14                   SAVES REGISTER 3 IN REG 14              000500
           AL        3,=R(MOD)              SAVES THE ADDRESS OF THE MODIFIABLE     000600
           USING     MOD,3                  SECTION IN REG 3.                       000700
           OPEN      UFB=UFBBEGIN           OPENS THE PRINT FILE                    000800
           MVC       UFBRECAREA,XYZ         MOVES XYZ TO THE REC AREA FOR PRINT     000900
CLEAR      MVC       CUTAREA,SPACES         CLEARS THE PRINTLINE TO SPACES          001000
           MVC       LNAME,LN               MOVES LN TO LNAME                       001100
           MVC       SALOUT,SOT             MOVES SOT TO SALOUT                     001200
           WRITE     UFB=UFBBEGIN           WRITES THE PRINTLINE                    001300
EOF        CLOSE     UFB=UFBBEGIN           CLOSES THE PRINTFILE                    001400
RETURN     RETURN    UNLINK,CODE=(0)        RETURNS CONTROL TO THE OPERATING     C  001500
                                            SYSTEM                                  001600
MOD        STATIC                           BEGINS THE MODIFIABLE SECTION           001700
           PRINT     NOGEN                  SUPRESSES THE PRINTING OF GENERATED  C  001800
                                            INSTRUCTIONS                            001900
XYZ        DC        A(OUTAREA)                                                     002000
LN         DC        CL15"JOE JONES"                                                002100
SOT        DC        CL5"12500"                                                     002200
           UFB       NODSECT                USER FILE BLOCK INFORMATION             002300
           ORG       UFBBEGIN                                                       002400
           UFBGEN    PRNAME=OUTFILE,DEVCLASS=PRT,MODE=OUT,FORG=CONSEC            C  002500
                     RECAREA=OUTAREA,RECSIZE=134                                    002600
SPACES     DC        CL1" "                                                         002700
OUTAREA    DS        OCL134                                                         002800
           DS        CL2                                                            002900
LNAME      DS        CL15                                                           003000
           DS        CL20                                                           003100
SALOUT     DS        CL5                                                            003200
           DS        CL92                                                           003300
           END                                                                     003400
```

*[handwritten: 6]*

## High-Level Languages *[handwritten: ① portable ② English-Like]*

Assembly language programs cannot be run by a computer without being translated by an assembler. However, as you can see from Figure 4.6, they are still not very meaningful to the programmer. They also are not portable; an assembly language program written for one computer will not run on another computer that is not of the same family.

These two disadvantages are eliminated in **high-level languages.** First, high-level languages are portable; they can be moved from one machine to another. Second, high-level languages are much more Englishlike, although they have their own syntax and vocabulary. People understand programs written in high-level languages more easily, but these programs still must be translated back into machine language for the computer to understand them. The translation is done by programs called *compilers* or *interpreters* (see Chapter 2). Many compilers are available; each translates the program into a different machine language, making it possible to run the same program on different machines. Compilers also issue **diagnostics,** error messages and other information that can help programmers find mistakes in their programs. *[handwritten: diagnostic-error messages.]*

High-level languages include FORTRAN, COBOL, BASIC, Pascal, C, and others, including report generators such as RPG. Closely related are query and natural languages. Many languages exist because each was designed to meet specific needs. FORTRAN was designed for scientific and mathematical applications; COBOL and RPG for businesss; Pascal, BASIC, and PL/1 for both scientific and business purposes. Query languages were intended to enable nonprogrammers to access data.

### *[handwritten: Sci]* FORTRAN *[handwritten: — math]*

**FORTRAN,** standing for FORmula TRANslator, was developed in 1955 for use by scientists, mathematicians, and engineers. Since it was designed for scientific applications, it is easy to write formulas (Figure 4.7) and to work with very large or very small numbers in FORTRAN. Its main disadvantage is that it is not designed to edit alphanumeric output easily. Most scientists and mathematicians are more interested in obtaining the correct solution than in elaborately editing their output. FORTRAN is still widely used, but many jobs once done in FORTRAN now may be written in BASIC or Pascal since both BASIC and Pascal were designed for scientific as well as business applications.

### *[handwritten: bus]* COBOL *[handwritten: — business]*

**COBOL,** standing for COmmon Business Oriented Language, was developed in 1959 by a group of people, including representatives from government agencies, education, and computer manufacturers. An influential member of this committee at its inception and for many years was Grace Hopper, an outstanding pioneer in computer languages. COBOL is similar to English and is designed for business applications (Figure 4.8).

**Figure 4.7**

Remember the formula about the relationship of the sides of a right triangle? Can you tell what this FORTRAN program is looking for?

```
        A = 3.0
        B = 4.0
        C = 0.0
        C = SQRT (A**2 + B**2)
        WRITE (G, 10)
   10   FORMAT (F5.3)
        STOP
        END
```

**FIGURE 4.8**

This section of a COBOL program produces a simple name and address listing. Can you read it more easily than the programs shown in Figures 4.5 and 4.6? Many programmers find COBOL easy to read but very slow to write because it is so wordy. (Its very wordiness limits the amount of COBOL program shown here; this is only one small section of the procedure division.)

```
WANG  VS  ANS COBOL COMPILER VO3.08.04

   00055   008010        MOVE CNT TO TOT-REC.
   00056   008020        MOVE "TOTAL RECORDS" TO MESSAGE.
   00057   008030        MOVE 2 TO VAR.
   00058   008040        PERFORM 900-WRITE-REC.
   00059   008100        CLOSE FILE-IN, FILE-OUT.
   00060   008200        STOP RUN.
   00061   009800   300-PROCESS.
   00062   009900        MOVE NAMEE TO 0-NAMEE.
   00063   011900        MOVE 2 TO VAR.
   00064   012000        PERFORM 900-WRITE-REC.
   00065   012010        MOVE STREET TO 0-NAMEE.
   00066   012020        MOVE 1 TO VAR.
   00067   012030        PERFORM 900-WRITE-REC.
   00068   012040        MOVE CITY TO PART-1.
   00069   012041        MOVE STATE TO PART-2.
   00070   012042        MOVE ZIP TO 0-ZIP.
   00071   012051        MOVE 1 TO VAR.
   00072   012055        PERFORM 900-WRITE-REC.
   00073   012060        ADD 1 TO CNT.
   00074   012100        READ FILE-IN AT END MOVE "NO" TO MORE-REC.
   00075   012200   900-WRITE-REC.
   00076   012300        WRITE REC-OUT AFTER ADVANCING VAR LINES.
   00077   012400        MOVE SPACES TO REC-OUT.
```

```
HARRY SMITH
5 HIGH POINT ROAD
ANDOVER          MA   01862

BARBARA LINEWEAVER
RT 1 BOX 17
BLAIRS           NC   25733

FREDERICK KLEINER
37 FOX HALL ROAD
PORTSMOUTH       NH   00378

TOTAL RECORDS                    3
```

Each COBOL program is divided into four sections called *divisions:* the identification, environment, data, and procedure divisions. The *identification division* names the program and author and provides other identifying information. The *environment division* describes the environment in which the program is to run. The *data division* describes the data used in and created by the program, and the *procedure division* describes how the data is to be manipulated.

Because COBOL programs resemble English, nonprogrammers can easily understand them. Another advantage is that COBOL provides the extensive editing capabilities required by business. The primary disadvantage with COBOL is that it is extremely wordy.

The newest release, COBOL85, is now out, and compilers for it are being validated by the National Bureau of Standards.

### RPG — business reports

**RPG,** or Report Program Generator, was developed by IBM in 1964. It was designed to generate business reports quickly and easily. Since then, it has been revised several times to enhance its capabilities. Current versions are called *RPG II* and *RPG III*. RPG II relies on a fixed logic cycle; that is, the RPG program is expected to read records, process them, and output the results. The programmer supplies the information that customizes this processing: which records are to be read, how they are to be processed, and what form the output is to take. This information is provided by filling in the forms that RPG requires. On each form, certain entries in particular columns cause RPG to perform specific functions (Figure 4.9). Eventually, limitations were discovered in following a fixed logic cycle and so instructions such as to perform subroutines were added.

RPG III, the newest version, is an **interactive language** that permits the user and computer to communicate conversationally. Because this language is not locked into the fixed logic cycle, the programmer has more freedom in describing how data is to be processed.

Business reports can be created rapidly in either RPG II or RPG III. The primary disadvantage is that writing programs that require unusual logic may be difficult in RPG II because the fixed logic cycle must be overridden. A second disadvantage is that neither RPG II nor RPG III is designed for mathematical and scientific applications; the user cannot handle very large numbers or code formulas easily.

### BASIC — beginners, or students

**BASIC,** standing for Beginners All-Purpose Symbolic Instruction Code, was developed for use by students. It also is designed to be used interactively on microcomputers, minicomputers, and mainframes. Novice programmers can easily read and write BASIC (Figure 4.10). One drawback to BASIC is that it is not a standardized language; there are a multitude of versions. In this wide multitude, however, some are designed for structured programming and some are even free form. BASIC is discussed in more detail in Appendix A.

**FIGURE 4.9**
RPG II is a fill-in-the-blank language: *(a)* the files are described on the F sheet, *(b)* the input on the I sheet, *(c)* calculations are entered on the C sheet, *(d)* output on the O sheet.

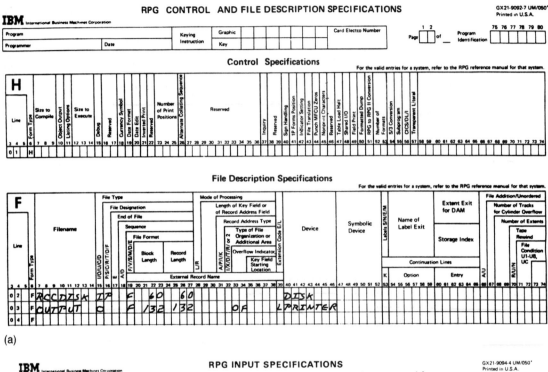

(a)

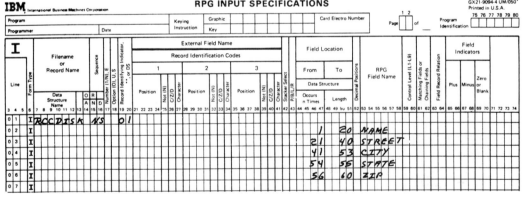

(b)

**FIGURE 4.9** *(concluded)*

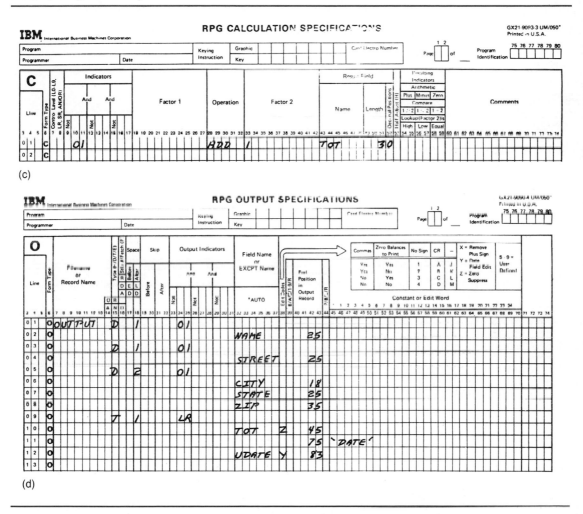

(c)

(d)

7. *Pascal* —bus +sci

**Pascal** is designed to use structured programming techniques, which increase a program's readability and reliability. It is appropriate for both the business and the scientific user because it has the extensive editing abilities the business programmer needs and the mathematical abilities scientists and mathematicians require. It has made better inroads into the university and scientific community than into the business community. Named for the French mathematician Blaise Pascal, it was developed in 1968 and is widely used in universities today (Figure 4.11).

**FIGURE 4.10**

Students often use BASIC. If you have the opportunity to use a microcomputer, you may want to do some BASIC programming yourself.

```
10 REM this program prints mailing labels
20 REM from data found in data statements
30 REM n$ = name
40 REM s$ = street
50 REM c$ = city
60 REM t$ = state
70 REM z  = zip
80 REM t  = total records processed
100 LET T = 0
120 READ N$
130 IF N$ = "the end" THE GOTO 300
140 READ S$,C$,T$,Z
150 PRINT N$
160 PRINT S$
170 PRINT C$, T$, Z
175 PRINT
180 LET T = T+1
190 GOTO 120
300 PRINT "total records", T
310 STOP
400 REM the following are the data records
410 DATA "harry smith","5 high pointroad","andover","ma",01862
420 DATA "barbara lineweaver","rt 1 box 17","blairs","nc",25733
430 DATA "fredrick kleiner","37 fox hall road","portsmount","nh",00378
440 DATA "the end"

RUN
harry smith
5 high pointroad
andover         ma              1862

barbara lineweaver
rt 1 box 17
blairs          nc              25733

frederick kleiner
37 fox hall road
portsmount      nh              378

total records   3
Break in 310
OK
```

## C

**C,** one of the newer programming languages (Figure 4.12), is rapidly increasing in popularity; experienced C programmers are in demand. C is considered more portable than most languages; programs can be moved from one machine to another with few or no modifications. Thus, it is attractive for developing applica-

**FIGURE 4.11**
Pascal, a powerful language for both business and scientific applications, is widely used on college campuses. It was developed to use structured coding techniques.

```
PROGRAM TOT;

VAR

        RATE, HOURS, AMT: REAL;

BEGIN

        READ (RATE, HOURS);
        AMT: = (RATE * HOURS);
        WRITE (AMT)

END
```

**FIGURE 4.12**
C, one of the newer languages, became popular in the early 1980s.

```
/* In C upper and lower case letters are distinct */

/* this program sums two integer values */
main ( )

        /* declare variables */
        int valu1, valu2, valu3;
        /* assign values */
        valu1 = 10;
        valu2 = 20;
        valu3 = valu1 + valu2;
        /* show results */
        printf ("The sum of %d and %d is %d\n",valu1,valu2,valu3);
```

tions software, systems software, and **proprietary software** (software written for sale to others).

## Object-Oriented Programming (OOP) Languages

— grouping similar or related commands.

One change from the procedural languages just discussed should be mentioned. **Object-oriented programming** languages are based on the concept of grouping similar and related commands together into what are referred to as "classes" or "objects." A class defines the data storage and data operations that may be performed on a particular data item or type. An object is a specific instance of a class and consists of a pointer to the class definition and some data storage. The relationship between classes and their objects is hierarchial; what is true of the class is true of all of its objects. This makes modification easier. Adding new objects requires only specifying what it unique; the other code can be inherited.

The programmer deals with these objects rather than with lines of code, which makes them easier to modify. Applications using these languages tend to be in the area of artificial intelligence and expert systems.

## Fourth-Generation Languages (4GLs) — high-level, non-procedural

Fourth-generation languages, commonly referred to as **4GLs,** are high-level, nonprocedural languages. Such 4GLs as PROLOG and FOCUS were developed to aid the move toward more systems development by end-users, although some other fourth-generation languages such as Natural were written primarily to be used by professional programmers developing large systems to be used on mainframes. They permit the end-user to execute complex procedures using only a few commands (Figure 4.13). Because there is a smaller set of commands to learn, the end-user can learn the language more rapidly and develop a program in significantly less time than with third-generation or low-level languages.

Programs written in 4GLs can often be developed interactively. This means that the commands may be edited as they are being written and before they are executed, rather than being all edited at once after the program is written.

A major disadvantage of 4GLs is their high machine resource requirements. Also, they may be incompatible with the existing database, and the user may already have a large investment in existing programs written and maintained in one of the earlier third-generation, high-level languages.

**FIGURE 4.13**
4GLs use higher-level, less procedural instructions than third-generation languages. In the following program, SELECT is used to determine which records to process. In a third-generation language, the programmer would need to write detailed instructions describing how to select.

```
FILE IS INVENTORY
LIST BY ITEM: ITEM DESC ONHAND
SELECT ONHAND < REORDER
TITLE: "INVENTORY BELOW REORDER POINT"
COLUMN HEADINGS; "ITEM NUMBER"; "ITEM DESCRIPTION"; "CURRENT BALANCE";
  "REORDER POINT"
```

## Natural Languages — *problems are due to idioms.*

**Natural languages** are the languages that we speak and understand, such as Spanish, English, and Japanese. They are nonprocedural; they do not require the writing of detailed procedures directing the operations of the computer. The user can tell the computer what is wanted rather than write a detailed set of procedures on how to obtain it.

*W.* The use of natural languages to access computers is still in the research stage. The same problems exist in attempting to use natural languages on a computer that exist in trying to automate the translation of any language. Most of the translation is easy, but enough idioms occur to make some translations nonsensical (Figure 4.14). The future use of natural languages is a part of the research being done in the area of artificial intelligence.

**FIGURE 4.14**
These phrases can be difficult for us to understand. Natural language translation of most speech is clear, but 10 to 20 percent of our speech is idiomatic, which, of course, can cause problems.

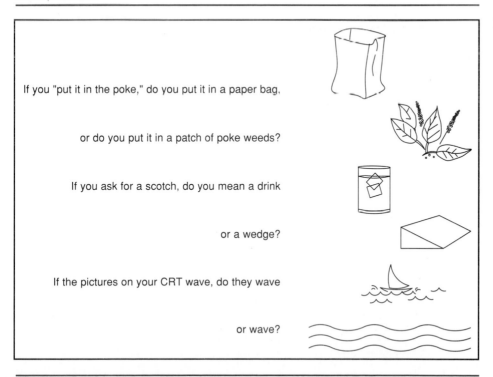

If you "put it in the poke," do you put it in a paper bag,

or do you put it in a patch of poke weeds?

If you ask for a scotch, do you mean a drink

or a wedge?

If the pictures on your CRT wave, do they wave

or wave?

9.    ## Query Languages — DBMS.

A **query language** is a part of most database management systems (DBMSs). It is a high-level, nonprocedural language that can easily be learned and used by nonprogrammers. Use of a query language enables the end-user to access or retrieve information on a database without having special programs written. Query languages are discussed further in Chapter 10 (Databases).

## SUMMARY

Purchased software is available to meet most data processing requirements, and the amount and types available for microcomputers are increasing daily. Three of the most popular types of purchased software are word processing packages, electronic spreadsheets, and multipurpose packages or integrated software.

Purchased software does not meet some needs; custom-written programs are sometimes necessary. Once a program is designed, the programmer can write it in any one of many languages: assembly language, COBOL, RPG, BASIC, Pascal, and so on. The trend today in programming languages is away from such procedural languages and toward natural, nonprocedural ones, including object-oriented languages, query languages, and 4GLs.

## VOCABULARY

Applications software    75

BASIC    89

Binary code    85

C    92

COBOL    87

Consultants    82

Custom software (custom programs)    75

Desktop publishing    79

Diagnostics    87

Electronic spreadsheets    77

FORTRAN    87

4GLs    94

Hexadecimal code    85

High-level languages    87

Integrated software    79

Interactive languages    89

Low-level languages    84

Natural languages    95

Object-oriented programming    93

Octal code    85

Pascal    91

Proprietary software    93

Purchased software packages    75

RPG    89

Spreadsheets    77

Symbolic code    86

Word processing    78

## EXERCISES

1. What is the advantage of multipurpose or integrated software over single-purpose packages such as spreadsheets?
2. Why must some software be customized?
3. What are the differences between low- and high-level languages?
4. In what ways were assembly languages an improvement over machine languages? What drawbacks still remained?
5. Why are there so many different languages?
6. What languages are used primarily for scientific and mathematical applications? Which are used primarily for business applications?
7. Which languages are designed to be multipurpose, appropriate for both business and scientific use?
8. Which languages are designed primarily for student use?
9. Who might use a query language? Why?
10. What is the greatest difficulty in the development of natural languages?

## PROJECTS

1. You are not a programmer but are required to use information stored in a computer. Describe the ideal way of obtaining that data. Use examples.
2. You are the dean of a school of engineering. Until now, your graduates have been required to take FORTRAN. Several instructors wish to change the requirement to BASIC; several others wish to keep FORTRAN. Find out more about both languages, and decide which should be the requirement. Defend your choice.
3. Do additional research on the current state of natural languages.
4. You are in the computer lab. A friend is using a word processing program. You think about the research papers you need to do and about how useful her program would be. You consider asking her to let you copy it. Would you? Why or why not?
5. Find out what public-domain software is. Would you copy your friend's program if she told you that it was in the public domain? Why or why not?

**5**

# Microcomputers

## CHAPTER OBJECTIVES

*After completing this chapter, you will be able to:*

1. Discuss the history of the microcomputer revolution.
2. Describe the unique hardware characteristics of the microcomputer.
3. Explain what a "supermicro" is.
4. Discuss the various uses of microcomputers.
5. Evaluate microcomputer hardware.
6. Evaluate software.
7. Know how to care for the microcomputer system.

## OVERVIEW

A child learning her multiplication tables, a farmer in the Midwest calculating optimal feed mix for his cattle, a small business owner tracking her accounts receivable, a teenager playing games, a house whose environment is being automatically monitored—what do they have in common? A microcomputer is at the heart of each of these activities.

Since 1976, microcomputers have grown into a multibillion- dollar business (Figure 5.1). In 1984, almost 4 million computers were sold for home use. By 1989, the market was projected to exceed $15 billion for microcomputer software alone.

This chapter presents an overview of microcomputers, their configuration, and the ways they are used. It will present in some detail the three most popular microcomputer applications; it will also discuss MIS, DSS, and the concept of information centers.

## BRIEF HISTORY OF MICROCOMPUTERS

*Computer whose processing component is a microprocessor.*

In 1971, Texas Instruments demonstrated the first fully operational microprocessor, a processor on a single silicon chip. Since then, microprocessors have been used in such diversified products as ovens, cars, and televisions.

Microcomputers, computers whose processing component is a microprocessor, have been available since 1976. At that time, Altair sold the first microcomputers in build-it-yourself kits to hobbyists and electronics buffs. This microcomputer did lure the hobbyist. However, it did not attract many people who wanted to use a microcomputer but were not interested in the electronics of building one.

A second revolutionary event occurred in 1976: Stephen Wozniak, a young hobbyist who worked for Hewlett-Packard, built a small computer. His friend, Steve Jobs, who worked for Atari, also saw the value of this computer. Small and inexpensive enough for the general public to buy and use, these "ready-made" computers could be made available to those who lacked the skill or interest to build their own. By 1982, the revenues of Apple Computer, Inc., exceeded $650 million.

**FIGURE 5.1**
Microcomputers have become a vital part of many homes, schools, and businesses. (Hank Morgan/Rainbow)

Apple was not alone in the microcomputer market. Commodore also introduced a microcomputer in 1977, the PET. The PET was a 4 K machine that could be programmed in the BASIC language. It used a cassette tape as secondary storage and was also designed for the general public.

## MICROCOMPUTER CHARACTERISTICS

Microcomputer sales are still booming. What are the characteristics of these machines?

### Hardware

A person could easily identify a microcomputer a few years ago, describing it by price, amount of internal storage, and designation for operation by one user at a time. Now, prices are falling, internal storage is being increased to unanticipated amounts, and some microcomputers are designed to serve more than one user at a time. What, then, is a microcomputer?

Basically, a microcomputer is a computer built around a single microprocessor chip. This single chip contains the arithmetic/logic unit (ALU), the control unit, and the primary storage unit (Figure 5.2). In addition to this chip, the computer has internal storage and facilities for some type of input/output—usually a keyboard and a video monitor.

The **video monitor** is the display screen used to show computer output. Monitors are available in both color and monochrome (the latter displaying only a single color—typically amber, white, or green—with black). Its **resolution** refers to the sharpness of the displayed image, determined by the number of addressable points on the screen. Each point is called a **pixel,** for picture element. The resolution is described in terms of the number of pixels in horizontal rows by vertical columns. That means a 320 × 200 resolution has 320 dots across by 200 dots down. **CGA** (color graphics adapter) monitors have a low resolution, **EGA** (enhanced graphics adapter) and **VGA** (video graphics array) have higher (see Figure 5.3).

*Sharpness of an image.*

Since microcomputers are typically used by one person at a time, they are also called **personal computers** (PCs). Microcomputers can vary from pocket to desktop sized. Auxiliary storage may be on cassette tape but more often is on floppy or hard disk.

The hardware components of a microcomputer system may be modified. Auxiliary storage devices may be added or removed, and control devices such as a joystick or mouse may also be added (Figure 5.4). These are usually attached through the serial port. Most PCs have printers attached; they are attached through the parallel port. If telecommunications are used, a modem may also be attached through the serial port.

In addition to the devices that are standard to the system, others may be added by using the existing expansion slots. **Expansion slots** are receptacles within the computer and connected to its bus that can be used to plug in additional printed circuit boards. The number of possible additions to the system is limited by the number of expansion slots.

Within limits, memory may also be increased by adding chips. The cost of memory continues to fall, making microcomputers increasingly more powerful without increasing the cost. During the last six months of 1989 alone, the cost of 1 megabyte of memory fell almost 50%, from just over $120 to just under $60.

The term **clone** is frequently used when talking about microcomputers. A clone is a compatible computer that can run the same software as the original computer. Unfortunately, clone is sometimes loosely used, and the computers it refers to may not be 100 percent compatible.

## Software

Hardware is only a part of the microcomputer system. What about the software: the operating system and applications software?

**FIGURE 5.2**

The microprocessor and other chips are mounted on a carrier that has standard pin connectors. The carriers are then attached to the *motherboard*, the main printed circuit board. (Fred Bodin)

**FIGURE 5.3**
The sharpness of the displayed image is determined by the resolution. CGA, EGA, and VGA are all common video display boards.

| Name | Text resolution | Graphics resolution | Colors |
|------|-----------------|---------------------|--------|
| CGA | 320 × 200 | 320 × 200 | 16 |
| EGA | 640 × 350 | 640 × 350 | 16 |
| VGA | 720 × 400 | 640 × 480 | 256 |

**FIGURE 5.4**
The mouse provides an easy method of moving the cursor across the CRT. As it is rolled across the desk's surface, the cursor is moved correspondingly across the screen. (Courtesy Logitech)

## Operating System

The operating system controls the software running on a computer and the hardware that comprises the system. It permits the operators to interact with the computer, allowing them to start and stop programs running on the system. It also enables the system to send messages to the operator. For example, "printer not ready" might appear if the user requested printed output without turning the printer on and stocking it with paper.

**FIGURE 5.5**

MS–DOS is one of the most popular PC operating systems. You can see how Englishlike its commands are.

```
COPY            Duplicates an existing file
COMP            Compares two files
DATE            Enables you to see or set the system date
DIR             Displays the contents of a directory
DISKCOMP        Compares two disks
DISKCOPY        Duplicates a disk
ERASE or DEL    Erases a file from the diskette
FORMAT          Formats a disk
RENAME          Enables you to change the name of an existing file
TIME            Enables you to see or set the system time
TYPE            Displays the contents of a file
```

The typical microcomputer user is not a professional computer operator; often, the microcomputer was purchased to do a job. This task is the important factor; the user wants to do it as quickly and easily as possible. Thus, the operating system makes the computer easy to operate. The system commands—such as LOCK, DELETE, RENAME, RUN, SAVE, LOAD, COPY, ERASE, and UN-LOCK—are logical, Englishlike, and easy to learn (see Figure 5.5).

The operating system of most microcomputers enables only one person to use the system at a time. However, **supermicros** have been developed that can multitask; that is, they have the ability to run more than one program at a time. These multiuser microcomputers are made up of several workstations that share the same microcomputer and peripheral devices. Each workstation consists of a keyboard and monitor. While a secretary uses one workstation to create a letter, an accountant might use another station to create a spreadsheet, and a different operator might use one to test a BASIC program.

### Applications Software

Microcomputer software is as varied as its users. Among the most popular software are word processing, database management, electronic spreadsheets, graphics, and communications. Integrated software, which performs multiple functions, is also extremely popular. Integrated software makes using a micro-computer even easier by allowing the user to take information created in one application and pass it to another application for use. A manager might create a spreadsheet and then pass the information contained in the spreadsheet to the graphics portion of the integrated package for conversion to a graph. Later, a secretary may pass the spreadsheet or graph over to the word processing program for inclusion in a memo or other document (see also Chapter 4). Database management is discussed in detail in Chapter 10; data communications are discussed in Chapter 11.

**FIGURE 5.6**
Input to a microcomputer can be through sensors as well as through keyboards. (Superstock)

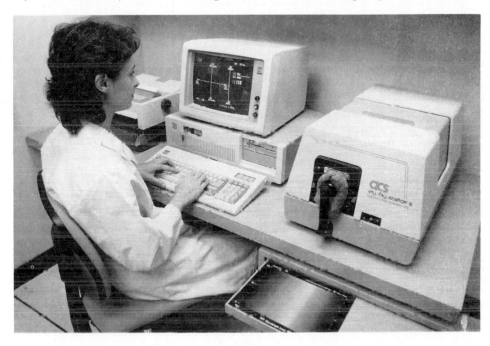

The microcomputer, originally viewed as a toy for the hobbyist or as a small, inexpensive computer for the individual user, has become much more important. Do you want a device to monitor the environment of your home, control heat and lights, and notify you that your lawn needs mowing or watering? Your microcomputer can do it with a sensor (Figure 5.6). Perhaps you want to play games, but no one is home tonight. Play against your microcomputer. Do you want to keep the books for a small business or records for a group? Keep them on your microcomputer.

Today, microcomputers are used in many locations, both likely and unlikely (see On the Job). Individuals and small businesses typically use them. Large companies use them either as stand-alone computers or as part of data networks. Linked to a mainframe computer as part of a network, the microcomputer may be used as a dumb terminal. It may also serve as an intelligent terminal; data may be downloaded from the mainframe to the microcomputer and processed there (see Chapter 3).

## THE USERS

As noted, individuals, educators and other professionals, and small and large businesses employ microcomputers.

## ON THE JOB

### A Bug in the Program or a Lizard in the Disk Drive?

Around the world, approximately 3,000 distinct language groups exist whose languages still have no written form. The Wycliff Bible Translators work to create written forms for these languages; then they translate the Bible into these forms. Their linguists are often pictured sitting in some village hut, pencil in hand, making notes as they listen to the villagers speak. This was once true, but today many sit, not hunched over a notepad, but over a portable computer.

Wycliff has been using computers for over 20 years. Like many organizations, their first computer application was accounting, followed by typesetting, but today every one of the more than 850 translation projects in process involves the computer in some way. JAARS, Jungle Aviation and Radio Service, whose hub of operations is located in Waxhaw, North Carolina, provides air travel and communications for those Wycliff Bible translators working with people in remote areas. In addition, JAARS evaluates computers for use by translators in the field.

Evaluation of computer durability in hazardous environments is strict. Computers must not only be battery operated, have appropriate software, and be easy to use; they must also be reliable in adverse climates. They must be able to withstand extremes of temperature, humidity, and dust. In addition to batteries, power may also be supplied by water or wind generators, or by solar panels.

Maintenance may be handled in the field, or the computer may be returned to Waxhaw for repairs. Recently, one was returned because a disk drive didn't work. Repair personnel quickly found the "bug": A lizard had moved into the drive and, unfortunately, died there.

### Individuals

Games have given way to word processing as the prime reason for purchasing many microcomputers, but many of us still try to fly our starships or try to outwit the computer at mazelike games or chess.

Many individuals, however, have found new computer tasks. They balance their checkbooks, file recipes, plan balanced menus, count calories, write letters, and design cards, invitations, and annoucements with the help of their microcomputer. A microcomputer was used in training Michael Spinks for his heavyweight championship match with Larry Holmes in 1985; it recorded play-by-play details of his training bouts. In addition, 1988 marked the first time presidential contenders campaigning in the primaries traveled with their own portable microcomputers.

Individuals have also found the value of hooking into commercial networks such as bulletin boards and other information services. Electronic **bulletin boards** can be used to post or exchange messages. The home computer can put one "in touch with the world" through the Dow Jones Information Service, CompuServe (Columbus, Ohio), The Source (McLean, Virginia), Bibliographic Research Service, and others. One of the more unusual databases accessed is Accu-Weather. Using an existing software package, Accu-Weather Forecaster, hobbyists, farmers, and people in such businesses as amusement park and ski resort management can import and analyze live weather data from the Accu-Weather service. Air pressure, fog, rain, wind direction, and speed can be obtained. Once the data is mapped, the user has a current weather forecast.

## Educators

Do you know anyone who teaches basic skills: defensive driving, basic reading, or math? What about teaching typing, physics, history, logic, wilderness survival, human anatomy, Spanish, algebra, Latin, geometry, human sexuality, or how photosynthesis really works? Microcomputer **courseware** is available on all these and many more subjects.

**Computer-aided instruction (CAI)** uses computers to teach course material. Although outside programmers develop most CAI material, many teachers are beginning to develop their own material using specialized, high-level programming languages such as Tutor. Material may be presented as **drills** in which little or no new information is offered. The student learns the contents by repeating them over and over, much as you once learned the multiplication tables. New material may also be presented in **tutorials** and the student then drilled on the contents. A third way CAI may teach is through **simulations,** which imitate the process to be learned but under the student's control (a method used in teaching flying).

Because the computer is interactive, the student's skill level can influence the material presented. Wrong answers may result in a review of material, whereas continued correct answers may cause a jump to more difficult material. Provided the computer courseware is relevant to the course, is sequenced properly (long division is not taught before addition), and is clear and appropriate in its feedback to the student, excellent results may be obtained.

One question always arises about even the best courseware: why not use a book, a lecture, or a film? The microcomputer should provide something not available from other media, such as the ability to proceed at one's own speed or to simulate potentially dangerous situations without exposing the inexperienced student to actual danger. For this reason, CAI is used extensively by the military as well as industrial organizations and educational institutions (Figure 5.7).

Microcomputers are also used for administrative purposes. Many schools are using automated telephoning to check on absentee students. Tests and crossword puzzles are automatically generated by computer (Figure 5.8), library

**FIGURE 5.7**

Preparing to land on a computer-generated airfield, this U.S. Marine Corps pilot is getting valuable training in the McDonnell Douglas AV-8B Harrier II operational flight trainer. The trainer does everything the short-takeoff and vertical-landing (STOVL) AV-8B does—turns, climbs, rolls, hovers—without taking the new pilot off the ground. (Courtesy McDonnell-Douglas)

catalogs are maintained, class rolls are kept, and gradebooks are averaged and graphed by computer. Even the reading level of material may be automatically calculated by keying in a brief selection from the material to be evaluated.

## Small Businesses

Small businesses perform almost all the functions of large businesses; they keep payrolls and the associated tax records, maintain and evaluate an inventory, and generate written communications such as letters and reports. They may also create graphs and signs announcing future sales and promotions. A microcomputer can assist in the performance of all these tasks. Many specialized business functions are also available for the microcomputer. The small construction business may use packaged programs in generating a bid, or a dairy farmer may decide how to cull his herd based on computerized records (Figure 5.9). Microcomputers are also used to keep medical records, locate lost dogs, maintain flight logs, monitor stock portfolios, and maintain real estate information.

## FIGURE 5.8

This crossword puzzle, reviewing some data processing terms, was computer generated and used in an Introduction to Data Processing test (answers are given below).

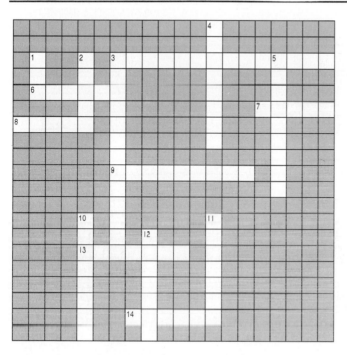

CROSSWORD PUZZLE CLUES

ACROSS CLUES:
  3) a processor-on-a-chip
  4) the physical components of a computer system
  6) the first commercially available electronic computer
  7) a language developed for business use by representatives of government and industry
  8) a general-purpose language developed at Dartmouth for student use
  9) a term for large computers
  13) an early scientific language
  14) a high-level language named for a seventeenth century mathematician

DOWN CLUES:
  1) another name for the arithmetic/logic unit
  2) the first computer to use the stored program concept
  3) a term describing the smallest class of computers
  5) storage that is not a part of main memory is sometimes called _____ storage
  10) the programs used on a computer are called _____
  11) the part of the central processing unit that directs the execution of instructions is called the _____ unit
  12) the step-by-step instructions that direct the computer

**FIGURE 5.9**
Many small businesses keep computerized records. Information that can be presented graphically is more readable. (A. M. Rosario/The Image Bank)

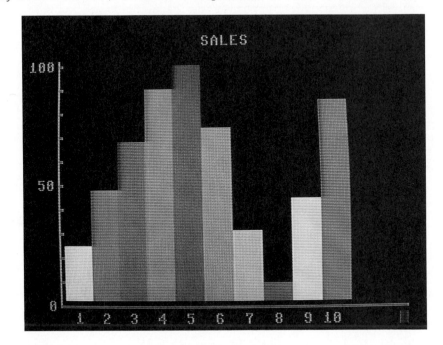

## Large Businesses

John V. Roach, chief executive officer of Tandy Corporation/Radio Shack, delivered the keynote address at the Data Processing Management Association meeting in Anaheim, California, in 1984. In that address, he said, "The time taken to define an optimum solution may, in fact, be too long to permit an optimum solution. . . . Fortunately though, a highly satisfactory solution can be arrived at by those who understand the alternatives and who react quickly and decisively."

He was speaking of the productivity gains made possible by technological advances, but he could as well have been describing the everyday challenge of any manager: how to make a decision in the face of rapidly changing circumstances.

A major problem in business has been that the information processing department can provide the information needed, but business needs the answer *now,* not six months from now when information processing can produce it. For many businesses, microcomputers have provided a partial answer to this problem. As a stand-alone device, the microcomputer provides computing power where it is needed—at the user's desk.

The great drawback of the stand-alone microcomputer is that the power is provided but often not the data. The information needed may be located at

**FIGURE 5.10**

Networking with microcomputers puts the resources of the mainframe on the desk of the user. (Courtesy "LANTechnology")

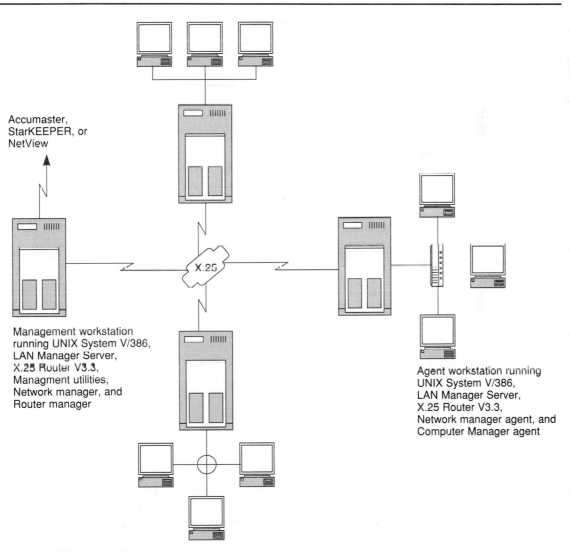

Accumaster,
StarKEEPER, or
NetView

Management workstation
running UNIX System V/386,
LAN Manager Server,
X.25 Router V3.3,
Managment utilities,
Network manager, and
Router manager

Agent workstation running
UNIX System V/386,
LAN Manager Server,
X.25 Router V3.3,
Network manager agent, and
Computer Manager agent

the mainframe. Interaction with the mainframe as part of a network gives the microcomputer both the power and the data (Figure 5.10). Easy access to data, however, carries problems of data security and integrity, as well as possible communication conflicts.

Despite these problems, data networks, varying in size from room-sized to global networks, are mushrooming.

## 6. CRITERIA FOR SELECTING AND EVALUATING A SYSTEM

Have all the possible uses discussed so far made you long to run out and purchase your own microcomputer? You could use the spreadsheets for work, the word processing for your research papers and club newsletters, and other software to maintain your budget or mailing lists for a small business you might own.

Stop for a minute. Would you buy a car only as the result of seeing what someone else had? You would probably first think about what you need it for and who was going to be driving it. Extensive commuting might demand a car with good gas mileage; using it only to shop and for vacations might make trunk size more important. If you were the only driver, a sports car might be fun; a son or daughter with only a new learner's permit, however, might make you hold off on the sports car a few years. Many of these same considerations are important in purchasing a computer system.

The most important question to ask yourself is: What do I want to *do* with the system? What jobs are to be performed? A computer used only to create reports for school will be quite a different system from one used to generate elaborate graphics, or one needed by a CPA for accounting applications.

Before you make any purchase, the first step is to determine the system's purpose: Why do you need a computer? The system is made up of both hardware and software, so the purchase of either one depends on the other. The perfect software package is useless if it cannot be run on your computer; the perfect computer is useless if no software is available to meet your needs. Remember; although the software you want may be available, it may not be available for the system you are considering.

Identifying the functions the computer is to perform is essential. You should do this *before* considering either software or hardware. Figure 5.11 identifies some functions. You may wish to add to the list. A second preliminary step is to establish your budget: How much can you afford to spend? What do you already have that could be used with the microcomputer to reduce the initial cost? For example, a TV set could be used as the video monitor. Once you establish the general functional requirements and budget, you can look in more detail at the software and hardware requirements.

## 7. Criteria for Evaluating Software

Once the computer is purchased, the search for software continues. How do you choose good software?

Software can be purchased either by mail or from a retail store. Usually, purchasing from a store is more expensive. Is it then better to purchase it by mail?

**FIGURE 5.11**

This checklist summarizes some of the functions of a micro. The most important consideration is: "What do I want to use it for?"

_____ Games
_____ Word processing
        _____ Letters and memos
        _____ Research papers and manuscripts
        _____ Specialized terminology and symbols
_____ Personal record-keeping
        _____ Appointment calendar
        _____ Address book or mailing lists
        _____ Stock market activity
        _____ Taxes
        _____ Itemized deductions
        _____ Cash management and budgeting
        _____ Other:
_____ Accounting
_____ Graphics
_____ Programming
_____ Educational packages and tutorials
_____ Communications with services such as CompuServe

The greatest advantage of purchasing from a store is that you can usually see a demonstration of the software. If it does not do what you anticipated, you can walk out without it. Mail order does not usually permit a demonstration; you base your choice on a written description or on prior familiarity with what the program does.

Once you see the package, how do you evaluate it? First, does the software need to be purchased, or will you need to write any of it? You may be a programmer—if the software is unavailable, you would be able to write it. Even if the software is available, you may choose to write the program anyway. Perhaps you have no interest in programming; in this case, everything you need must be available for purchase.

Second, if you purchase the software, does it do what you need? Does it meet all your requirements? If you are buying a program that keeps track of the checks you write, can it handle the number of checks you write annually? Will it flag those checks affecting your tax returns?

Third, how efficiently does the package handle data? If you purchase the check-balancing program mentioned above, how many times do you have to enter the same information? Do you enter it only once? Is it used for both balancing and taxes, or do you have to enter the data once for each? The latter would be very inefficient and would likely result in errors. Can you perhaps use the data collected for another program without rekeying it?

Fourth, what is the quality of the package? Does it do what it says it will? What if requirements change? Will the vendor modify the program, or can you trade it in against a newer version? This is particularly important for business software.

Fifth, what about the documentation? Is it clear—can you follow the instructions? Is it concise—is all the information you need stated clearly but briefly? Is it well organized—can you find the information you need? Is it easy to use— does it have an index? Is it accurate—does it tell you to insert card D into port C, but you find that there is no port C in the illustration? Documentation should be written for the user. Good documentation is written for you, is clear to you, and is accurate when you follow the instructions.

Finally, the best source is other users of the package you are considering buying. Again, computer clubs, fairs, and magazine articles provide invaluable information. You may want to prepare a checklist of software requirements before you go shopping. When evaluating a software package, consider these questions:

1. Do you need a demonstration? If so, you will probably want to buy from a store, not by mail. If not, mail order is cheaper.
2. Does it meet your requirements?
3. How efficiently does it handle data? Will it work with other packages you own or may purchase?
4. Is it a quality package? Will it do what is claimed? What about revisions and modifications?
5. How good is the documentation?
6. How do other users like it?

## Criteria for Evaluating Hardware

A first consideration in choosing hardware is deciding what the computer's functions will be. Reports probably require a good printer, whereas games may never produce printed output. A black-and-white monitor is fine for reviewing written material, whereas Battle between the Galaxies really loses something when it is not in full color.

A second consideration is who is going to be using it? What is the user's background? The electronics hobbyist may love to tinker with the machine and figure out how it works on her own, whereas another user may just want to get the job done quickly and efficiently and forget it. The latter needs good, clear documentation; the former wants to know only how to put the microcomputer back together after she has taken it completely apart.

How much money do you have to spend? Can you buy what you want? Perhaps you are willing to give up some features to save money. Perhaps the cost is less than you anticipated; you might even be able to get some of those "nice but can live without" features.

Finally, what is the vendor's reputation? Many manufacturers make microcomputers. Some probably will be around in five years; others probably will not. The quality of the microcomputer may have little to do with the success of the company producing it. How important is it to you for the vendor to be here next year, in two years, or in 10 years from now? What are you willing to pay for that security?

Many people are now selecting portable PCs. Several additional concerns should be addressed when selecting a portable PC. Some screens are reflective; that means that they use the room light to reflect back, illuminating the words on the screen. If you plan to use the portable in low-light conditions, backlit LCDs are better. Laptops are available both with and without a hard disk. If you need to carry much data with you, the hard disk is very convenient. Remember, also, that weights of portables vary from 15 pounds down. A 15-pound portable is not as convenient to carry as a 5 pound one. You also want to consider the battery that will be used as the alternative power source; the life of the battery as well as its weight become important if you will be using the computer in the field.

Remember that your needs are unique. As a user, you are unique, and the choice of a microcomputer has to be as individual as you and those needs are. As you make that choice, take advantage of exhibits, courses, magazine articles, computer clubs, fairs, workshops, and so on. Remember also that whatever you selected was your best choice *at the time*. Both computer hardware and software are constantly being improved. A month or a year after you make your selection, something better will come on the market. You cannot wait for the perfect solution to your computing needs. Don't be disappointed. Familiarize yourself with what is new. You will make other purchases in the future. For the present, however, learn all you can about what you now own. By doing so, you will get the maximum out of whatever you have available.

## CARING FOR YOUR SYSTEM

Modern microcomputers are relatively maintenance free and perform well in environments that would have been unfriendly to older computers. For example, in the past, computers had to be used in heavily air-conditioned rooms. This is no longer necessary.

It is a good idea to keep the computer clean and free of dust by using plastic dust covers that slip over the VDT or printer when the computer is not in use.

Be sure to install the computer properly and to attach all peripheral devices according to the instructions provided. If you are concerned that surges on the electrical line providing power to the computer may occur, you can purchase adaptors to regulate the power supply.

If your system uses diskettes, handle them carefully. (For further information, refer back to Using Floppy Disks on page 61.)

## TRENDS IN MICROCOMPUTERS

Microcomputers are changing rapidly; the hand-held microcomputer is now available, and the supermicro is coming into the marketplace. What, then, are the trends in hardware and software development, in sales, and in usage?

### Trends in Development

Trends in the development of microcomputer hardware and software include the growth of larger and more powerful microcomputers—16-bit and 32-bit word supermicros. These supermicros are also capable of something new for microcomputers: multitasking, the concurrent execution of more than one job. They are also multiuser, capable of supporting more than one user at a time.

The CRT screens are becoming sharper, with more pixels to the square inch. They are also becoming more interactive and friendly as touch screens and graphics pads grow in popularity.

Software is also becoming more friendly as more and more programs are icon-driven. An icon is an image; in an **icon-driven program,** each activity on the menu is represented by a picture of the activity.

As memory size continues to grow, more languages formerly used exclusively on mainframes are being used on microcomputers: COBOL, FORTRAN, and Pascal, as well as a growing number of fourth-generation languages (see Chapters 1 and 4).

More portable operating systems also are being developed. These portable operating systems can move from one machine to another rather than being exclusive to one machine. This eases the problems encountered when a new machine is purchased and the software bought to run under one operating system is no longer supported under the new one. If the operating system itself is portable, there is a much greater chance that software will run on it.

### Trends in Usage

One current trend is using microcomputers as productivity enhancement tools for managers. Early microcomputer users were usually clerks or secretaries. Today, the trend is toward the manager using a personal microcomputer, often to compare alternatives when making management decisions. The clerks and secretaries are not losing their access, however; microcomputers are a significant tool in office automation (see Chapter 11).

Another trend is toward the use of microcomputers in communications networks. As the processing of data becomes more widely distributed, microcomputers in the branch locations are being used both to communicate with the host computer and to process data locally.

Software is being written to serve broader applications. More integrated packages are being developed.

One problem with the increasing use of microcomputers is the lack of standardization. This causes problems both in communications between machines and in portability of software. A major trend should be toward standardization and portability.

Microcomputers are ceasing to be only personal computers; they are becoming more of a shared resource. One recent study found that the average office personal computer is shared by two or three persons and that one fourth of all business personal computers are used by 10 or more persons. This is not concurrent use but refers to many individuals using the same computer at various times.

Microcomputers are increasingly being used to form **local area networks (LANs)**, where they are able not only to handle their own processing but also to talk to other microcomputers as well as to the mainframe.

The amount and variety of software continue to grow. With the availability of more and easier-to-use software, more professionals in fields other than data processing are using microcomputers. Information centers that provide help for these users are springing up in many companies.

Today, many articles discuss the ethics of making illegal copies of software. Much is written about how to regulate the reproduction of software and eliminate illegal copies. Data processing personnel want the ability to make backup copies of purchased software in case originals are destroyed. The authors of software want to receive their just profits from the sales. How can backup copies be permitted while prohibiting copies that may be used by someone unauthorized to do so? The conflict has yet to be solved to everyone's satisfaction.

### Trends in Sales

Microcomputer sales continue to increase, bringing many companies into the competition. In 1984, approximately 350 companies were producing microcomputers. This crowding of the market suggests that producers will thin out.

### SUMMARY

Since 1976, microcomputers have grown into a multibillion dollar business. Microcomputer sales are booming. As the machines become more powerful, it is becoming more difficult to distinguish between a powerful microcomputer and a small minicomputer. Basically, a microcomputer is a computer built around a single microprocessor chip. They vary from pocket to desktop-sized machines.

Most PC operating systems are intended to be used by a single user, but more and more, PCs are capable of multitasking. The typical microcomputer system is made up of the microcomputer, a video monitor, and a keyboard. The video monitor is available in both color and monochrome. Its resolution refers to the number of pixels. The hardware components can be modified; standard devices attached through the serial and parallel ports, and others added by using the existing expansion slots. A clone is a compatible computer that can run the same software as the original.

Hobbyists, big and small businesses, educators, and many others use micros. Although we once thought of them as stand-alone personal computers, we are now beginning to see more of them used as a shared resource, with several co-workers using one microcomputer. Rather than being used as stand-alone devices, many microcomputers are now used with a mainframe or with other microcomputers as part of a network.

In selecting a computer system, the first question is, "What do I want it to do?" Based on the answer to that question, the software and the hardware may be selected.

Evaluation of software is important. The user must decide if it does what is needed. Is it efficient? What is the quality—will it be supported? How good is the documentation? What do other users say about it?

Selecting the hardware also requires several considerations: Who is going to be using it? What is their background? What is the budget? What is the vendor's reputation?

Trends are toward the development of larger and more powerful microprocessors, greater resolution of monitors, and more user-friendly software, often icon-driven. There is also a trend toward using microcomputers as production-enhancement tools.

## VOCABULARY

## EXERCISES

1. What is a microcomputer?
2. What is a supermicro?
3. What is meant by resolution?
4. How are microcomputers being used as parts of networks?
5. What is an expansion slot?
6. List the things you would consider before purchasing a microcomputer.
7. What would you consider before purchasing software?
8. Describe any special care a microcomputer and its peripheral equipment require.

## PROJECTS

1. Visit a local microcomputer vendor. Find out all you can about one brand of the hardware they sell. If possible, talk to some owners of that type of equipment. Report on what you find out.
2. Visit a local computer club. Talk to some of the members to find out what goes on at the meetings. Report on what you find.
3. Select one microcomputer manufacturer who is on the New York or American Stock Exchange. Graph the sales history of its stock for the past year or two. If you find any large change in the selling price of the stock, try to find out what happened at that time to cause it.
4. Visit your computer lab. What microcomputers are available? What software is used on them? Are they networked? What information is provided there on the ethical use (including copying) of software?

# 6

# Microcomputer Applications

## CHAPTER OBJECTIVES

*After completing this chapter, you will be able to:*

1. Describe what an integrated software package is.
2. Explain what a spreadsheet is and how it is used.
3. Describe word processing and its advantages over both typing and using a memory typewriter.
4. Discuss ways that a database is used on a microcomputer.
5. Define graphics and describe how they are used in a microcomputer environment.
6. Discuss some features such as windowing that are used in software packages.
7. Discuss communications programs and describe how they are used by microcomputer users.

## OVERVIEW

Today, microcomputers perform most of the same functions as mainframes. They communicate with each other through networks, which are systems of computers connected by communications equipment. Through their databases, they permit electronic shopping and banking. They monitor security systems and environmental control systems and offer everything (see On the Job 1) from communication systems for the disabled to games for the entire family.

In business, microcomputers are most often used for five basic applications: (1) to produce spreadsheets, (2) to handle word processing, (3) to create graphics, (4) to oversee database management (see also Chapter 10), and to provide communications facilities (see Chapter 11).

There are many software applications packages available to perform these tasks (Figure 6.1). This chapter discusses the five basic microcomputer applications as they are offered in one package called **Microsoft Works.**

## MICROSOFT WORKS

Single-purpose applications software has been available for microcomputers for years. In 1983, Lotus Development Corporation introduced a program called 1-2-3® from Lotus. Its popularity boomed as buyers discovered 1-2-3 could perform multiple functions, since it possessed electronic spreadsheet, graphics, and database management capabilities. Many other software packages that are able to share their resources among multiple users have been developed. These collections of programs that are able to share their resources and to easily pass information back and forth are called integrated software packages.

This chapter uses Microsoft Works, an integrated package from Microsoft, to illustrate how spreadsheets, word processors, databases, graphics, and communications programs work.

## ON THE JOB 1

Tracking a Cattle Drive

In the summer of 1989, more than 3,500 horses, 2,500 riders, 2,700 head of cattle, and almost 200 covered wagons celebrated the 100th anniversary of Montana's statehood by participating in recreating a traditional cattle drive. The drive, through the rugged Bull Mountains to Billings, 58 miles distant, took six days, traveling about 10 miles per day. Enroute, cattle had to be examined by veterinarians, over 1,200 tons of feed disbursed, and over a million gallons of water supplied to horses, riders, cattle, and wagons. Waivers had to be obtained before the crossing of private land, and liability releases also had to be acquired from the participants. As with any group this size, there were periodic medical incidents and emergency messages needed to be sent to some of the participants. The logistics of the drive were successfully handled by six computers, including two portables.

**FIGURE 6.1**
This is only a partial list of some of the most popular software packages available.

| **Word processing** | **Business graphics** |
|---|---|
| WordPerfect | Harvard Presentation Graphics |
| WordStar | Microsoft Chart |
| Microsoft Word | Freelance Plus |
| Multimate Advantage | Chart-Master |
| PC-Write | |
| | **Drawing graphics** |
| **Spreadsheets** | PC Paintbrush |
| Lotus 1-2-3 | Freelance Plus |
| VisiCalc | PC Paint |
| Multiplan | Publisher's Paintbrush |
| SuperCalc | |
| VP-Planner | |
| | **Integrated** |
| **Data management** | Microsoft Works |
| dBASE III and III Plus | Framework II |
| R:base | Lotus 1-2-3 |
| Paradox | Enable |
| Reflex: The Analyst | Jazz |
| | |
| **Communications** | |
| Crosstalk XVI | |
| Smartcom II | |
| PC-Talk III | |

As we are looking at Microsoft Works, remember that all applications packages do not function alike, any more than all computers do. The specifics, such as how to move the cursor or insert words, vary from one machine to another and from one package to another.

## WORD PROCESSING

The first thing that many people learn to do on a microcomputer is to use a word processor. Typewritten documents have been used in business since the late 1800s. Word processing functions, however, go far beyond simple typing. What typewriter can insert, delete, and modify text, or search for strings of characters, replacing those strings with others of equal or unequal length? What typewriter can change the margins and line spacing after the document is written, automatically number the pages, or change the typeface and type size without retyping?

A word processor can do all this. It allows you to create a document, edit it, and store it as a text file until it is needed again. The document in a word processing package first appears as an almost blank screen. Across the top is a line indicating tasks such as File, Edit, and Print (Figure 6.2). These prompt

**FIGURE 6.2**
The word processing screen at first looks almost like a blank sheet of paper. A menu of possible tasks appears at the top of the screen.

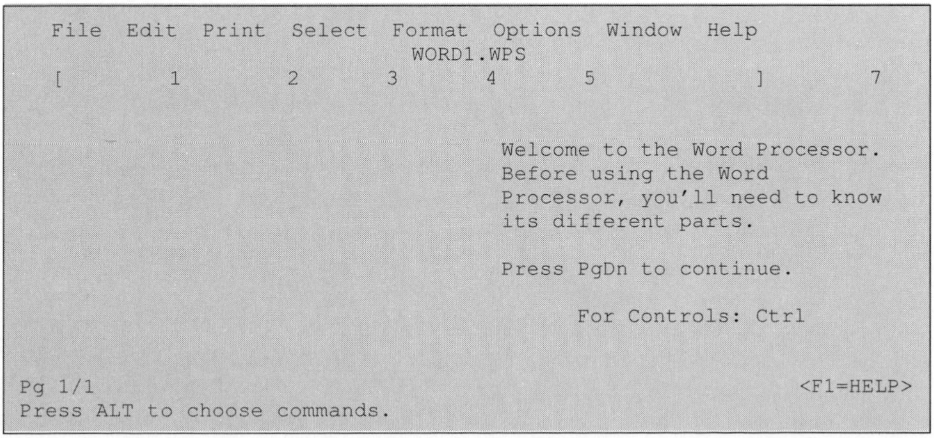

```
   File   Edit   Print   Select   Format   Options   Window   Help
                           WORD1.WPS
   [          1          2        3        4        5               ]          7



                                      Welcome to the Word Processor.
                                      Before using the Word
                                      Processor, you'll need to know
                                      its different parts.

                                      Press PgDn to continue.

                                          For Controls: Ctrl


 Pg 1/1                                                      <F1=HELP>
 Press ALT to choose commands.
```

you to select the task you want to perform. It is as simple to create the document using a word processor as it would be to type it. First, you key in the text. You do not have to be concerned with dividing words at the end of lines or with returning the carriage at the end of each line. Whenever the right margin is reached, the word processor automatically moves the cursor to the next line. This is referred to as **word wrap** or **wrap around.** New paragraphs and blank lines are indicated by pressing the ENTER key.

Once the text is created, you can view it by scrolling through the document. **Scrolling** causes the text to roll up or down the monitor. You may also advance to a given line number or page without scrolling through all the preceding text. (You may even locate a section of the document by searching for a key word or words found in the document.)

It is easy to make changes as well as insert or delete text since you may enter insertions without rekeying what you have already typed. Titles or other text can be centered or justified (adjusted so that they align on either the right or the left margin) with simple commands. If the writer decides that a different arrangement of paragraphs might make the meaning of the text more clear, text may be moved. If some text appears unnecessary, it may be eliminated. If repetition might help clarify the meaning, text may be copied to another location.

With integrated software such as Microsoft Works, data may be entered into the text from other programs within the package. Each Works file can appear in a different window on the monitor. A **window** is a separate viewing area on the monitor. The ability to window is provided by the software; having multiple windows permits the user to keep several application programs visible at the same time. Information may be moved from window to window to create the document you need (Figure 6.3).

Once the document is created, you can save it by storing it on a disk or tape. When you need the document again, you may retrieve it from the library, modify it if necessary, and reuse it.

Word processors are used to create letters and other documents. They are very useful in the production of the personalized form letters used in mass mailings.

In a mass mailing, a standard letter is created, then merged with a file of names and addresses. Each letter is addressed to one of the names found on the file. The body of the letter may remain the same; it may also be varied by inserting variable information from the file.

Once the document is created, it may be printed with a wide variety of fonts, a set of characters of a given size and style. Since the printing is separate from document creation, it can be altered by changing fonts, margins, pagination, and so forth (Figure 6.4). A word processor's ability to do electronic filing greatly enhances its usefulness by enabling it to store documents for later retrieval, modification, and use.

**FIGURE 6.3**
Using windows permits you to see what is on several files or what is on nonadjacent areas of the same file.

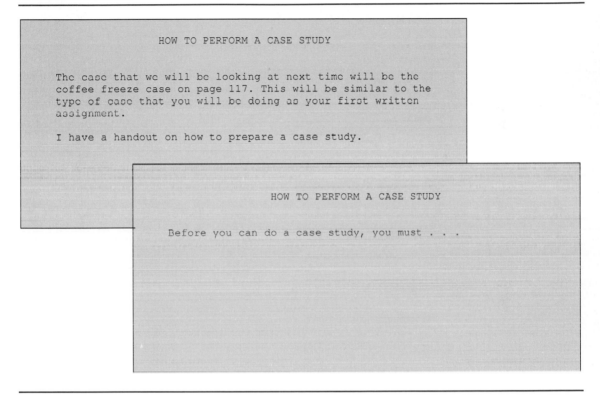

## SPREADSHEETS

A spreadsheet program simulates a paper spreadsheet or columnar pad. Spreadsheets are used to post columns of numbers that are then mathematically manipulated. Electronic spreadsheets originated with the introduction of VisiCalc in 1978. Electronic spreadsheets are used for recording historical data as well as for forecasting. They also are an integral part of decision support systems (DSSs) (Figure 6.5). They are used for any purpose that might employ a paper spreadsheet.

**FIGURE 6.4**

The appearance of this memo is changed significantly by altering the margins and fonts.

(a)

## WRITING A RESEARCH PAPER

Be sure that you understand the assignment before you begin, and that the paper is written to the assignment. Selection of topic is the basis of a good research paper. Choose your topic early. Be sure that it is of interest to you—you are going to be spending a lot of time studying it.

*Research*

Remember that all research is not reading—interviews, news programs, etc., may also expand your knowledge of the topic. The earlier you select a topic, the sooner you will recognize the opportunities for these types of research.

Do your research carefully: take notes on the material you read, hear, etc. Be sure to note the source: program, interviewee, date, publication, author, page number, etc. Organize your notes in such a way that they can be easily related to the sections of your paper.

Read/hear your sources critically. Everything will not necessarily be true or complete. We all have our biases; try to discern those of the authors. If your topic is controversial, study the opinions of those you agree with and those you don't, then let your paper reflect your own opinion. You can't disagree effectively if you don't understand opposing views.

OUTLINE

An outline enables you to structure your material into a logical order. This logical order makes all arguments in support of your theses more effective.

(b)

## WRITING A RESEARCH PAPER

Be sure that you understand the assignment before you begin, and that the paper is written to the assignment. Selection of topic is the basis of a good research paper. Choose your topic early. Be sure that it is of interest to you—you are going to be spending a lot of time studying it.

*Research*

Remember that all research is not reading—interviews, news programs, etc., may also expand your knowledge of the topic. The earlier you select a topic, the sooner you will recognize the opportunities for these types of research.

Do your research carefully: take notes on the material you read, hear, etc. Be sure to note the source: program, interviewee, date, publication, author, page number, etc. Organize your notes in such a way that they can be easily related to the sections of your paper.

Read/hear your sources critically. Everything will not necessarily be true or complete. We all have our biases; try to discern those of the authors. If your topic is controversial, study the opinions of those you agree with and those you don't, then let your paper reflect your own opinion. You can't disagree effectively if you don't understand opposing views.

**FIGURE 6.5**
Decision support systems (DSSs) are used to analyze unstructured types of problems. Spreadsheets aid managers in decision making by presenting alternative "what ifs." The bottom spreadsheet shows the effect of changing the unit cost of Part 3 from $5 to $4 for each of the 30 Part 3s used.

|              | PROD 1 | PROD 2 | PROD 3 | PROD 4 |
|--------------|--------|--------|--------|--------|
| PART 1       | 3      | 2      | 2      | 3      |
| PART 2       | 0      | 1      | 3      | 5      |
| PART 3       | 30     | 20     | 45     | 48     |
| PART 4       | 4      | 2      | 4      | 1      |
| PART 5       | 4      | 8      | 3      | 0      |
| COST BY PARTS |       |        |        |        |
| PART 1       | 3      | 2      | 2      | 3      |
| PART 2       | 0      | 2      | 6      | 10     |
| PART 3       | 150    | 100    | 225    | 240    |
| PART 4       | 8      | 4      | 8      | 2      |
| PART 5       | 24     | 48     | 18     | 0      |
| TOTAL COST BY PROD | 185 | 156 | 259 | 255 |

|              | PROD 1 | PROD 2 | PROD 3 | PROD 4 |
|--------------|--------|--------|--------|--------|
| PART 1       | 3      | 2      | 2      | 3      |
| PART 2       | 0      | 1      | 3      | 5      |
| PART 3       | 30     | 20     | 45     | 48     |
| PART 4       | 4      | 2      | 4      | 1      |
| PART 5       | 4      | 8      | 3      | 0      |
| COST BY PARTS |       |        |        |        |
| PART 1       | 3      | 2      | 2      | 3      |
| PART 2       | 0      | 2      | 6      | 10     |
| PART 3       | 120    | 80     | 180    | 192    |
| PART 4       | 8      | 4      | 8      | 2      |
| PART 5       | 24     | 48     | 18     | 0      |
| TOTAL COST BY PROD | 155 | 136 | 214 | 207 |

## Layout

With the spreadsheet program loaded, the CRT screen becomes a blank sheet. This sheet is made up of a matrix of columns and rows. The intersection of a column and a row forms a **cell** (Figure 6.6). A series of cells, called a **range,** may also be referenced as a group.

**FIGURE 6.6**

*The spreadsheet cell holds one unit of information.*

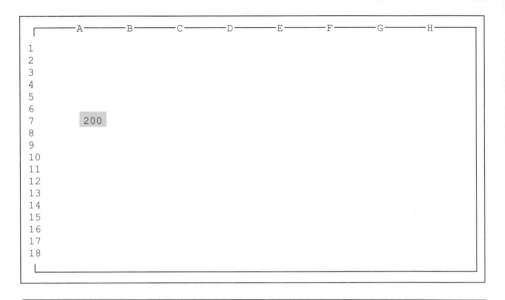

The **cell pointer,** which indicates the location on the screen as a cursor would, may be moved up, down, left, or right, often by means of the arrow keys. Each time the arrow key is pressed, the pointer moves one cell in that direction.

Spreadsheets may contain both data and the labels that identify that data (Figure 6.7). Either the labels, in the form of row and column headings, or the data may be entered into any cell.

## Spreadsheet Windows

Microsoft Works allows the user to create a spreadsheet too large to fit on a CRT screen. For this reason, the spreadsheet may be viewed through windows, views of particular sections of the spreadsheet.

## How the Spreadsheet Is Used

If a spreadsheet allowed you only to enter data and labels, its use would be very limited. The real value of a spreadsheet lies in its ability to manipulate the data through **formulas.**

**FIGURE 6.7**

Row and column headings identify the contents in a spreadsheet window. In this window, the word *cost* is in column E, row 3.

```
      ┌────A───────B───────C───────D───────E───────F───────G───────H──┐
   1  │  JOB                                                           │
   2  │                                                                │
   3  │  NUMBER              HOURS    RATE     COST                     │
   4  │                                                                │
   5  │                                                                │
   6  │                                                                │
   7  │       200             11     47.32    520.52                   │
   8  │       225             15     48.25    723.75                   │
   9  │       250              7     50.25    351.75                   │
  10  │       275             13     50.47    656.11                   │
  11  │                                                                │
  12  │                                                                │
  13  │                                                                │
  14  │                                                                │
  15  │                                                                │
  16  │                                                                │
  17  │                                                                │
  18  │                                                                │
      └────────────────────────────────────────────────────────────────┘
```

Suppose you want to sell items for a predetermined markup of the cost of materials. The markups are found in column B of the spreadsheet, and the cost of materials is found in column D. You wish to place the answer in column C. You enter the formula into column C. Formulas can contain the mathematical operators such as +, −, /, and *. They can also contain values or cell and range references (see Figure 6.8).

You can also multiply all the entries in column B by all the corresponding entries in column D and place all newly calculated selling prices in column C. Of course, much more complex computations are possible. The ability to manipulate values easily makes spreadsheets extremely useful in decision making.

Another valuable feature is the ability to split the screen. If this month's sales figures were found in column E and sales for the same month last year were in column Q, it would help to be able to view them side by side. Splitting the screen permits this viewing of nonadjacent columns and rows next to each other (see Figure 6.9). Note that the correct row and column titles remain visible.

Spreadsheets have many applications. They are frequently used to solve "what ifs": What if I could reduce the cost of each case by $.15? How would that affect profits? If we opened another warehouse in Des Moines, how would storage costs be affected? What if I bought the seed for $29.45 per bag? Could

**FIGURE 6.8**
This formula causes the contents of cell B7 to be multiplied by the contents of cell D7. The result is put in cell C7.

$$C7: +B7*D7$$

**FIGURE 6.9**
Split screens can also be used on a spreadsheet. This permits the user to see the contents of column E next to column A for comparison purposes.

|     | A         | E     | F     | G     | H      | I | J | K |
|-----|-----------|-------|-------|-------|--------|---|---|---|
| 1   |           | APRIL | MAY   | JUNE  |        |   |   |   |
| 2   |           |       |       |       |        |   |   |   |
| 3   | PRODUCT 1 | 1564  | 8932  | 7322  | 38559  |   |   |   |
| 4   | PRODUCT 2 | 2978  | 3064  | 4222  | 24015  |   |   |   |
| 5   | PRODUCT 3 | 2980  | 1987  | 3976  | 18932  |   |   |   |
| 6   | PRODUCT 4 | 3089  | 2347  | 2096  | 17241  |   |   |   |
| 7   | PRODUCT 5 | 5067  | 4568  | 3789  | 20503  |   |   |   |
| 8   |           |       |       |       |        |   |   |   |
| 9   | TOTAL     |       |       |       |        |   |   |   |
| 10  | COSTS     | 15678 | 20898 | 21405 | 119250 |   |   |   |
| 11  |           |       |       |       |        |   |   |   |
| 12  |           |       |       |       |        |   |   |   |
| 13  |           |       |       |       |        |   |   |   |
| 14  |           |       |       |       |        |   |   |   |
| 15  |           |       |       |       |        |   |   |   |
| 16  |           |       |       |       |        |   |   |   |
| 17  |           |       |       |       |        |   |   |   |
| 18  |           |       |       |       |        |   |   |   |

I sell it at a profit if it cost me $.75 per bag to store each month and $8.13 per hundredweight to ship?

Used in conjunction with other programs, spreadsheet information may be employed to produce graphs or may be included as part of textual reports.

## GRAPHICS

Although graphs may be made from any information, **graphics** are particularly useful for representing spreadsheet information. For many people, a picture is much more meaningful than any spreadsheet.

**FIGURE 6.10**
Several different types of graphs can be produced. The most frequently used are *(a)* the bar graph, *(b)* the line graph, and *(c)* the pie graph.

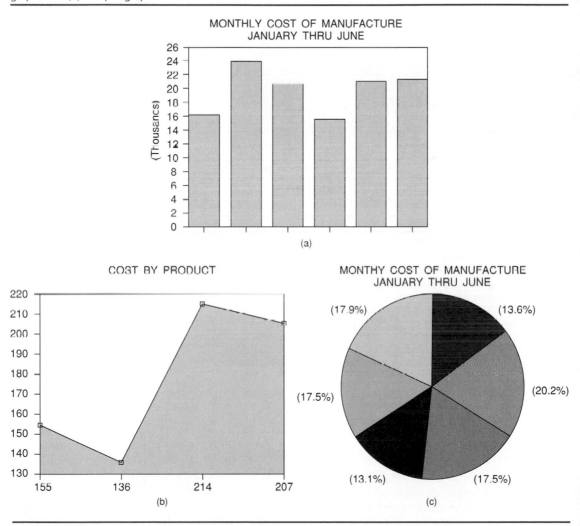

Microsoft Works can produce eight types of graphs: high-low graphs, two types of line graphs, three types of bar graphs, pie graphs, and XY (scatter) graphs (Figure 6.10). Bar, pie, and line graphs can be used for most applications. High-low graphs indicate a range, whether of temperature or stock market selling prices. XY charts indicate each occurrence and are helpful when individual activity is to be shown rather than trends. For example, an XY or scatter chart of the final grades of all class members would clearly indicate clusters of grades.

**FIGURE 6.11**
The range, selected through menu options, indicates what is to be graphed. B5 . . . M5 indicates that the contents of cells B5, C5, D5, E5, F5, G5, H5, I5, J5, K5, L5, and M5 are to be graphed.

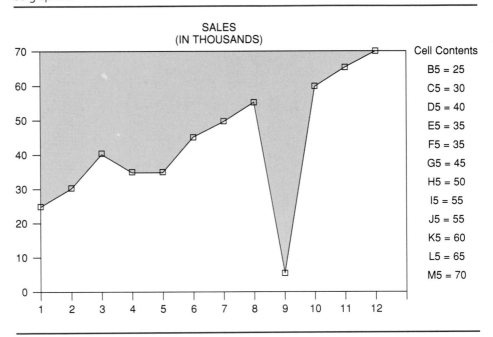

To create a graph, the user takes an existing spreadsheet and, using menu-driven options, indicates the type of graph to be created and its range. The range refers to which cell's contents are to be graphed (Figure 6.11).

With the data available and the graph type and range indicated, the graph is produced. Titles also may be created. These titles, along the axes of the graph, clarify the graph's meaning. The operator can also enter explanatory data labels at points along the graph, although too many labels tend to clutter and confuse the graph (Figure 6.12).

Once created, these graphs may be either viewed on the screen or printed. They may also be saved on disk for later use. Special equipment enables copies of the spreadsheets to be created on slides or transparencies for use in presentations.

## DATABASES

**Databases** are structured collections of information used for multiple purposes; they will be covered more fully in Chapter 10. Many database packages exist for microcomputers, but this section discusses only the one provided in Microsoft Works.

**FIGURE 6.12**

*(a)* Putting titles on each axis clarifies the meaning of the graph. *(b)* Although the use of many labels is confusing, an occasional data label (HOLIDAY) may help clarify the graph.

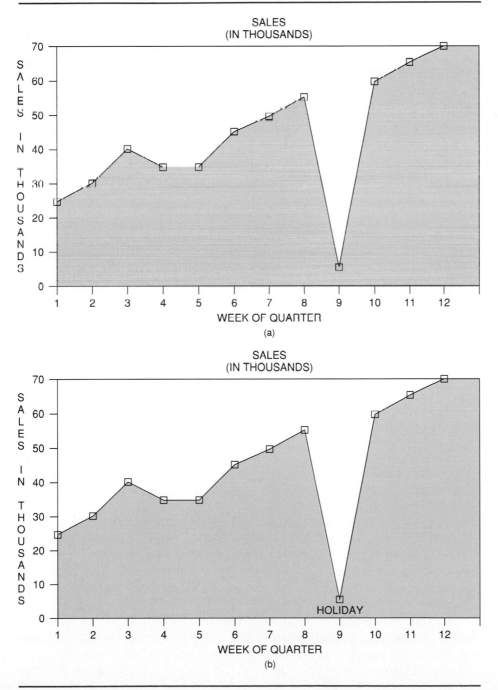

**FIGURE 6.13**

Think of each field within the database record as a cell. In this case, the item number is one field and the supplier is another.

| ITEM # NUMBER | SUPPLIER | QUANTITY ON HAND | REORDER POINT |
|---|---|---|---|
| 11010 | XYZ CORP | 126 | 50 |
| 11020 | XYZ CORP | 273 | 225 |
| 11030 | ABC LTD | 10 | 150 |
| 11040 | XYZ CORP | 128 | 150 |
| 11050 | NPAL INC | 1895 | 550 |
| 11060 | NPAL INC | 27089 | 25000 |
| 11070 | XYZ CORP | 57 | 100 |
| 11080 | ABC LTD | 1976 | 550 |

**FIGURE 6.14**

If the name of each column represents the field stored within it, finding and manipulating data will be easy. Item number 11070 can be located quickly by scanning the item number column.

| ITEM # NUMBER | SUPPLIER | QUANTITY ON HAND | REORDER POINT |
|---|---|---|---|
| 11010 | XYZ CORP | 126 | 50 |
| 11020 | XYZ CORP | 273 | 225 |
| 11030 | ABC LTD | 10 | 150 |
| 11040 | XYZ CORP | 128 | 150 |
| 11050 | NPAL INC | 1895 | 550 |
| 11060 | NPAL INC | 27089 | 25000 |
| 11070 | XYZ CORP | 57 | 100 |
| 11080 | ABC LTD | 1976 | 550 |

Think of the spreadsheet as you try to picture the database. Each record contains all of the information about one person, item, or event. A **record** is a single row. Each entry within that record is referred to as a *field*. It is single cell or group of adjacent cells within that row (Figure 6.13). Still thinking of the spreadsheet, picture the name of the field as the label at the top of each column.

Once the data is stored, it can be manipulated. Knowing the name of each field is the key to manipulating the data found within the database (Figure

**FIGURE 6.15**

The user can also easily select all data with a range of values. If column B represents the supplier, all items from NPAL, Inc., may be selected for display or listing.

| ITEM # NUMBER | SUPPLIER | QUANTITY ON HAND | REORDER POINT |
|---|---|---|---|
| 11010 | XYZ CORP | 126 | 50 |
| 11020 | XYZ CORP | 273 | 225 |
| 11030 | ABC LTD | 10 | 150 |
| 11040 | XYZ CORP | 128 | 150 |
| 11050 | NPAL INC | 1895 | 550 |
| 11060 | NPAL INC | 27089 | 25000 |
| 11070 | XYZ CORP | 57 | 100 |
| 11080 | ABC LTD | 1976 | 550 |

6.14). Specific data can be displayed, listed, counted, or located. The ability to manipulate that data goes far beyond simple counting. Statistical functions such as finding the highest or lowest value or calculating the average or the standard deviation may also be performed.

New records may be inserted and old records deleted or modified. The user may browse through existing records; certain ones may be selected and displayed based on any criteria the user chooses (Figure 6.15). For example, all persons living in Boston or all personnel having a job classification code of S25 may be displayed. Data may be selected by range as well, such as all persons with an S15 to S30 job class.

The user may also rearrange records within the file by sorting them in whatever order needed—ascending or descending. Once the needed information is selected and sorted, it may also be printed. With this ease and flexibility of use, database files can meet many organizational needs.

## COMMUNICATIONS

**Communications programs** transmit data to and receive data from terminals or other computers. With a communications program, you can connect your computer to another computer to exchange information. You can join bulletin boards, computer systems that are made available to many users with a common interest, which provide a centralized source of information and a message exchange. Your computer can automatically answer the call from another computer, and you may transfer data between computers.

## OTHER APPLICATIONS

Microcomputers use word processing, graphics, databases, and spreadsheets in a variety of ways. For instance, owners of rental property use them for recording rental information and producing reports of late rents, vacant apartments, current income, and so on. Air charter services use microcomputers to compare costs using different routes and aircraft. Churches record membership statistics, pledges, and donations.

At a local mall, someone in a booth may be selling computerized horoscopes, handwriting analyses, or even computer-generated pictures. Sports leagues find microcomputers useful for scheduling games and referees.

Medical personnel may use microcomputers for storing patient histories or communicating with expert systems in diagnosis. (Expert systems contain the knowledge of human experts; the knowledge is converted to rules and strategies, which are used as advice and guidance for decision making.) For many disabled persons, microcomputers serve as communications devices (see On the Job 2). The applications are endless.

## MICROCOMPUTERS AND THE DECISION–MAKING PROCESS

Most microcomputers are used for stand-alone applications (word processing, spreadsheets, and simple databases), which are useful in managerial decision making. However, as microcomputers are increasingly linked into networks with access to companywide databases, they are becoming even more important as tools for high-level decision making. A growing trend is toward the use of microcomputers in information centers, management information systems, and decision support systems.

### Information Centers

The term **information center (IC)** describes a facility that helps users interact with computers. As users become aware of more ways in which they can utilize computers to obtain useful information, they become more active in their efforts to obtain it.

An information center provides the hardware, software, and technical services that enable users to become active in obtaining their own information. Hardware would normally include microcomputers and/or terminals that may be linked to a host computer. Software would include application packages to meet user needs. Technical services include (but are not limited to) consulting, training, and troubleshooting.

One advantage to the IC concept is that users become more aware of what the computer can and cannot do. Also, ICs reduce costs of obtaining information and provide users with some control over developmental backlogs. Unfortu-

## ON THE JOB 2

*The Eyegaze System*

In June 1989, 10 Computerworld Smithsonian awards were given to honor innovative uses of information technology to help mankind. One recipient, L. C. Technologies—a small company in Fairfax, Virginia—won for its Eyegaze Computer system.

The system is designed to be run by profoundly disabled people. No external device is attached to the body of the system user, who may be spinal cord injured or suffer from a severe neurological deficit. Most DOS-compatible software can be operated by anyone who is able to focus his or her eyes on a "keyboard" shown on the screen of the computer's visual display terminal. The computer utilizes a mounted camera and an infrared light source to interpret where the eye is focused. The user then can visually issue commands that enable him or her to operate word processors, spreadsheets, databases, and so on. The system can also be used for environmental control activities such as turning on lights, operating telephones, and synthesizing speech.

In addition, the system has an optional HeadTracker portion that follows the user's eye movement across a wide range, enabling even those with poor head control or severe spasticity to communicate through the computer.

nately, the loss of central control over data results in some redundancy of data and a tendency of systems developed independently to not interact properly or be consistent with companywide systems.

## Management Information Systems

A **management information system (MIS)** means different things to different people. To some, it includes all managerial decision making, including decision support systems (DSSs). To others, it means a computer-based system that provides the user with information to support routine decision making; these people would distinguish it from a DSS, assigning to DSS systems the less routine decisions. We will separate MIS from DSS at this point and discuss them separately in spite of their close relationship.

If two main components of an MIS system are the user and the computer, a third and no less significant part is the data being processed. Databases (discussed in Chapter 10) enable data to be shared across applications. The data may be accessed quickly and inexpensively by many different users. Although many of the decisions made using an MIS are routine, they can be made much more rapidly than before; they can also be revised as alternatives are presented.

One routine decision frequently made in business involves inventory levels. These can be calculated by hand but that is time-consuming since calculations involve the rate of resupply, cost of each item held, cost of storing it, and usage rate. If any of these factors change, the economical ordering quantity will also change. Suppose you are the inventory manager. You normally order 500 XYZs each month at a cost of $100 each. You are offered the opportunity to buy 5,000 at a cost of $75 each but must take delivery on all of them this month. Is this a good buy? Rapid access to information to support your decision is essential. Other common uses of an MIS include sales analysis, production scheduling, and evaluation of investment alternatives.

## Decision Support Systems

A **decision support system (DSS)** uses data and technology to improve the decision-making process. Managers spend most of their time obtaining information, analyzing it, and attempting to make the best possible decisions based on the information available. Decision support systems, employing information that crosses departmental and divisional lines, include spreadsheets, graphics packages, statistical packages, and a query language.

However, it is not enough to obtain the correct information; the information must also be timely and must be analyzed accurately. To succeed, managers need as much help as possible. DSSs provide information from a variety of functional areas.

### Components

We often make decisions after considering the current situation and then saying "what if." What if sales increase 3 percent? What if I use part of my current plant capacity to manufacture a new product? What if the cost of a gasket used in our mixers increases $.02?

These "what ifs" can be quickly answered using modeling techniques. We build a model, perhaps of what the mixer costs the manufacturer now. Next, changes are made to individual figures: the cost of a gasket, the number of mixers sold, and so on. The computer is used to process these new figures to forecast the result of possible changes. Often, spreadsheet programs are used to create the model and to make rapid changes to it. So used, the spreadsheet becomes an integral part of a DSS.

For many people, a picture is really worth more than any number of words. Graphics packages are usually included in a DSS so that the results may be displayed graphically.

Because managers may need to obtain statistics from the data, statistical packages also are often an important part of decision support systems. The user of a DSS may also need to retrieve data quickly. Thus, a query language is normally a part of the system.

## Uses

The only purpose of a DSS is to solve problems; however, the uses are as varied as the problems it solves. All these problems have one point in common: they are not routine problems, and no established solution exists. Often, the problems occur only once; perhaps no one has faced such a decision before, and there are no precedents for making it. A solution must be created as the problem arises.

For example, the DSS can build models to compare the results of varying items used in assemblies, making various investments of available cash, or calculating the impact of taxes owed on these various investments. A food packer might ask, "How can I cut a mushroom for greatest profit? How many stems and pieces can I sell? How many buttons? How many should I broil in butter sauce?" All these questions can be forecast on a spreadsheet to show the resulting impact on profits.

Although the DSS aids the decision-making process, it does not provide a solution or suggest which solution should be chosen. It simply provides the ability to build a model, compare the alternatives, and supply the information necessary to evaluate them.

The future of DSS, as well as of most of data processing, lies in more and more integration of information. Databases shared among the various users through networking will permit rapid access to the most accurate and timely data.

## SUMMARY

The switch from single-purpose software to integrated software is occurring rapidly. An integrated software package provides the ability to easily exchange data between individual programs. Microsoft Works is an integrated package that provides five of the basic microcomputer application capabilities: word processing, spreadsheet, graphics, database, and communications.

Word processing is a major microcomputer application. It permits the keying in of textual information, easy modifications within the text, and electronic storage and retrieval. Word processing documents may also be integrated with spreadsheet data (Figure 6.16).

The spreadsheet is divided into rows and columns that form cells, each of which can contain one item of data. The user can move from one cell to another by means of the cell pointer. Because the spreadsheet is usually too large to fit on a CRT screen all at one time, it is viewed through windows. The screen may be split to enable one to view nonadjacent data simultaneously. The strength of the spreadsheet is that a change to one or more fields can be propagated throughout the entire spreadsheet easily.

Because spreadsheet information may often be more clearly expressed with visuals, the graphics section of the package permits the user to generate bar, line, pie, XY (scatter), and high-low graphs from existing spreadsheet data.

**FIGURE 6.16**

The usefulness of both spreadsheets and word processing is increased by their integration. In this figure, spreadsheet sales figures have been included in a word processed memo.

```
From: N. Hillard

Subject: First quarter sales

I have completed the analysis of first quarter sales. The overall
sales picture is good. There was an upward trend all quarter with
the exception of week nine, the holiday when the plant was closed
except for rush orders.

Sales were (in thousands)

Week 1          25
Week 2          30
Week 3          40
Week 4          35
    . . .
Week 12         70

I am pleased with your efforts so far and expect the good work to
continue throughout the remainder of the year.
```

Database storage resembles storage of spreadsheet information. Each record resembles a row, and each field within the record resembles a cell. Once the data is stored, it can be located, displayed, listed, or counted. Some statistical functions can also be performed within the database.

Communications programs enable one computer to communicate with another to exchange information.

As microcomputers increasingly have access to companywide databases, they are becoming more useful in decision making. ICs, or information centers, enable users to interact creatively with computers. Management information systems (MISs) aid managers in making the more routine decisions, whereas decision support systems (DSSs) provide a way to answer the what-if questions managers frequently face. Rapid access to and sharing of information across organizational boundaries will become even more important in the future.

## VOCABULARY

Cell   *127*

Cell pointer   *128*

Communications program   *135*

Database   *132*

Decision support system (DSS)   *138*

Formula   *128*

Graphics   *130*

Information center (IC)   *136*

Management information system (MIS)   *137*

Microsoft Works   *121*

Range   *127*

Record   *134*

Scrolling   *124*

Window   *124*

Word wrap (wrap around)   *124*

## EXERCISES

1. What is the difference between single-purpose and integrated packages?
2. What is a spreadsheet?
3. Explain the concept of rows, columns, and cells.
4. What does a cell contain?
5. How is the cell pointer used?
6. What is a window?
7. Can graphics be created from spreadsheet data? If so, can a graph be created from only a portion of the data?
8. What is a data label?
9. Describe each of the following types of graphs: bar, line, XY (scatter), pie, and high-low. What might be a use of each?
10. What are the advantages of word processing over typing?
11. Can you change margins, tabs, or page length after a document is written on a word processor?
12. What is meant by electronic filing?
13. Describe the layout of a Microsoft Works database.
14. Can the database portion of Microsoft Works do any manipulation of the data? If so, what can it do?
15. What is the difference between DSSs and MISs?
16. What is an information center?
17. What types of software might be used for MISs and DSSs?

## PROJECTS

1. Research and report on how microcomputers are used in one local business.

2. Using whichever word processing package is available to you, produce the report for project 1.

3. Select one business application of a spreadsheet. Describe how the spreadsheet would be used. Two possible applications are as follows: (1) What will happen to our profits if transportation costs increase 1 percent? (2) I need to compare this year's earnings to last year's, quarter by quarter. A graph would help; I could make a transparency and use it at the meeting.

4. Using whichever spreadsheet package is available to you, create a spreadsheet. Each column represents a product. There are four rows: the first row contains the name of the product (product 1 through product 5); the second row contains the original cost of the product ($152, $375, $250, $198, and $273). Use the spreadsheet function to calculate row 3, the overhead, if it is 35 percent of the original cost of each product. Also calculate row 4, the total cost, which is the original cost plus overhead.

5. How might a business use a DSS? What advantages would a DSS have over calculations made by hand?

6. You are a new user of an information center. What services would you expect to find?

# 7

# The Systems Approach

## CHAPTER OBJECTIVES

*After completing this chapter, you will be able to:*

1. Identify where requests for systems service originate.
2. Describe the systems life cycle.
3. Recognize several fact-finding techniques (questionnaires, observation, and interviews) and discuss the advantages and disadvantages of each.
4. Recognize and understand the purpose of systems flowcharts, data flow diagrams, and data dictionaries.
5. Describe the steps in creating a new system: designing files, output, input, and system controls.

## OVERVIEW

*study + solution of problems*

**Systems analysis** is the study and solution of problems. This solution often, although not always, involves the use of computers. It always involves people: the users. The analysis may suggest that the problem could be solved by writing or modifying one program, a group of related programs, or an entire system.

Additional writing may not be required; instead, the solution may be to purchase existing software, to issue reports at a different time, or to distribute existing reports differently. Whatever changes are made, users will be affected. Good systems design involves users from the earliest research stages through final training.

## WHAT IS THE SYSTEMS APPROACH?

*group of elements that perform a task.*

A **system** is a group of interrelated elements that work together to perform a specific task. There are many business systems. For example, a payroll system is made up of all the programs and procedures that work together to create a payroll and to produce the information associated with it. This includes, among other things, time cards, the personnel file, deduction information, a program to calculate earnings and taxes, a program to print checks, error reports, and programs to produce government reports such as 941s and W-2s (Figure 7.1). This union of individual elements gives the system itself a value exceeding that of the sum of its elements.

A system is usually developed to satisfy a request made either by an end-user or by data processing personnel. The request may result from the need to obtain information not currently available, such as, "We need to know how our telephones are being used. Can the computer monitor our telephone usage?" It may also originate because of something that is not occurring or is not occurring correctly: "Our inventory system needs to be upgraded. The inventory list is obsolete by the time we receive it. If we could update the inventory as changes occur, we could display a current inventory on our CRTs. That would let us schedule our production more efficiently."

Because the value of the system is dependent on how well its elements relate to each other, the systems approach is designed to ensure that all elements—data, programs, information, and users—will work together meticulously.

**FIGURE 7.1**

Payroll activity begins with the employee clocking in. Time cards are verified against the master file and the rate of pay obtained. After earnings are calculated, checks and a payroll register are produced.

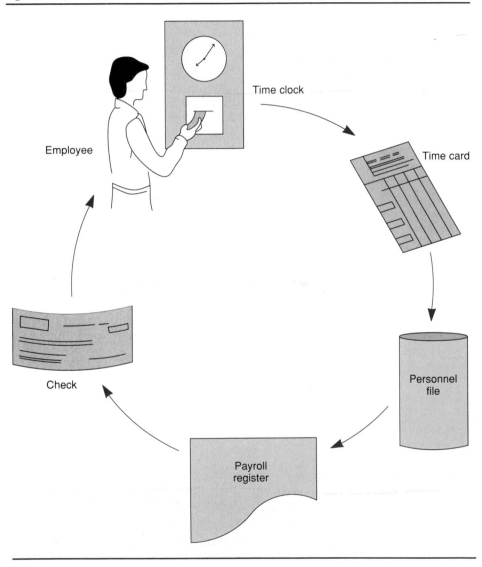

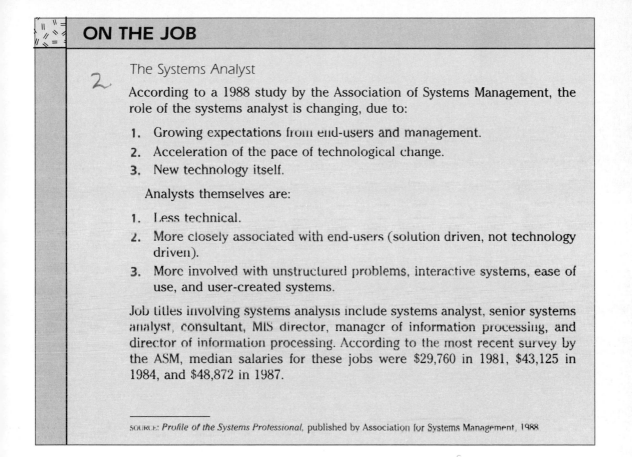

## ON THE JOB

2

The Systems Analyst

According to a 1988 study by the Association of Systems Management, the role of the systems analyst is changing, due to:

1. Growing expectations from end-users and management.
2. Acceleration of the pace of technological change.
3. New technology itself.

Analysts themselves are:

1. Less technical.
2. More closely associated with end-users (solution driven, not technology driven).
3. More involved with unstructured problems, interactive systems, ease of use, and user-created systems.

Job titles involving systems analysis include systems analyst, senior systems analyst, consultant, MIS director, manager of information processing, and director of information processing. According to the most recent survey by the ASM, median salaries for these jobs were $29,760 in 1981, $43,125 in 1984, and $48,872 in 1987.

SOURCE: *Profile of the Systems Professional,* published by Association for Systems Management, 1988.

## The Systems Analyst

*— person who makes a system work.*

*① elicit info*
*② involve the users*
*③ work with people at all levels*
*④ gain support.*

The person who is responsible for making these elements work together is the **systems analyst.** The analyst must have the technical skills necessary to develop creative solutions to problems, evaluate alternative solutions, manage the resulting project, and implement the new system. Technical skills alone are not enough, however; he or she must also possess interpersonal skills to complement those technical skills (see On the Job).

For most of us, change is a frightening experience. The analyst almost always introduces changes in existing work patterns, and many people perceive these changes as a threat. The analyst must be able to: (1) elicit valid information from people in spite of this perceived threat, (2) involve the users in creating

**FIGURE 7.2**

After the payroll system is broken into its primary components *(a)*, each of those components may be further broken down *(b)*.

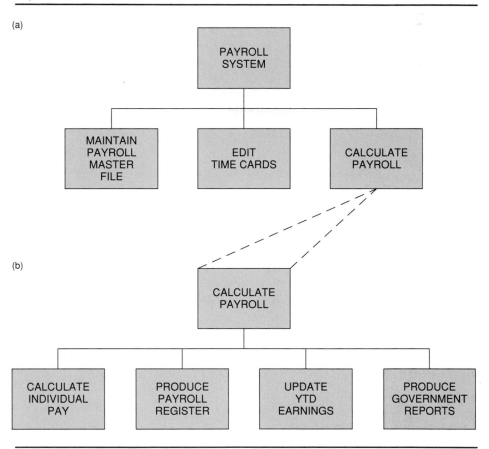

change, (3) work with people at all levels of an organization, and (4) gain their support in effecting change. Later in this chapter, we'll take a closer look at the tools the analyst uses and the skills he or she applies during the process of developing a new system.

## Structured Systems Development

It is crucial that systems design follow an orderly process. Users must remain involved to ensure that the final system will meet their needs. Costs must be carefully monitored continuously throughout systems development to ensure that they do not exceed benefits. Management should insist that good development practices be followed in order to protect their investment.

*① designing the system.*

Attempts to meet these criteria have led to a methodology of systems development referred to as **structured systems development.** A component of structured systems development is **structured systems design,** whereby all functions are analyzed in minute detail.

When a system is designed, each of the major functions of the system is identified and described. For example, in a payroll system, some major functions are to maintain the payroll master file, to edit hours worked each week, and to calculate the payroll, as shown in Figure 7.2(a).

These major functions are then broken down into their subfunctions. To continue our payroll example, calculating the payroll would consist of calculating gross and net pay, producing the payroll register, updating year-to-date earnings, and producing government reports such as W-2s and 941s, as shown in Figure 7.2(b). These subfunctions could be further broken down, as necessary, into their own subfunctions.

Finally, the system is described as a series of elementary functions called modules. Each module should perform one function independently so that a change in one module does not affect any other.

Armed with this methodology, the systems analyst is ready to begin the series of procedures that constitute the systems development life cycle.

*1.*

# THE SYSTEMS DEVELOPMENT LIFE CYCLE

*① initial request ⑤ creation of system*
*② survey ⑥ installation*
*③ def'n of users ⑦ evaluation.*
*④ alternatives*

The **systems development life cycle (SDLC)** consists of the initial request, a preliminary feasibility survey, definition of the users' requirements, evaluation of alternative solutions, creation of the new system, installation of that system, and, finally, evaluation of the results.

## Initial Request

*4.*

Many occurrences prompt the initiation of a systems project: a difficulty may be encountered in the running of an existing system; one of the managers may attend a conference where he hears what a competitor is doing and wants to do something similar; another manager may look over her budget, realize that costs must be cut, and suggest changes.

The original request may come from a user, the computer operations department, or the data processing department itself. It may come via a telephone call or be written on a preprinted form or on memo paper (Figure 7.3). Regardless of where the request originates, a decision must be made about how to act on it.

## Preliminary Feasibility Survey

Most systems departments receive more requests for service than they have the time or personnel to fulfill. Some requests are trivial but originate from influential people or departments. Other requests may provide real cost-saving

**FIGURE 7.3**
An initial request for systems development may be quite simple and informal.

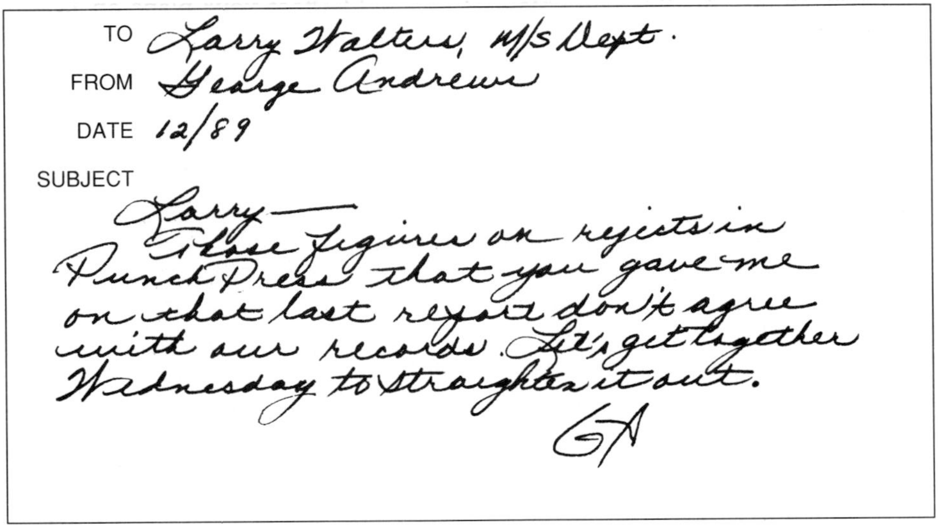

TO Larry Walters, M/S Dept.
FROM George Andrews
DATE 12/89
SUBJECT

Larry—
Those figures on rejects in Punch Press that you gave me on that last report don't agree with our records. Let's get together Wednesday to straighten it out.

GA

opportunities but be too expensive to complete given the current budget. Some requests may lack management support, while still others may define as a problem what is only a symptom of a greater problem. Somehow, all these requests must be prioritized.

Many organizations have a steering committee that prioritizes requests. This committee is most often made up of people from several areas in the organization, not just from the systems area itself. This committee decides which requests will be studied, postponed, or dropped entirely. (Those that are to be studied must also be prioritized in some way.) When a request is approved, the **preliminary feasibility study** begins.

The preliminary feasibility study has several purposes. One is to determine if the perceived problem is, in fact, the real problem. Other purposes include determining how urgent the problem is, whether the problem merits the time, effort, and money necessary to solve it, and what possible cost/benefits may arise from the solution.

Feasibility is determined not once but repeatedly throughout the development cycle. It is necessary to determine at the beginning of any project whether or not to proceed. It is equally necessary to continue to look at the feasibility as the project progresses since new information is continually uncovered. This new information may reveal as unprofitable projects that at first glance appeared feasible.

Suppose you have a project in mind that you estimate will cost $50,000 and will return $250,000 over the next five years. After you've spent $25,000, further study indicates that it will really cost $500,000 and will return only $250,000. Obviously, this new information would affect your plans and cause you to change directions. For that reason, the feasibility of a project should continually be reviewed.

## Definition of User Requirements

Another crucial step in a systems study is to define the user requirements: what does the user need from the system? Often, users don't really know what is needed; they may perceive problems with the current way of doing things yet have only the vaguest idea of how to do it better. Even if they know what output is needed at present from the new system, they may be unaware of long-term future needs.

It is the analyst's job to study the current system, determining what works and should be retained as well as what should be added or changed. The analyst must also determine how a proposed system will affect other areas of the business, since sometimes the needs of one department conflict with those of another. How the current system works is recorded by the analyst using such tools as system flowcharts and data flow diagrams (which will be discussed later in this chapter).

## Evaluation of Alternative Solutions

Once the current way of doing things is understood, alternative solutions to the problem are considered. Perhaps the old system should remain in place (maybe the real problem is the personnel using it or the way it is being used). Another solution may be to purchase an available packaged system and install it. Still other solutions might be to develop the system in-house, to purchase new, more efficient equipment, or to convert an existing batch system to an on-line one.

In evaluating alternative solutions, there must be agreement about what constitutes the *best* solution. Is best the least expensive? The most sophisticated? The most machine efficient? Some questions must be answered before a system can be considered feasible: Can we do it with the people and equipment we have? If not, can we afford to replace either people or equipment? Will the system meet the users' requirements? How will it affect current jobs and the people holding them? What will the system cost, and what will the benefits be? (See Figure 7.4.) Both tangible (easily measured) and intangible (difficult or impossible to quantify) costs and benefits must be considered. One system may cost less to develop but be more expensive to run; another may be inexpensive to run but require extensive training of users.

**FIGURE 7.4**

There are many costs and benefits associated with change. These are only a few.

|  | Tangible | Intangible |
|---|---|---|
| *Costs* | | |
| | Additional equipment purchased | Lowering of employee morale |
| | Overtime during conversion | Poorer service during conversion |
| | Additional training | Negative public relations |
| | Additional supplies | Loss of control |
| | Higher operating costs | Loss of efficiency due to learning curve |
| *Benefits* | | |
| | Decreased response time | Improved goodwill |
| | Decreased error rate | Improved employee morale |
| | Reduced expenses | Improved company image |
| | Elimination of job steps | Improved control |
| | Increased profits | Improved decision making |
| | Faster turnaround | Increased operating efficiency |
| | Faster decision making | |
| | Decreased computer time | |
| | Decreased personnel costs | |
| | Sale of replaced equipment | |
| | Increased accuracy | |
| | Reduced maintenance | |

After each possible solution is evaluated, one is recommended to the requesting user. Acceptance of this recommendation is up to the user, since his or her budget will be paying for it. Ideally, the analyst is not the creator of a new system but a collaborator with the user in its creation.

## Creation of the New System

Once a recommendation for a new system is approved, implementation plans must be made.

If the system is to be purchased (as many are today), files, reports, and internal controls may already be designed. It may be possible to modify the purchased system, customizing it to specialized needs. External controls such as password access to information or controls over distribution of printed information must still be designed. And, of course, user training will be required.

If the new system is not purchased, the analyst must develop it in-house. This will require the design of output, files, input, and controls.

6.

### Design of Output

*find out what the user needs.*

First, the output is designed. Why start with the output? Why not start at the beginning, with the input? The first step in designing any system is to know what the user needs from the system, and these user needs are the results—the output. Only when you are sure of the output can the input be determined.

First, the analyst looks at the content and purpose of the output. Is it going to be used within the organization or outside it? Is it meant to show detailed activity, to summarize it, or to call attention to exceptions? These are the types of questions that must be addressed in output design.

### Design of Files

Once the output has been determined, files must be designed. These files will contain all data necessary to produce the output. Elimination of redundant data is a primary consideration, and, ideally, an item of information should appear in only one file. Redundant data items use more storage space; moreover, when data is updated, it must be changed in each location, increasing the chance that the redundant fields could contain different values for the same data item, thus destroying the data's integrity.

### Design of Input

Where does the data in these files come from? How can we capture it? How do we input it to the computer? Once again, the analyst first determines what input is required by the system and what is already available. Next, the media, method, and format of that input must be selected. The media might be magnetic tape or disk, optical mark, bar code, or a CRT terminal. The method may be batch or on-line. Accurate data input is essential, since, of course, the quality of the input affects the quality of the resultant output.

### Design of Controls

Throughout the entire design phase, the analyst stresses the need for data accuracy and integrity. Measures must be taken to prevent the loss or corruption of data, to detect such loss or corruption when it does occur, and to recover from it.

The organization's own internal auditors may be involved in designing controls. Their concerns include security, emergency and fallback (recovery) procedures, and the existence of an acceptable **audit trail,** or record of transactions.

## Installation

Installation involves placing the new system into operation. Before a system can be turned over to operations or to the user department, several things must occur: files must be converted, users trained, and the system itself converted from old to new.

**FIGURE 7.5**
A follow-up evaluation should occur after the new system has been in operation for some time.

TO Larry
FROM George
DATE 6/89
SUBJECT The New Inventory System
It's been running great! When we went to run the quarterly reports, though Anna noticed that the last employee was missing from the 941s. We typed him up, but you'd better correct the program by next quarter.
GA

One major activity is the retraining of users. Ideally, the users have been involved in the entire systems development life cycle. Who knows more about what the system will be used for? But whether or not these people have been involved previously, they must be involved now. Users must be taught to use new equipment, follow new procedures, and interpret new reports. The most critical factor in the success or failure of a systems project is people. Users may be highly skilled—even expert—at using current equipment. Change makes them beginners again, as unfamiliar with the procedures as the newest person hired. Training must be designed to meet these users' needs. It must also be scheduled so that users are able to attend. Those who work from 11 P.M. to 7 A.M. need training that meets their schedule. Moreover, because some users may be reluctant to attend, training should be not just available but actually required. Ongoing support after installation must also be made available—through manuals, self-help features in the programs themselves, and the availability of support personnel on a long-term or permanent basis.

## Evaluation

Implementation doesn't mark the end of the systems cycle. It does, however, mark the time when the systems analyst and the development team can look back and evaluate what happened. A successful installation means different things to different people. To some, it may mean that the system was installed on time, that it was error-free, and that cost projections were not exceeded. To others, it may mean that it was easy to learn, that documentation was clear, that training was adequate, and that installation was not disruptive to normal operations.

Regardless of what determines a successful system, evaluation is necessary. Frequently, this evaluation takes place in two stages. The first may occur immediately after installation. At this time, the systems development team is still together; events—both good and bad—are fresh in their memories. This is the time to look back on the experience and see what went well and should be repeated, as well as what mistakes were made and should be avoided. The second stage of the evaluation may take place much later, perhaps after six months. This distancing permits additional problems to surface. Users, having become familiar with the system by using it for several months, may now be able to suggest further refinements, corrections, and improvements (Figure 7.5).

## AN ANALYST'S SPECIAL TOOLS

During the course of the systems development life cycle, the analyst needs to record what is being done currently as well as to describe what will be done in the future. To do this, the analyst uses specialized tools to document existing systems and to design new ones. These tools include systems flowcharts, data flow diagrams, and data dictionaries. Other aids in systems design include proto typing and the use of CASE packages.

### Systems Flowcharts

A **systems flowchart** is a diagram showing the overall flow of data through a system. It shows where the data originates, how it is manipulated, and where it goes in its final output form. The data and processes are indicated using graphic symbols and flow lines (Figure 7.6).

### Data Flow Diagrams

**Data flow diagrams (DFDs)** are also used to show the overall flow of data throughout a system. This overview is recorded using four types of symbols: **process, external entity, data store,** and **data flow** (Figure 7.7, bottom).

Unlike systems flowcharts, which usually only show an overview of the system, data flow diagrams are often layered. This means that the first diagram drawn reflects the analyst's original overview of the system. As the analyst learns

**FIGURE 7.6**
Each symbol has a meaning in a systems flowchart. The flow is from top to bottom.

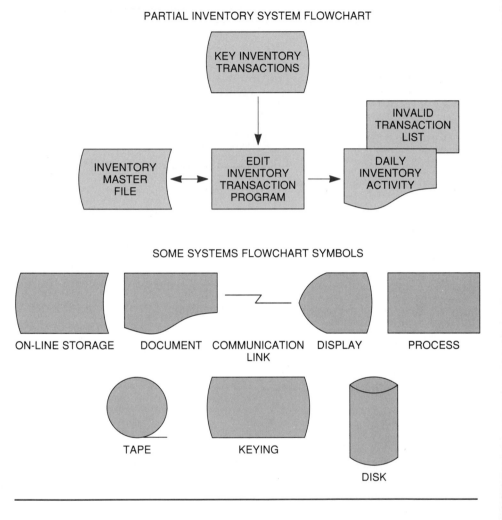

PARTIAL INVENTORY SYSTEM FLOWCHART

SOME SYSTEMS FLOWCHART SYMBOLS

more and more about the details of the system, he or she can draw a series of more detailed diagrams. For example, in the DFD in Figure 7.7 (top), the analyst identifies one activity as the creation of the invoice. In a second layer (not shown), this would be expanded to describe the individual tasks that go into the creation of that invoice: checking the credit rating, typing the invoice, forwarding the invoice to warehouse for item selection, and mailing the invoice with items ordered.

**FIGURE 7.7**

In a data flow diagram, external entities are people and organizations outside the system; data flows include forms, reports, letters, data transmissions, and so on; data stores are files, reference books, logs, and so on; a process is an action performed on a data flow.

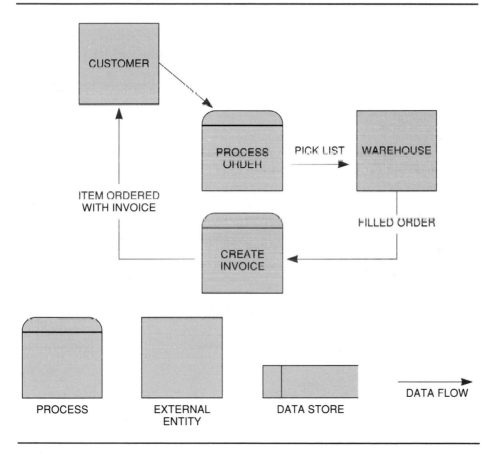

## Data Dictionaries

A **data dictionary** contains information about data elements and data groups within the system. The content of each data store and each data flow is also described (Figure 7.8). The data dictionary is used throughout systems development to keep track of all the details about each data item: its size, structure, components, usage, and so on.

**FIGURE 7.8**
Data dictionary.

| | |
|---|---|
| NAME OF FILE OR RECORD: | *CUSTOMER-CREDIT* |
| PREPARED BY: *N. FLOYD* | DATE: |

ACCESS AND ORGANIZATION

| PROGRAM PROCESS NAME | ACTIVITY RATIO | UPDATE? | ACCESS METHOD |
|---|---|---|---|
| *INVOICES* | *1:50* | *YES* | *RANDOM* |
| | | | |

The data store CUSTOMER-CREDIT is a collection of records that describe customer accounts.

An occurrence of CUSTOMER-CREDIT is uniquely identified by the element CUSTOMER ID.

The CUSTOMER-CREDIT data store contains 1,000 occurrences with an anticipated growth of 15 percent per year.

A CUSTOMER-CREDIT consists of the following data elements:

    CUSTOMER ID

    CUSTOMER NAME

## 3. Prototyping

One trend in systems design is **prototyping.** What better way could there be to reassure users that a change will work than to show it working, or at least to show a sample of how it will work? Prototyping is the creation of a sample—a working system that will illustrate the proposed system. The user then may approve the model or may ask that it be modified. The process of sample creation and modification continues until the user is satisfied with the prototype that illustrates the final system.

Two factors have influenced the rise of prototyping: the increasing involvement of users in the design of their systems and the development of special-purpose software that makes rapid prototyping possible. Frequently, users know what is needed but are unable to clearly specify their requirements. Through prototyping, the requirements can evolve during the design phase. In addition, continuous participation increases user involvement in and commitment to successful systems implementation. Special-purpose software used in prototyping includes fourth-generation languages and program code generators.

## CASE Packages

**CASE (computer-aided software engineering) packages** are used by many organizations as an aid in systems design. Using a CASE package, the analyst enters preliminary system specifications; data and process specifications are then generated and verified by users and other involved personnel for completeness, accuracy, and consistency

Additions and modifications can be made and new specifications generated much more quickly than with manual methods. This ease of modification encourages a much more interactive approach to systems design. In addition to being used in systems design, many CASE packages also include automated code generators.

## MANAGEMENT SKILLS FOR THE ANALYST

Clearly, the analyst is not only a designer but also a manager. Budgets are developed and adhered to. Information is gathered from users. Relationships among users, programmers, analysts, and operations personnel are managed. The systems analyst must apply many management skills including project management, fact-finding techniques, and cost/benefit analysis.

### Project Management

Technical design skills are not enough for the analyst. The systems development project must be managed: users must be interviewed; the system must be designed, developed, and installed; users must be trained; follow-up evaluation must be conducted. Not only must all these steps be completed; they must be completed on time and within budget. Thus, people, money, and time are all managed. Two tools that the analyst uses to help manage time are Gantt and PERT charts.

**Gantt charts** were developed by Henry Gantt in 1917. They permit the analyst to measure actual performance time against the original schedule. Although the technique is both simple and old, Gantt charts are still widely used because they are effective (Figure 7.9).

**PERT (program evaluation and review technique) charts** were developed in the late 1950s. Their strength is their ability to indicate the interrelationship of tasks and the critical path(s) through the project (Figure 7.10). A critical

*[handwritten margin notes: "9." ; "measures perfor. time against original schedule" ; "indicates relationships + paths."]*

**FIGURE 7.9**

Gantt charts compare estimated times to actual times.

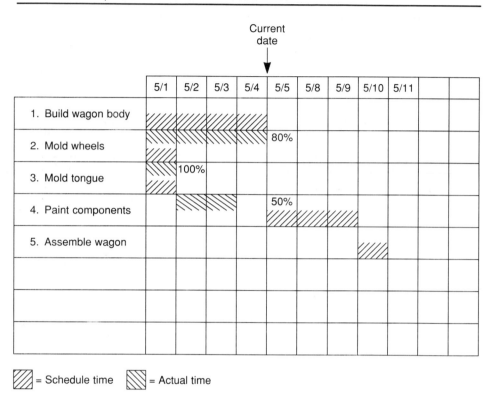

path is a path along which any delay will cause the completion date of the entire project to be missed.

Gantt charts are simpler, but PERT charts better illustrate the interdependency of tasks. In practice, the two types are often used together—the Gantt to indicate progress and the PERT to indicate the critical path(s) and the interdependency of tasks.

## Fact-Finding Techniques

The analyst must gather information throughout the entire SDLC. To do so, he or she uses several fact-finding techniques, including (but not limited to) observation, interviews, and questionnaires.

Although observation may seem at first to be a very reliable method, it has several drawbacks. First, people are sensitive about being observed, and this sensitivity often affects their performance. Second, the work being observed

**FIGURE 7.10**

PERT charts illustrate interdependencies. Note that the length of the line does not reflect the time involved. Tasks A, D, and E make up the critical path.

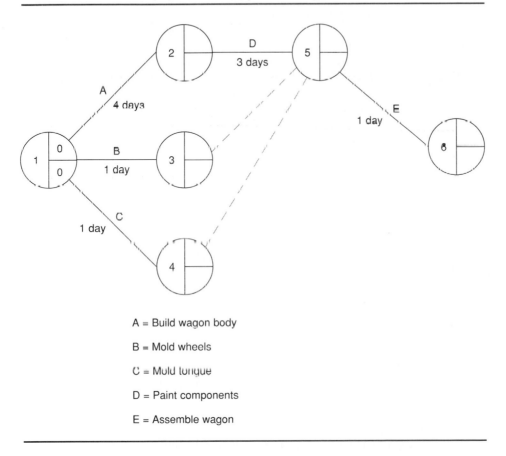

A = Build wagon body

B = Mold wheels

C = Mold tongue

D = Paint components

E = Assemble wagon

at any point in time may not be typical; some activities may not occur at all, and the workload may not reflect normal volumes. Third, it may be necessary to observe at inconvenient times (for example, during the third shift), or unpredictable times (for example, during emergency procedures).

Interviews enable the systems analyst to collect information and opinions from individuals face to face. The interviewee can respond freely to questions, reword questions, and provide more information than was requested. This technique also permits the interviewer to respond to the interviewee's body language and to restructure the interview while it is in progress. The disadvantages are that interviews are costly, time-consuming, and sometimes not feasible due to the diversity of locations of the interviewees.

Questionnaires are the least expensive method of information gathering. If well designed, they are easy to tabulate and analyze. They also permit anonymity, which may increase the honesty of the answers. However, there are drawbacks to this technique. First, many people do not respond at all or do not answer all the questions. Second, since questionnaires are usually mailed out, there is no opportunity to clarify a question or to elaborate on an answer. Third, it is very difficult to prepare a clear, concise questionnaire that is also easy to tabulate.

## Cost/Benefit Analysis

As mentioned previously, the feasibility of a systems project is measured not just at the beginning of the project but throughout development. One critical factor in the value of any project is a measure of the cost of completing the project compared with the anticipated benefits that will arise from its completion.

Benefits and costs are both tangible (easily measured) and intangible, as discussed earlier. Many methods exist for evaluating the value of a project. They include payback analysis and return-on-investment analysis.

**Payback analysis** looks at the development and operating costs—that is, how much they are and when they will occur. The analyst then determines the benefits that will accrue and when they will occur. Finally, the analyst determines when the benefits will begin to exceed the costs. The results of this evaluation might be, for example: "In two and one-half years, we will have repaid the cost of doing this project. In the following six months after we repay all costs, we will save an additional $25,000 because we installed this system."

**Return-on-investment analysis** looks at the savings potential of a project (lifetime benefits minus lifetime costs) and relates these savings to the original cost in an attempt to measure the relationship between the benefits and the original cost. This process provides the analyst with ways of comparing alternative actions requiring different investments. For example, one option may cost $10,000 and have lifetime benefits of $25,000. A second option may have lifetime benefits of only $22,000 but cost $7,500. Which is the better choice? Return-on-investment analysis would indicate that the first option had a return of:

$$\$25,000 - \$10,000 = \$15,000$$

$$\$15,000/\$10,000 = 150 \text{ percent}$$

The second option would return:

$$\$22,000 - \$7,500 = \$14,500$$

$$\$14,500/\$7,500 = 193 \text{ percent}$$

*When* the costs and benefits occur is also important. **Present value analysis** converts future costs and benefits to today's dollars and is also a major part of cost/benefit analysis.

## TRENDS

The trend in systems analysis is toward an increasing use of prototypes for systems development as well as increased use of program generators. More systems will be on-line, real-time, and distributed. This will require analysts to continually consider the security, privacy, and audit trail of systems as they are developed.

## SUMMARY

A system is a group of interrelated elements that work together to perform a specific task. Systems analysis is the study and solution of problems in a system, often involving the use of computers and always involving the users of the system. The person responsible for developing these solutions, evaluating alternative ones, managing the resulting project, and implementing the changes is the systems analyst.

The systems development life cycle, the series of procedures that leads to this implementation, includes the initial request, a preliminary feasibility study, definition of user requirements, evaluation of alternative solutions, creation of the new system, implementation of the system, and analysis of the results.

The analyst uses specific tools to carry out these procedures. These include systems flowcharts, data flow diagrams, data dictionaries, prototyping, and the use of CASE packages. Managerial skills are also required. These include time management skills, fact-finding techniques, and cost/benefit analysis.

## VOCABULARY

## ▣ EXERCISES

1. What is meant by the systems development life cycle? List its steps.
2. Discuss the interpersonal skills needed by a systems analyst.
3. What is prototyping? Why are more organizations using it?
4. Where do requests for systems service originate?
5. When is project feasibility evaluated?
6. Why is output designed first?
7. What is the difference between tangible and intangible costs? Tangible and intangible benefits?
8. What is a systems flowchart?
9. What is the difference between Gantt and PERT charts?
10. What are the advantages and disadvantages of observation, interviews, and questionnaires as fact-finding methods?

## ▣ PROJECTS

1. Design a method of gathering information about your college's registration process. Collect forms, and describe how you would study the current system (interviews, questionnaires, and so on).
2. You have been asked by a very small business to help select an inventory system. Since they will purchase the system, they see no reason to spend any time studying their current one. Write them a memo describing why you want to go through the entire systems development life cycle.
3. You have been asked to design a new time card. From whom might you want to gather information? Why? What techniques would you use to gather this information? Why?

# 8

# The Programming Process

## CHAPTER OBJECTIVES

*After completing this chapter, you will be able to:*

1. Discuss why some logic design is needed before you begin programming.
2. Differentiate between flowcharts and structure charts.
3. Identify the five basic flowcharting symbols.
4. Design a simple flowchart.
5. Discuss the advantages of top-down design.
6. List the objectives of structured programming.
7. Discuss the advantages of structured programming.
8. Identify the three permissible structures in structured programming.
9. Identify a loop and a branch.
10. Identify an IPO chart and explain its purpose.
11. Define pseudocode and describe its purpose.
12. Describe the relationship between logic design and coding.
13. Explain the purpose of testing.
14. Differentiate between syntax and logic errors.
15. Discuss the purpose of documentation, who needs it, and why.

## OVERVIEW

When you begin planning your vacation, you decide where you want to go and collect maps, travel guides, and folders describing the scenic attractions. You determine how many days you have, how much money you can spend, and who will be going with you. Before you go, you develop plans for how to get there and what to do when you arrive.

Writing a program is similar to planning a vacation. Before the program itself can be written, plans have to be made. This chapter covers how those plans are made and then how they are turned into a computer program. It discusses the design of a program: how we solve problems, how the solutions are documented and then converted into a program, and how the program is tested and then documented for the users.

## WHAT IS PROGRAMMING?

*[handwritten annotation: List of instructions for the computer to follow in performing a task]*

Programming is more than putting words on paper or typing them into a terminal. A program is a list of instructions, called **code,** for the computer to follow in performing a task. Programming is the creation of that list. It involves knowing not only the statements used in a language but also how to choose and arrange those statements so that the task will be performed logically.

The languages in which we program, whether BASIC, Pascal, COBOL, or some other language, are relatively easy to learn. That is, learning what statement to use when you want to read a record is easy; the hard part is knowing *when* to read.

## SYSTEMS ANALYSIS AND PROGRAMMING

You should be aware that most programs are written to run as a part of a system. A system is a group of interrelated elements that work together to perform a specific task. In data processing, there are many systems: inventory, production control, payroll, and so on. Each program must run properly not only when it is run alone but also when it is run with all other programs in the system.

## ON THE JOB 1

Conversions

In 1985, the Internal Revenue Service of the United States was embarrassed by being unable to deliver tax refunds in a timely manner to millions of citizens. It has been suggested that the IRS had taken a chance on their data processing conversion being completed on time and, like many other smaller organizations, were caught short.

Given the magnitude of the operation, it was possible that no one was fully aware of the number and complexity of the tasks involved in converting the IRS database and so the time involved was underestimated. Millions of lines of code were tested, but that wasn't enough—much parallel testing hadn't been undertaken. When the conversion finally occurred, the processing of tax returns had been slowed down and the issuance of refund checks delayed, making the processing problems visible to the entire country.

Systems analysis is the study and solution of problems. The solution may or may not involve the use of computers. The study or analysis might suggest writing one program, a group of programs, or an entire system; it might also recommend only that reports be issued at another time or be distributed differently.

Faulty understanding of the users' needs results in poor programming. More computer programs have been failures because they produce the correct answer to the wrong problem than because they produce the wrong answer to the right problem. Sometimes, the correct solution is obtained but is embarrassingly late (see On the Job 1), or perhaps the cost of obtaining it exceeds the value of the information.

Although programming and systems analysis cannot be separated, we have tried to do so here. Systems analysis is discussed in greater detail in Chapter 7.

## PROGRAMMING LOGIC

We solve problems daily. From deciding which route to use driving to work to how to best invest some savings, we consider options, select the best one, and then determine how to carry it out.

We also do this "thinking" for the computer. Although new, nonprocedural languages are being developed, much programming is done with third-generation procedural languages such as BASIC or COBOL. Using these languages, the programmer determines the steps or procedures that the computer must perform to solve the problem: when to read, when to multiply, and so on.

We do not need complete instructions to carry out a task; we bring our judgment to unclear or incomplete instructions and are able to determine what needs to be done. For example, if a friend invited you to a movie, saying "I'll meet you at the movie at 3:00," you would know he meant 3 P.M. and not 3 A.M. If a tornado was seen in the neighborhood at 2:30, you would assume that your friend would not be standing in front of the theater; if you both had learned that the theater burned the night before, you would know not to go.

No one told you those things; as a thinking person, you exercised judgment. However, because it lacks judgment, a computer needs much more explicit instructions. It needs to know exactly what it must do and exactly under what conditions it must do it. Before you can code a program, you must think through the **logic flow** the computer needs. You must also understand the purpose of the program, such as whether to update an inventory file or list items that need reordering.

The two most common methods of representing program logic are flowcharts and structure charts. The choice of method is not either/or. Many programmers do their overview or general logic design using structure charts and their detail logic using flowcharts. Other combinations of techniques are also used.

## FLOWCHARTS

A **flowchart** is a pictorial representation of the steps a computer must take to solve a problem. Because it only illustrates what is to be done to solve the problem, the program can be written in any language to run on any computer.

Since flowcharts describe the solution to the problem, they are written before the program. When you take a trip, you consult the map first to decide the best route. Any errors in the route are most easily corrected before the trip starts; any errors in the flowchart are most easily corrected before coding is begun.

### Flowcharting Symbols

Five basic symbols are used in program flowcharts: an oval, a diamond, a parallelogram, a rectangle, and a circle. Three of these symbols (the rectangle, the parallelogram, and the diamond) represent basic functions of the computer: the rectangle is used for processing, the parallelogram for input/output, and the diamond for decision making. The horizontal oval represents either starting or stopping (where the program begins and ends), and the circle represents continuation of the flowchart to another location.

Although these symbols can be sketched freehand, many programmers use commercially available **flowcharting templates** with patterns to guide them in drawing the symbols (see Figure 8.1). In addition to these five basic programming symbols, the template contains other symbols used in system flowcharts.

**FIGURE 8.1**

Although the flowcharting template contains many symbols, only five are commonly used in program flowcharting. In addition, flow lines are used to indicate the logical flow of the program.

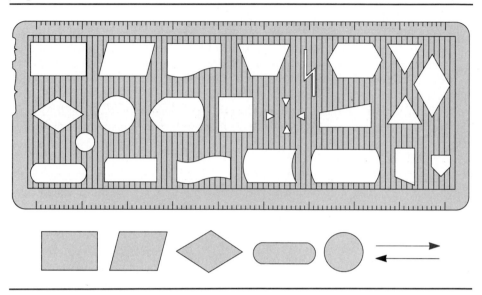

**FIGURE 8.2**

Each of these rectangular blocks represents a process.

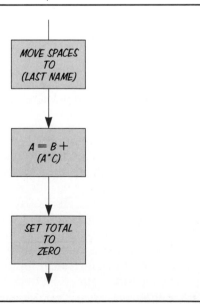

The **process block** is a rectangle used to represent processes. These processes may be moves or computations (Figure 8.2). Within these process blocks, computations use common mathematical symbols:

+ Addition
− Subtraction
* Multiplication
/ Division
** Exponentiation

The **input/output block,** represented by a parallelogram, contains the request to read or to write (Figure 8.3). It often also indicates what information is to be read or written.

The **decision block,** also called the **decision diamond,** is used whenever a decision is to be made (Figure 8.4). For example, is the account number equal to 5? Are YTD earnings greater than the FICA limit?

## Logic Flow

When designing a flowchart, the programmer describes the task from beginning to end, although some of the logic may represent predefined activities described in detail elsewhere. The flow normally goes from top to bottom or from left to right. When the flow reverses these directions, arrows are used on the flow lines to indicate direction (Figure 8.5).

**FIGURE 8.3**
Whether you call it READ and WRITE or GET and PUT, input or output is represented by a parallelogram.

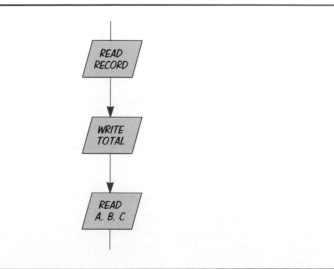

**FIGURE 8.4**

The ability to make comparisons and decisions and to perform different functions based on the results is the foundation of data processing.

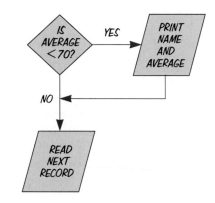

**FIGURE 8.5**

Although some programmers use arrows on all lines, they *must* be used when the normal flow is reversed (from right to left or from bottom to top).

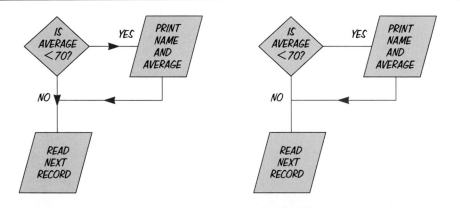

## Loops —pepitition

One of the great advantages of data processing with a computer is that, once a series of activities is determined, the sequence can be repeated over and over without additional coding. This repetition is referred to as a **loop** (Figure 8.6). Most loops involve decisions. The series of instructions is to be repeated until some event occurs; then another series of instructions usually begins (Figure 8.7).

**FIGURE 8.6**
Without the ability to loop, programming would be hopelessly inefficient. This loop, however, would repeat forever. A decision must be included to indicate when to end the looping.

**FIGURE 8.7**
Notice how a decision changes the flow of this loop.

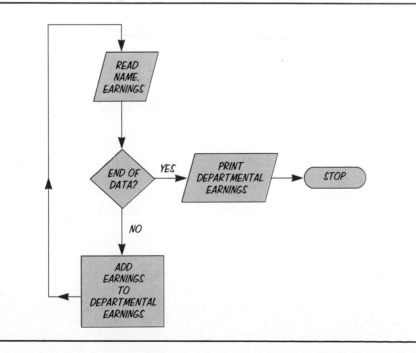

**FIGURE 8.8**

A change in the logic flow caused by a decision is known as a branch. In this example, a 1 percent commission is paid when sales are less than $5,000; for sales of $5,000 or more, the commission is 2 percent.

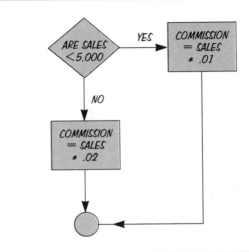

## Branches

**Branches** are changes in the direction of the logic flow, often based on some decision (Figure 8.8). A branch causes the logic flow to change directions and go to another location in the flowchart to perform the instructions found there. Once the symbols, statements, and loops of the flowchart are written, the entire solution is visible (Figure 8.9).

The greatest disadvantage to flowcharting is that the solution to the problem proceeds from beginning to end. If anything interrupts your chain of thought, you can easily omit essential steps in the flowchart. When a decision is made, the programmer must flowchart one course of action while remembering to go back later to flowchart the alternative. With the multitude of choices in many programs, the amount to remember to do later is enormous.

A second disadvantage to flowcharting is that one person's structure of the solution may differ significantly from another's. Later, when **maintenance** is needed on the program, it may be difficult to follow the logic, especially when many loops and branches are involved.

To avoid these difficulties, programmers use a modular approach to developing large programs. This approach, called **modular programming,** breaks down the program into logical components. These separate sections can be defined, written, and tested separately. In very large projects, they may even be written by different people. Once written and tested individually, the individual modules can be merged together.

**FIGURE 8.9**
Putting all the techniques in Figures 8.2 through 8.8 together results in a program flowchart.

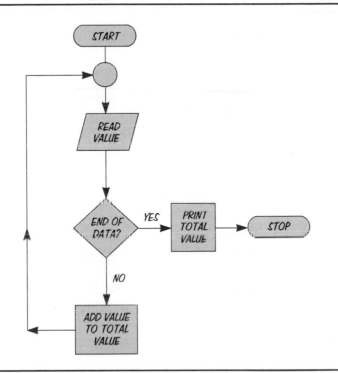

## STRUCTURED PROGRAMMING

*[handwritten: ① increase productivity*
*② " clarity*
*③ reduce testing + maintenance time]*

**Structured programming** began in 1966, when Bohm and Jacopini published a paper proving mathematically that any problem could be solved using only three control structures: sequence, selection, and iteration (defined later in this chapter). Two years later, E. Dijkstra published a letter in *Communications of the ACM* (Association for Computing Machinery) criticizing the complexity caused by too much branching within programs. He suggested that using the GOTO statement to cause this branching confused the logic of many programs. Reducing branching by reducing the number of GOTOs would make programs more understandable. Because the programs could thus be more easily understood, they would also be more reliable and easier to maintain. (Dijkstra likened GOTO-laden programs to tangled bowls of spaghetti.)

Structured programming techniques developed from this beginning. These standardized techniques are designed to make it easier to debug—to go through a program in order to locate and remove errors—and modify existing programs as well as to create programs written by teams of programmers. The objectives of structured programming are (1) to increase productivity, (2) to increase clarity, and (3) to reduce testing and maintenance time. Structured techniques include top-down design and structure charts, IPO charts, pseudocode, and structured code.

## Structure Charts

Structured design approaches a problem from the top down. The programmer first attempts to divide the program into its major functions or modules (level 1 of a tree). Each of these functions in turn may be divided into its major functions (level 2 of the tree). These in turn continue to be subdivided until each module performs only one unique function (Figure 8.10). This chart is referred to as a **structure chart, tree diagram,** or **hierarchy chart.** The combination of a structure chart with its related IPO charts is referred to as *HIPO* or hierarchy plus input, processing, and output.

## IPO Charts    — input, processing, output.

Information found in the structure chart is supplemented by a type of module documentation called an **IPO (input, processing, and output) chart.** The IPO chart describes in detail the input to a module, the processing of that input, and the output from a module (Figure 8.11).

**FIGURE 8.10**
Note how the structure of this chart resembles a tree.

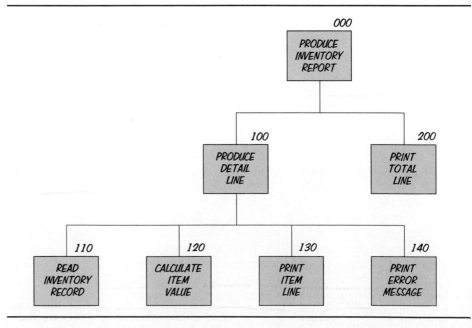

**FIGURE 8.11**
Only with the IPO chart can the programmer see exactly what happens in each module.

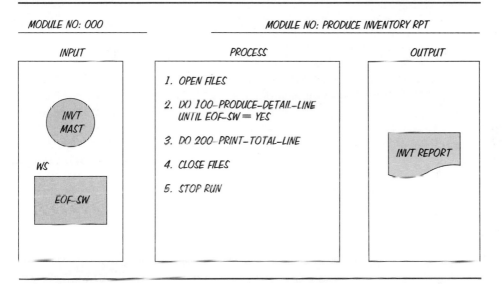

| MODULE NO: 000 | MODULE NO: PRODUCE INVENTORY RPT | |
|---|---|---|
| INPUT | PROCESS | OUTPUT |

Process:
1. OPEN FILES
2. DO 100-PRODUCE-DETAIL-LINE UNTIL EOF-SW = YES
3. DO 200-PRINT-TOTAL-LINE
4. CLOSE FILES
5. STOP RUN

Input: INVT MAST, WS, EOF-SW
Output: INVT REPORT

*8.* **Pseudocode** — *highly structured version of English.*

**Pseudocode** is a highly structured version of English used to describe program logic. Since it closely resembles a programming language, it clearly describes the logical steps that must occur in the program. Also, although it is structured and logical, it is independent of any programming language; thus, it can be quickly translated to actual coding in any language.

Pseudocode is used in an IPO chart to describe the logical steps that must occur within that module. It is also used independently of IPO charts to describe both program and systems logic (see Figure 8.12).

*4.* **Structured Code** ① *sequence – activities one after the other* ② *selection – choice between two actions* ③ *iteration – "do while" or "do until"*

Structured programming was defined earlier as a collection of programming techniques used to produce programs that are easy to understand and maintain. **Structured coding,** one of these techniques, includes patterns of coding to increase clarity. The only functions permitted in structured code are sequence, selection, and iteration.

In a **sequence structure,** activities are performed one after another. In the **selection structure,** a choice is made between two actions. One action is performed if a statement is true, whereas another action is taken if it is false. The **iteration structure** may be either a "do while" or a "do until" structure. In a "do while" structure, a test is made immediately after entering the loop.

**FIGURE 8.12**
The logic shown earlier by the flowchart in Figure 8.7 can also be shown by this pseudocode.

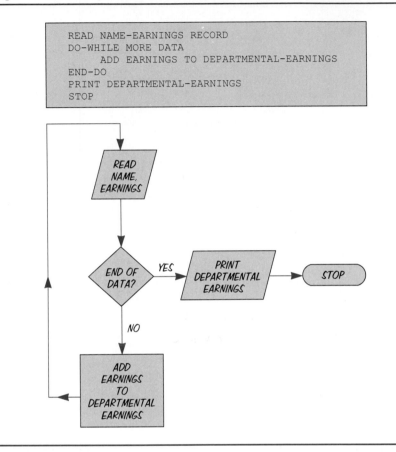

```
READ NAME-EARNINGS RECORD
DO-WHILE MORE DATA
     ADD EARNINGS TO DEPARTMENTAL-EARNINGS
END-DO
PRINT DEPARTMENTAL-EARNINGS
STOP
```

The process is executed only if the tested condition is true. In a "do until" structure, the process is executed once and then the test made. The process will continue as long as the tested condition is false (Figure 8.13).

**Nested structures** may also be used, which means that any structure may replace any box within any other structure (Figure 8.14).

## CODING THE PROGRAM

Once the program is designed, whether by flowchart or by structure chart, the next step is to convert the activities represented by the chart into some

**FIGURE 8.13**

An iteration may be expressed as either a "do while" or a "do until." In a "do while," the test precedes the activity. In a "do until," the activity is always performed at least once because the activity precedes the test.

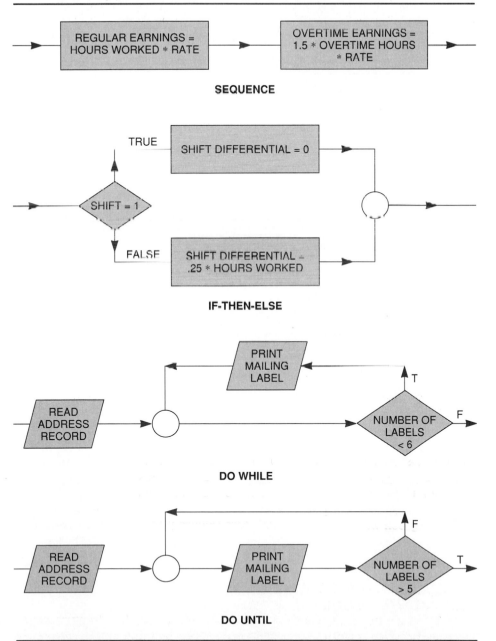

**FIGURE 8.14**

To describe a program with these structures, the programmer must be able to "nest" the structures. (In the second figure, a "do while" replaces the activity II process box.)

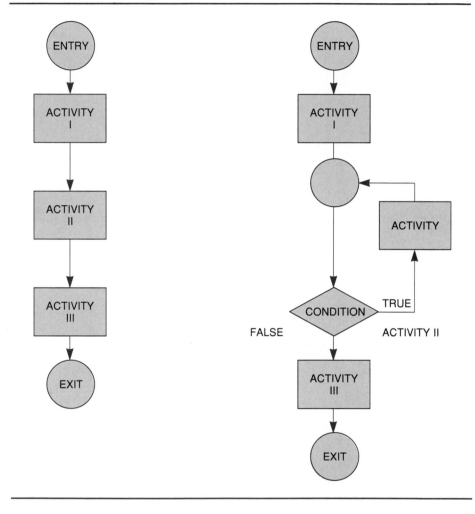

programming language (Figures 8.15 and 8.16). If the steps to be performed are correctly described in the design step, the resultant coding should be logically correct.

## TESTING THE PROGRAM

Once the program is written, it must be tested. Testing is intended to guarantee the accuracy of the results. Errors fall into two categories: syntactical and logical.

**FIGURE 8.15**
This figure illustrates how the flowchart would look when translated into BASIC.

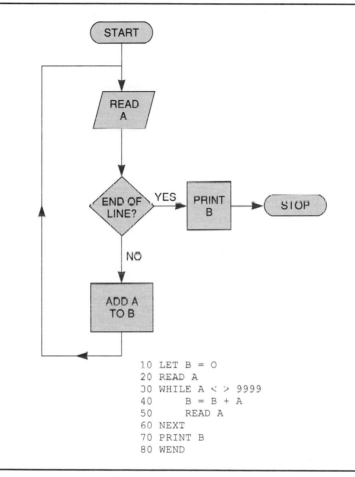

```
10 LET B = 0
20 READ A
30 WHILE A < > 9999
40     B = B + A
50     READ A
60 NEXT
70 PRINT B
80 WEND
```

## Syntax Errors

As with any language, programming languages have a vocabulary, grammar, and punctuation. Violation of the language rules results in **syntax errors,** or errors caused by the incorrect use of the language. These errors are most often found when the program is translated to machine language (Figure 8.17).

## Logic Errors

Even if the program has no syntax errors, it still may be incorrect (see On the Job 2). The programmer may have clearly described the steps the computer

**FIGURE 8.16**

Because logic design is language independent, the flowchart in Figure 8.15 could be translated into this segment of a COBOL program.

```
BEGN.
        OPEN INPUT FILIN, OUTPUT FILOUT.
        READ FILIN AT END MOVE "NO" TO
          MORE-REC.
        PERFORM PARA-1 UNTIL MORE-REC =
          "NO".
        MOVE B TO TOT-FIELD OF OUT-REC.
        WRITE OUT-REC.
        CLOSE FILIN, FILOUT.
        STOP RUN.
PARA-1.
        ADD A TO B.
        READ FILIN AT END MOVE "NO" TO
          MORE-REC.
```

**FIGURE 8.17**

In BASIC, remarks are indicated by REM, not REMARKS. The use of REMARKS in line 10 would be a syntax error.

```
10 REMARKS     THIS PROGRAM CONVERTS
20 REM         FEET TO INCHES
30 INPUT       "ENTER NUMBER OF FEET";N
40 A = N * 12
50 PRINT "THE NUMBER OF INCHES IS ";A
60 END
```

**FIGURE 8.18**

If the programmer had intended the program to print the names of all students whose grades were *below* 70, this program would contain a logic error. What would print? Do you see any other problems with the logic?

```
10 INPUT "ENTER GRADE AND NAME";A,N$
20 IF A< 70 THEN GO TO 10
40               ELSE PRINT N$
50 GO TO 10
```

## ON THE JOB 2

Computer Gliches

Phobos I

In 1988, Phobos 1, a Soviet satellite, was lost on its way to Mars. According to *Science* magazine, a ground controller omitted a single letter in a series of digital commands sent to the spacecraft. This omission caused the code to be mistranslated, and as a result, Phobos went into a tumble from which it never recovered.

AT&T

In January of 1990, AT&T suffered its largest service outage ever. The outage was blamed on an error in a new system designed to improve its long-distance network.

During the nine hours between discovery of the problem and its correction, more than one half of the calls placed in the United States did not go through. The problem stemmed from a logic error or "bug" in the software, which affected more than 100 switching centers

was to perform, but the steps could be incorrect (Figure 8.18). These are referred to as **logic errors.** Because programmers want to be sure that the program will run correctly under all circumstances, they test the program for logic errors and debug any they find.

To test the program, programmers and users create **test data**—sample data that meets all possible conditions. The data is designed to make the program fail, if it is going to, in a test situation where it can be corrected easily, without causing the damage that might result if the program failed while running "live" data.

When the program is finally correct, it is put into production. When programmers write programs for personal use, they are usually the only people who will run their programs for whatever purpose they intended. However, if the program was written for regular and repetitive use in a business, it is turned over to production so the computer operator can run it on a regular basis on the mainframe computer or network. Because the operator may be unfamiliar with the procedures involved in running the program, the operating procedures must be documented before the program is turned over.

## MARKING THE TRAIL—DOCUMENTATION

The operator may not be the only one who must be familiar with the program. People other than the programmer may use the program by providing input to it or using the output from it. Furthermore, the program may need to be changed because of changing government regulations, company policy, or errors found within the program. Each of these situations requires that a trail be left showing what the program does and how it does it. This trail is called **documentation.**

### Documentation for Maintenance

Because most programs require change at some time and the person changing the program may not be the person who wrote it, it is necessary to document the program for those who will maintain it. The flowchart or structure chart is one source of information about what the program does and what module does it. Other documentation may include systems flowcharts showing how all the programs within a system relate to one another (Figure 8.19). It may also include descriptions of record layouts and brief descriptions of what each program does (Figure 8.20).

### Documentation for Operators

To be able to run a program, operators must know where files are located, what to do when errors occur, how to distribute reports, what forms to use, and so on. Operators also must know if the program can send any messages to them on the console and, if so, how they are to respond to them.

This information may be included in the program itself; in the **job control language (JCL),** which consists of the statements that tell the computer which job to run and machine-specific instructions about the job; or in written operator instructions.

### Documentation for Users

Users must know how to prepare input data and also how to interpret output reports. Again, information aiding the user may be presented on the CRT screen as data is being entered, or it may be presented in written instructions. With the increasing number of video display terminals being used, more programs are driven by menus (a list of choices from which the user may select). The screen itself often contains prompts and instructions to assist the user. The most important thing is that the user has a reference available when it is needed.

**FIGURE 8.19**
A systems flowchart indicates how all programs within a system interrelate.

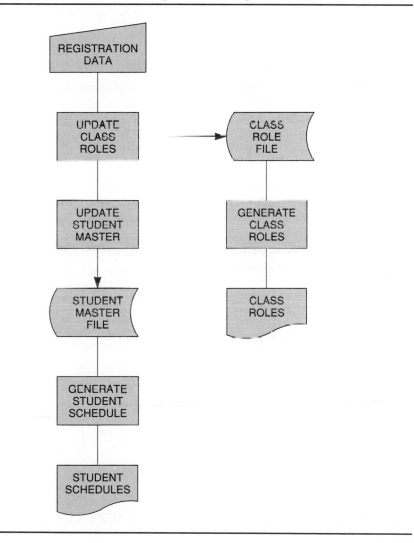

## Training Operators and End-Users

Before programmers release the program, they must be sure that users and operators are trained in how to run it. When you first sat at a computer or terminal, countless questions probably went through your head. What should

**FIGURE 8.20**

A programmer should produce a brief written description of what a program does *(a)*. This saves someone unfamiliar with the program from having to read the coding to see what the program does. The programmer will also create other documentation, for example, a printer spacing chart *(b)* to show where each field will appear on the output.

---

This program prints a monthly sales and commission report. There is one file to be read in; it contains 36 characters. Two tables are prepared; one for commissions and the other for selling prices. These tables contain the product number and either the commission rate or selling price.

The program will process each data record utilizing both tables to calculate the commission for each salesperson.

The output record contains 90 characters. The final output reports the number of units sold and the amount of sales of each product by salesperson and by territory. There is also an overall sales total.

(a)

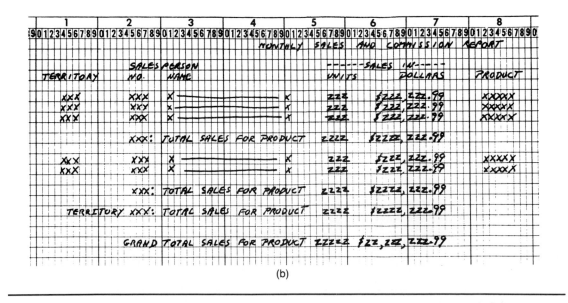

(b)

---

I do first? How do I turn it on? What do I do next? What if nothing appears on the screen? What should appear? How long will it take? What does that little red light mean?

Training may be unnecessary; the programmer may be the only user. If the program will be sold to the public, the only training available may be the written manual. At other times, when the program is custom written for use at one site, training may be extensive. Lectures, practice, seminars, and on-the-job training may be made available to operators and end-users (those people who will have contact with the system—that is, provide the input or use the output).

## SUMMARY

A program is a list of instructions for the computer to follow in performing a task. Programming is the creation of that list. Most programs are written to run as a part of a system.

Regardless of the language in which the program is written, the logic must first be determined and then documented.

The two most common methods of representing program logic are flowcharts and structure charts. A flowchart is a pictorial representation of the steps a computer must take to solve a problem. Five basic symbols are used in program flowcharts: a rectangle, a parallelogram, a diamond, an oval, and a circle.

Structured design approaches a problem from the top down. The programmer first attempts to divide the program into its major functions or modules. These, in turn, continue to be subdivided until each module performs only one unique function. This chart is referred to as a structure chart.

Structured coding includes patterns of coding to increase clarity. The only functions permitted in structured code are sequence, selection, and iteration.

To test the program, the person creates test data. Violations of the language rules results in syntax errors. Even after the coding is completed correctly, the program itself may not be correct; these are called logic errors. Syntax errors are caused by incorrect use of the language. Logic errors result from telling the computer to do the wrong thing or not telling it to do the right thing.

After the program is written and tested, it still must be documented to provide a trail for users, operators, and the next programmer to use it.

## VOCABULARY

Branch    174

Code    167

Decision block (decision diamond)    171

Documentation    184

Flowchart    169

Flowcharting template    169

## EXERCISES

1.  Why is program logic described in some formal way before the program is coded?
2.  Does the form of logic design used depend on the language the program is to be coded in?
3.  What are the advantages of structured design?
4.  What are the three structures permitted in structured coding? What is the purpose of each structure?
5.  What are the five basic symbols in program flowcharting? What is the purpose of each?
6.  What is a loop? A branch? Why are they needed?
7.  What is an IPO chart? What purpose does it serve in structured design?
8.  What is pseudocode? Where and how is it used?

## PROJECTS

1.  Design a flowchart that will read student records containing name and average grade and then print the name and grade of all students who have an average below 75.
2.  Design test data, or describe what the test data should contain, in order to test a program written from the flowchart in project 1.
3.  If you have access to a computer and computer lab, write the documentation that would enable a new user to both "log on" and "log off" (sign on and sign off) the system.

# 9

# File Organizations

## CHAPTER OBJECTIVES

*After completing this chapter, you will be able to:*

1. Describe how data is structured.
2. Discuss batch versus interactive-oriented processing.
3. Discuss blocking and packing and explain how they are used to save space on a file.
4. Differentiate between fixed- and variable-length records and discuss why each might be used.
5. Compare four methods of file organization: sequential, direct, relative, and indexed.
6. Contrast sequential and direct access and discuss when each might be used.

## OVERVIEW

Most companies have a multitude of files. When you enter a hospital, the admitting clerk probably checks the patient master file to see if you have ever been there before. When you register for a class, the student master file is checked to see if you are enrolled in the school. When you purchase a hamburger, the cash register may update the inventory file as well as issue your bill.

What are these files? How are they organized? Why are there so many types of file organizations? This chapter discusses the answers to these questions.

## DATA STRUCTURE

Data—the letters, numbers, and special symbols the computer processes—becomes organized information stored on a file. The data is composed of characters, fields, records, and files. Each individual letter, number, or special symbol is referred to as a **character.** These characters are grouped to create items of information called *fields*. On an inventory file, one field might be the inventory number; another field might be the reorder point or reorder quantity. Another name for a field is a **data element.** Related fields are also grouped together to form records (Figure 9.1). In the inventory file just mentioned, all the fields related to one inventory item would be grouped together to form that item's inventory record. The record would contain all the information about that one item: item number, balance on hand, reorder point, reorder quantity, vendor, and any other information about it.

Finally, the related records are grouped into a **file**—in the example here, a collection of all of the records relating to inventory.

**FIGURE 9.1**
The computer records on a class roll file might look like this.

| Class No. | Section No. | Name | | Student ID | Grade |
|-----------|-------------|------|------|------------|-------|
|           |             | First | Last |            |       |

191

Files represent the basic organization of business information. Inventory information such as item number, description, balance on hand, vendor, and reorder point is stored on an inventory file. Personnel files contain all the information kept on each employee. Any information may be stored on a file; how that information is used determines how it is stored and processed.

The database, a type of file structure in which the data is integrated and related so that redundancy is minimized, is discussed in Chapter 10.

## SPACE CONSIDERATIONS

Files usually contain many records. Any space saved on one record saves many times the space on an entire file. Three usual ways of saving space include (1) using the appropriate record type, (2) blocking records, and (3) packing numerical fields.

### Record Types: Fixed versus Variable

The records on the inventory file just discussed are probably all of the same length; they each contain an inventory number, balance on hand, and so on. These records are referred to as **fixed-length records.**

For some files, however, it is not convenient for all records to be of the same length. Some fields might appear on all records on a real estate file: owner's name, address, and so on. Other fields may differ from one record to another. Some individuals may own only one piece of property; they would need only enough space to hold one location and one property value. Others might own several lots of land and buildings; their records would need to show the location of each piece of property and its value on their tax record (Figure 9.2). To save enough space on each record to hold the maximum property entries would waste space on most records. Therefore, it is helpful to let the record size vary. Records of varying sizes are referred to as **variable-length records.** Although records may be of various sizes, each field usually has the same number of characters in all records within the same file. Each inventory item number field might be six characters long on the inventory master discussed, and each vendor field might be 20 characters long.

**FIGURE 9.2**
The variable-length real estate record might have a different number of characters stored in it, depending on how many properties a person owns.

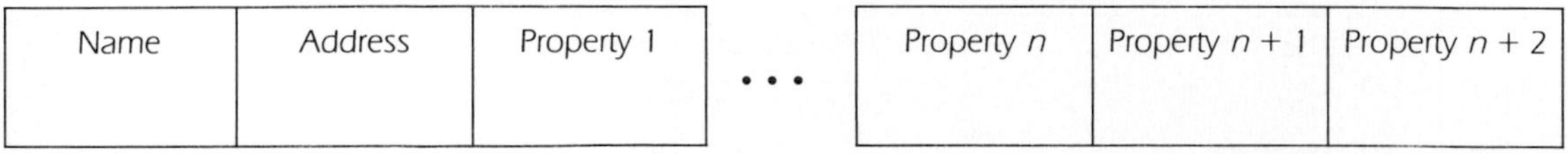

| Name | Address | Property 1 | | Property $n$ | Property $n + 1$ | Property $n + 2$ |
|------|---------|-----------|---|-----------|--------------|--------------|
|      |         |           | • • • |           |              |              |

All the available field space may not be used. Consider people's names; one person may have a short name such as Ann Smith, whereas another may have a much longer name such as Tabitha Twilinger. Although the name field must be large enough to hold the longest name, always saving that many bytes of data wastes valuable space (a byte is the smallest addressable unit in a computer memory, usually six or eight bits). Data compression may be used to eliminate unnecessary character positions (Figure 9.3).

## Blocking — recoding a group of records as though it were one

With **blocking,** groups of records are processed as though each group was one record. This decreases both wasted space and wasted time because fewer "gaps" are needed (Figure 9.4).

**FIGURE 9.3**

Compression permits more information to be stored in a given record size.

| Name (25 bytes) | Address (25 bytes) | Zip (9) |
|---|---|---|
| **Uncompressed Records** | | |
| Joe Jones | Menominee, MI | 49858 |
| Tabitha Twilinger | Salem, MA | 01970 |
| Barbara Wilson | Effingham, IL | 62401 |
| . . . | . . . | . . . |

59 bytes

**Compressed Records**

Joe Jones | Menominee, MI | 49858
Tabitha Twilinger | Salem, MA | 01970
Barbara Wilson | Effingham, IL | 62401

45 bytes

**FIGURE 9.4**

Only one READ instruction is necessary to copy these five records, stored as one block, into memory.

| Record 1 | Record 2 | Record 3 | Record 4 | Record 5 |
|---|---|---|---|---|

Block

When a record is written on magnetic tape, a space called an *interrecord gap (IRG)* or *interblock gap (IBG)* is left between each record. This space is necessary to enable the tape drive to reach processing speed before it begins to read the record. Although necessary, such gap space is wasted. By logically grouping records into blocks, also called *physical records,* the computer can read the entire group at one time. An IRG is necessary only between each group, thus saving space. You may want to refer back to Figures 3.13 and 3.14 for illustrations.

Time is also saved by processing blocks of records. Since an entire block can be read at one time, time is saved by decreasing the total number of READs and WRITEs.

### Character Representation

Characters—letters, numbers, and special symbols—are usually stored in a byte of data; one byte represents one character. A byte is made up of eight bits (each containing a 0 or 1) grouped together. These bytes are then grouped into fields, or units of information. Further information about the codes used to represent characters and the various methods of storing numeric data, such as **packed numbers,** is found in Appendix B.

Each field is described in one of three ways: numeric, alphabetic, or alphanumeric. A **numeric field** is one that contains only numbers and can be used numerically, such as for mathematical computations. Year-to-date earnings or inventory reorder points would be examples of numeric fields. Alphabetic fields contain only letters or spaces. Few fields will always contain only letters or spaces; even names often contain numbers (for example, John Jones, 3rd). Thus, alphabetic fields are rarely used. **Alphanumeric fields** may contain letters, numbers, or special symbols and are used very frequently.

Each occurrence of a field is described in the same way to the program regardless of the actual contents. For example, a field containing an employee's name would always be described as alphanumeric even though one record might contain John Jones 3rd in the name field and another record might contain Sally Smith.

## PROCESSING METHODS

All transactions are not processed the same way. Think of some of the transactions you may be familiar with; the processing of some was transaction oriented, the processing of others was batch. This section discusses these two processing methods.

## Batch Processing *— records prepared at one time.*

At the telephone company, all the charges on one person's bill are listed, followed by all the next customer's charges, followed in turn by the next one's charges. All the bills are probably prepared at one time, one after the other. This is called **batch processing.** The entire batch of charges was collected for processing at one time.

Batch processing requires that all data be accumulated for a given period and then processed together. The time involved may be an hour, a day, a week, or any other period, but during that time, the individual data entries are not processed but are collected for processing later at one time.

This method of processing implies that the results of the processing are not urgent; information does not need to be more current than the time that the last batch was run.

Another example of this type of processing would be the printing of your grade reports at the end of this course. During the time this course takes, your grades are accumulated. At the end of the quarter or semester, the grades are averaged, grade reports are printed, and these reports are mailed to you.

### Transaction-Oriented Processing

Think about the last time you made a purchase using your credit card. At that time, the validity of your card and your credit status were checked. There was no waiting for processing later. Sometimes, it is critical that information be available as soon as possible. If a police officer stops you for speeding and routinely checks your license to see if there are any outstanding warrants against you, he cannot wait until evening for a group of license numbers to be batch processed. He needs to know immediately.

In both these cases, processing takes place at the time the transaction occurs. This is referred to as **transaction-oriented processing.** When the data is processed as the transactions occur and this processing produces results quickly enough to affect the activity producing the data, it is called **real-time processing.** For processing to be real-time, the user and the data must be **on-line;** that is, the user must be connected to and interacting with the computer, usually through a terminal. Examples include an airline reservation system, the stock-trading system, and automatic teller machine (ATM) processing.

## FILE ORGANIZATIONS

Files are made up of related records. How those records are organized and how they are accessed depend on the purpose and use of the information stored on the file. The method by which the data is stored is referred to as

## ON THE JOB

*There's Money in the Method*

A medium-sized company located in North Carolina has found a real value in accessing methods. Their computer was heavily used; upgrading to a more powerful system seemed inevitable. A newly hired systems analyst was assigned the task of looking at the current workload, seeing if time savings could be made, and projecting future use requirements.

What he found astonished him. Much of the problem could be resolved by better utilizing the equipment on hand. One outstanding example was an indexed file that was batch-updated regularly. Many changes were made to the file each evening; in fact, most records were updated each evening. The updating was taking approximately five hours each day.

The systems analyst found that the incoming data was not sorted and the update was by random access. Further investigation revealed that the file had its index on the same disk pack as the data portion of the file, causing the read/write head to cross the pack each time a record was looked up in the index and again when the record was read from the file.

Because the use was so heavy, the analyst suggested that the company try moving the index to a different pack from the body of the file to reduce the physical movement of the access arm. He further suggested that they try sorting the incoming data and accessing the indexed file sequentially when they updated, reducing accessing time. Despite now reading all the records on the file instead of just those being updated, running time was reduced to under two hours. Money and time were saved by selecting the correct access method.

the *file organization*. Four methods of file organization are discussed here: sequential, direct, relative, and indexed. A fifth type of organization, the database, is discussed in Chapter 10.

### Sequential File Organization

In a **sequential file,** one record follows another, usually in a specified order according to a **key field** (a field that exists on all records whose contents are used to recognize that record). On an inventory file, that field might be the inventory number; on a payroll master file, the social security number. To find a particular record, the computer must read all records and compare the value of their user key field with that of the key being sought.

When a sequential file lacks a key field, the records are usually stored in the order in which they are received. A sequential file may be stored on disk or tape.

Sequential files are efficient in using space and, if many or most records are to be processed, may provide the most rapid access (see On the Job).

## Direct File Organization

In a **direct file,** the location of the record within the file is determined by the key of the record. A direct relationship exists between a record's key and its physical location.

One example might be a payroll master file. Imagine a factory that issued new employees a four-digit employee number when they were hired. All employees would have an identification number between 0001 and 9999. Now suppose that the payroll master file was created as a direct file. Employee 0003 would be the third record on the file, whereas employee number 2999 would be the 2999th record on the file.

With this organization, you could easily locate any record on the file. Once you knew the employee number, you could go immediately to where that record was located, increasing processing speed tremendously.

Direct file organization provides rapid access but, unless the keys are a group of continuous numbers and almost all keys represent records on the file, direct organization wastes space.

Another method of directly relating the key of the record to its physical location involves the use of **randomizing,** or **hashing.** This type of file organization is also referred to as **relative file organization.**

## Relative File Organization

In randomizing or hashing techniques, the key is used to calculate the location on the file (Figure 9.5). Hashing or randomizing techniques apply a formula to the key. The calculations generate a number that represents the location. Many formulas may be applied, but a common one involves division by a prime number (a number that cannot be divided evenly by any number except 1 and itself). Examples of prime numbers are 7 and 13.

When the record is stored, its location is calculated using the same techniques. To retrieve the record, the program need only have the key and the formula so it can reapply the formula to regenerate the storage location.

The disadvantage of relative file organization is that it is not always possible to take the keys and generate storage locations that are evenly distributed across the file and not redundant. In fact, identical addresses are regularly generated, and the address points only to the track. Redundancy becomes a problem when some tracks are full and still need to have records added while other tracks are empty or used only sporadically. Also, because direct and

**FIGURE 9.5**

*In a relative file, a randomizing technique is used to locate the record.*

Using the randomizing technique, take the key, divide it by the next lowest prime number, and store the record at a location equal to the remainder plus 1. The track location of a record with the key 21 would be 3. It is calculated as follows:

$$
\begin{array}{r}
1R2 \\
\hline
19\,|21
\end{array}
$$

next $\longrightarrow$ 19 $|$ 21 $\longleftarrow$   key
lower
prime    2 + 1 = 3 $\leftarrow$   track location
number     $\uparrow$

remainder

relative files can be accessed by key, they must be located on direct access storage devices such as a disk.

## Indexed File Organization

As the name implies, **indexed file** organization uses an index to locate a record within the file. As the file is created or updated, an index to the records is also created or updated. This organization is a compromise between sequential and direct file organizations.

In indexed file organization, a record is found by looking for the key in the index. Once the key is found, the index points to the location of the record in the file. Locating the record is thus a two-step process: (1) finding the entry in the index, and then (2) finding the record in the file.

Indexed files are created with their records in sequential order. After this, records may be added in any order. As the file is created, each track is loaded in sequence with some space saved for additions. When the track is full except for this overflow area, the key of the last record on the track is recorded in the index (see Figure 9.6). Later, as the file is updated, records are added and the index is used to determine on which track to place the record. The record is then placed in its sequential location on that track, and records having higher keys are pushed farther down the track. As records are added, the tracks gradually become full. Records having the highest keys are bumped off the track into the overflow area; pointers are created to point from the track to these records in the overflow area. The index is changed to point to the highest record still physically on the track and to the highest record still associated with that track. This latter record formerly was the highest record on the track itself but now resides in the overflow area.

Because finding a record is at least a two-step process, indexed file processing is very slow, particularly when a large number of records are located in the overflow area.

**FIGURE 9.6**

In an indexed file, records are found by looking for their locations in an index. A record with the key 87 would be found on track 2; one with the key 110 would be in the overflow area.

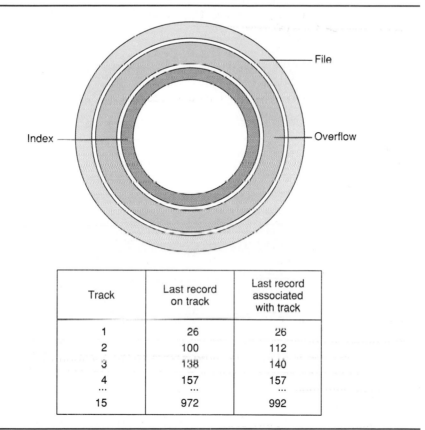

| Track | Last record on track | Last record associated with track |
|-------|----------------------|-----------------------------------|
| 1 | 26 | 26 |
| 2 | 100 | 112 |
| 3 | 138 | 140 |
| 4 | 157 | 157 |
| ... | ... | ... |
| 15 | 972 | 992 |

As with direct and relative files, indexed files may be accessed either sequentially or randomly, and they must be located on direct access storage devices such as a disk.

_____

## ACCESS METHODS

*5.* The file access method is limited by the type of file organization chosen.

### Accessing Sequential Files

Sequential files may be read only sequentially—that is, one record after another. If you must locate a particular record, that record must have a key. As each record is read, its key is compared to the key of the record being sought. To match two sequential files (for example, to update one by the transactions on the other), both files must be in order by their key.

Although sequential access is rapid when the records to be located are in order and when many records on a file are needed, it is a slow method of locating only a few records because the preceding records must also be read and their user keys compared.

### Accessing Direct and Relative Files

Direct and relative files may also be accessed sequentially, with the records read in the order in which they physically appear on the file. In addition, they may be read randomly.

To read a direct or relative file randomly, you only need to know the key of the record you are searching for and recalculate the location of the record on the file from that key. Locating the record this way is rapid; no preceding records must be read, nor is any time spent looking up the address in an index. The only time required is the time needed to position the read/write head over the correct track and locate the correct record. Being able to access a file randomly rather than sequentially permits the file to be used for transaction-oriented, on-line processing.

### Accessing Indexed Files

Indexed files, like sequential, direct, and relative files, may be read sequentially. However, it is often more useful to read them randomly.

To locate any record, you only need to know the key, look this key up in the index, obtain the location from the index, and then look in this location to obtain the record.

The disadvantage of this method is that another step is added in reading a record—reading the index to locate the record. This makes it a slower access method than either sequential processing or the random reading of direct and relative files.

Regardless of whether a file is read sequentially or randomly and whether the file is sequential, direct, relative, or indexed, the programmer has help in reading the file. This help comes from the access method programs.

### Access Method Programs

Each time programmers use a program to ask that a record be read from or written to a file, they are making a logical request. That logical request has to be translated into the actual "physical" request before the record can be obtained. The way in which the **physical request,** or physical means by which the record is obtained, is made differs for each file type. Programmers do not have to give explicit physical instructions to read a record. A part of the operating system, a series of programs called the **access method programs,** takes the logical request and translates it into the physical request.

---

## SUMMARY

The information stored by a computer consists of characters, fields, records, and files. Because storage space within the peripheral devices is limited, it is necessary to save space by using variable-length records or by blocking records. Space may also be saved with compression.

Several methods of file organization are available. The most popular today is the database, discussed in Chapter 10. Others include sequential, direct, relative, and indexed organization. Sequentially organized files may be read only sequentially; the other types may be read either sequentially or randomly. With the use of the random method, much processing has become transaction oriented.

The programmer does not need to give detailed instructions on how to read the file; the access method programs convert the logical request to the actual physical request, which depends on the file organization.

## ▨ VOCABULARY

| | | | |
|---|---|---|---|
| Access method programs | *201* | Blocking | 193 |
| Alphanumeric field | *194* | Character | 191 |
| Batch processing | 195 | Data element | 191 |

## EXERCISES

1. What is blocking? Why is it used?
2. What is data compression? Why is it used?
3. Explain the difference between variable- and fixed-length records. Give an example of when each might be used.
4. Differentiate between real-time and batch processing. Give an example of when each might best be used.
5. What is the purpose of an access method program?
6. Explain sequential file organization. Does a sequential file have to be in any order?
7. How are records located on an indexed file?
8. Differentiate between direct and relative file organization.
9. What is a database?

## PROJECTS

1. Describe one application that would best be stored on a file having each of the following organizations. Why is that organization your choice?
   a. Sequential.
   b. Direct or relative.
   c. Indexed.
   d. Database.
2. Answer the following questions concerning storage:
   a. If a section of magnetic tape is 1-foot long and storage is 2,400 bpi, how many bytes can be stored?
   b. If those bytes are grouped into records of 1,200 bytes and there is a 1-inch IRG, how many bytes can be stored? How many records?
   c. If those 1,200-byte records are in blocks of 4 and the IRG is 1 inch, how many bytes can be stored? How many records?

# 10

# Databases

## CHAPTER OBJECTIVES

*After completing this chapter, you will be able to:*

1. Define the term *database.*
2. Discuss why databases evolved.
3. Describe the purpose of a query language.
4. List the main functions of a database management system.
5. Name the three most common types of database organizations and describe their structure.
6. Discuss the problems arising from the collection of large banks of data in a central location and problems with privacy, security, and ethics.

## OVERVIEW

"Why do we have all these files? When Sara Thompson changed her name to Sara Bower, we got it right on the payroll file but she's still Sara Thompson on the personnel file."

"I want some biographical information on Joan Rivers. Where can I find it?"

"I have a rash on my arms and a low-grade fever in the evening. Where can I get some information about it?"

Both public and private databases exist to help answer these questions. For years, the public has accessed information by using libraries or other services. Today, much of the same information can be accessed from a person's home by using a home computer, a telephone, and a commercial database.

For example, The Source, a subsidiary of *Reader's Digest,* provides current news. CompuServe's HealthTex provides medical emergency information to the general public through its database. Other services provide financial reports and professional information on medicine, law, and agriculture.

"What are these databases?" "Why did they develop?" "What effect will they have on me?" These are some of the questions this chapter answers.

---

## WHY DID DATABASES EVOLVE?

Many companies have multiple files with information duplicated on them. Marketing wants to know who buys from them, credit wants to know the credit history of these customers, and accounting is most interested in the outstanding bills.

If each department maintained its own files, the duplication of effort and equipment would be tremendous. For instance, when customer A moves from East 42nd Street, New York City, to Appleton Drive in Los Angeles, each file would have to be changed. In addition to the duplication of effort, inaccuracies could creep into the files. Changing a data element stored in only one location would be easier and safer. Databases were developed to do this.

In addition, there was the problem of security. Conventional files permitted the user to access any data on the file if they could access the file at all. Database management systems (DBMSs) provide improved security features.

Finally, because of the ease of adding data to existing databases, DBMSs provide much more flexibility as information requirements change.

## WHAT IS A DATABASE?

*— Collection of related files.*

A database is often described as a collection of integrated data or of related files that are created and managed by a database management system. The database can be used for a variety of applications.

*specialized → focussing on one subject*

A **commercial database** is specialized; an organization develops it to cover a particular subject. The information within this database is then made available to others, usually for a fee. Such well-known databases as The Source, Compu-Serve, and the Dow Jones financial service (see On the Job 1) are examples.

Commercial databases provide organizations and individuals with demographic data, statistics, abstracts, current news, professional information, and medical information. The user, using a home computer, modem, and telecommunications software, signs on to the service, searches the database using a query language, and is charged (usually based on connect time). In addition, the user is responsible for any long-distance charges incurred. The cost of maintaining correct and up-to-date information is borne by the vendor of the database service.

Creation of a **centralized database** file involves determining all the information needed by all users. It also requires defining the fields and the relationships among various items of information.

## ADVANTAGES OF A DATABASE ORGANIZATION

The database type of organization has several advantages, including reduced data redundancy, increased data integrity, more effective security, and easier sharing of data across functional areas.

### Data Redundancy

One significant advantage of a database organization is that it reduces **data redundancy.** In the previously described file organizations, each department or functional area (personnel, payroll, inventory, production) probably had its own files. If inventory kept track of the items on hand and ordered, and production kept track of the items as they were used, each area had separate files. If each file contained information about inventory items, much information was duplicated. What if a physical inventory revealed that the balance on hand was incorrect and it had to be adjusted? Again, if the personnel department

# ON THE JOB 1

On-Line Services

One way in which many individuals and companies keep current is by using on-line databases. The user can access information from his or her home or office, often 24 hours a day, by creating a search statement. The search statement identifies the topic looked for—for example: How is the current emphasis on health affecting Americans' lifestyles? Key words from the statement are *current, health, American,* and *lifestyles.* The search looks for articles or references to any one or combination of these words.

Several of the leading services providing business information are listed below. (Hours of access, fees for services, and databases accessed may change.)

BRKTHRU (arts, humanities, education, science, medical, and technologies)
   BRS Information Technology
   1200 Route 7
   Latham, N.Y. 12110

CompuServe (consumer and business services, electronic mail)
   5000 Arlington Center Boulevard
   Columbus, Ohio 43220

Dialog Information Services (business, technical, and scientific)
   3460 Hillview Avenue
   Palo Alto, Calif. 94304

Dow Jones News/Retrieval (business, investments, stocks, and world news)
   P.O. Box 300
   Princeton, N.J. 08540

Mead Data Central (news, business, and law)
   P.O. Box 933
   Dayton, Ohio 45401

Source Telecomputing (consumer services)
   1616 Anderson Road
   McLean, Va. 22102

kept track of employees, there was an entry showing an employee's name on the personnel master file. The name also was kept on the payroll master file. What happened when an employee was married and changed her name? With duplication of information came the problem of it not having the same value in all locations.

## Data Integrity

Closely linked to the problem of redundancy is data integrity. **Data integrity** refers not to whether or not the data is correct; it refers to whether or not it is consistent. If identical data is found in more than one location, the data may easily be changed at one place without being changed at other locations. For example, if an employee married and changed her name, or another moved and changed his address, the change would have to be made on both the personnel and the payroll files. With the integration of data in a database organization, names and addresses would be in only one location.

## Data Security

When data was stored on the older types of files, access to the data was controlled by monitoring who would access the entire file. In some cases, certain fields on one file contained sensitive information; other fields did not. In the payroll file, for example, no one usually cared who accessed the addresses, but the pay rates were much more sensitive. Unfortunately, the user either could access the file and see all fields or could not access the file at all. With databases, security is by field rather than by file, making it easier to handle the file's security.

   **Data security** prevents unauthorized access to data. A common method of limiting access is the use of **passwords.** Passwords may limit access to the system, as in sign-on passwords; here, they are validated by the operating system. They may also further limit access after the user is signed on. The DBMS itself may also check for passwords; here, passwords may be used to determine how much of the database the user may access. They may enable the user to access the entire database or they may be used to limit access to certain subsets of the database. These partial views of a database are referred to as **subschema.** (Security is further discussed in Decentralization and the Ethical Use of Data, later in this chapter.)

## Shared Data

Because many functional areas share data, information that crosses departmental lines is more easily provided with a database organization (see On the Job 2). With past file organizations, the information existed but on several files. Retrieving the needed information from multiple files was a difficult and time-consuming task. With the integrated data of a computer database, the task is much simpler.

## ON THE JOB 2

### Environmental Databases

Great Britain's Natural Environmental Research Council (NERC), headquartered in Swinburne, England, performs research on a wide variety of ecological concerns including marine geology, acid rain, and the tracking and preservation of the world's whale population. NERC maintains over 80 different ecological and environmental databases in diverse locations worldwide. These databases are maintained and accessed by mainframes, minis, and microcomputers. They have a dual architecture policy (IBM and VAX) and use ORACLE as their DBMS. Currently, they are expanding to a triple architecture by adding Sun and Apollo workstations running UNIX.

The data originates when the scientists record the results of their observations or experiments. This information is put into some electronic form. Once it is in electronic form, it can be stored on a database, analyzed, or later retrieved from the database. Most of the databases are archival but data is also retrieved and analyzed using statistical or graphical modeling packages.

## DATABASE MANAGEMENT SYSTEM

*Series of programs to create, modify + control access to database.*

Software is necessary to maintain and use a database. A **database management system (DBMS)** is a series of programs that create, modify, and control access to the database.

### Purpose

The DBMS permits the user to access the information contained within the database. The DBMS is almost always a purchased package consisting of (1) a data dictionary, containing information about the database; (2) a query language, used to access the database; and (3) the access method programs, which permit the user to access the database with the user's own applications programs or through the DBMS's own query language.

Well-known stand-alone database management systems include Integrated Data Management System (IDMS), developed by Cullinet; Information Management System (IMS), which is a hierarchical system used by IBM; and such others as dBase III and IV, Progress, Plus, Adalos, SQL, ORACLE, and R:base. In addition, there are several software packages such as Lotus 1-2-3 and Symphony that contain database components.

### Data Dictionary

*— description of the data.*

The data dictionary is a file within the DBMS. Since data items in a database are shared among applications, it is necessary that information about the data item be available. A data dictionary contains a description of the data within the database. This includes common names for the fields, the field's format and size, and details about whether the information is numeric, alphanumeric, or alphabetical. Alphanumeric data is also referred to as character data when contrasted with numeric data (Figure 10.1). The security of the field is also described: Who has the right to access or change the field's contents? The data dictionary is referenced by users who need to know whether a needed data item is already available on the database or must be captured and added to it. If the item is already available, the dictionary lets the users know the name of the item, the characteristics, and—most importantly—the other applications that access the item.

### Query Language

*— allows user to retrieve info easily or generate reports.*

Because the purpose of any file is to make information available for use, most DBMSs include a query language, which permits the user to retrieve information easily from the file. The query language can also be used to generate reports. The user can provide the title that will appear on the report, as well as the names of the fields. The contents of these fields may also be manipulated mathematically to produce new information such as totals or averages (Figure 10.2).

**FIGURE 10.1**
The data dictionary provides information on the data stored within the database.

| FILE | DATA ITEM | MEANING | LENGTH | TYPE |
|------|-----------|---------|--------|------|
| INVENTORY | ITEM-NO | ITEM IDENT NUMBER | 8 BYTES | NUMERIC |
| | ITEM-DESC | DESCRIPTION OF ITEM | 15 BYTES | CHARACTER |
| | ON-HAND | NUMBER IN WAREHOUSE | 4 BYTES | NUMERIC |
| | ENROUTE | NUMBER RELEASED/SHIPPED | 4 BYTES | NUMERIC |
| | RE-PT | REORDER POINT | 4 BYTES | NUMERIC |
| | RE-QTY | REDORDER QUANTITY | 4 BYTES | NUMERIC |
| | SUPPLIER | SUPPLIER CODE | 3 BYTES | CHARACTER |

MAIN

**FIGURE 10.2**
A query language allows a nonprogrammer to generate a report quickly. In this example, the manager wants a list of the names and the salaries of all employees who belong to salary class A.

FILE:
EMPLMASTER = A
LIST NAME, SALARY

## SHARED FILES

Whereas a computer may make use of its own database file, computers in a network may also share files. In a network, the database may be stored on a mainframe to make it available to all users. Another computer, communicating with the mainframe, may make a copy of **(download)** the file or a selected portion of the file from the mainframe. The data then can be manipulated locally.

## TYPES OF DATABASES

*[handwritten: ① hierarchical ② relational ③ network.]*

*[handwritten in margin: 6.]*

Several approaches to database design have been attempted. Of these, three models have emerged: hierarchical, network, and relational.

Hierarchical and network models reflect how their data is logically related. Rapid access to the data is possible—an important feature of many applications such as airline reservation systems.

The performance of a relational database is usually much slower, but a relational database does permit **ad hoc** (special-purpose) queries. The ability to query for a specific purpose or situation is important to managers who use computers for decision making.

### Hierarchical Databases

*[handwritten: —one parent for each child entry]*

*[handwritten in margin: 8.]*

The **hierarchical database** forms a treelike structure, a series of nodes connected by branches. Each entry has only one **parent entry,** although an entry may have many subordinate **child entries.** No references exist across the tree. Data must go from the top of the tree downward along a unique path until it reaches its destination. All references between two items follow the path from the first item to some common **node** or point on the tree where the paths intersect, and then follow the path back down to the second item.

In Figure 10.3, the relationship between supervisors and production workers is shown. Supervisors are a higher-level entry; the workstations they supervise are subordinate to them. Subordinate to the workstations are the production workers assigned to each station. If a production worker's station is changed, the entry on the file also must be changed.

### Network Databases

*[handwritten: —multiple parents for each child.]*

*[handwritten in margin: 9.]*

The **network database** resembles the hierarchical one in that a parent node can have many subordinate child nodes. However, unlike in the hierarchical model, a child can have more than one parent in the network.

These complex relationships are handled by **pointers.** The pointers, which can be updated, indicate which child or subordinate nodes are related to which parent or owner nodes in the database. Of course, since these pointers must be saved, network databases do require additional space for the overhead required by these pointers.

In Figure 10.4, the relationship between supervisors and production workers is followed by linking production workers to workstations, linking supervisors

**FIGURE 10.3**

To relate two subordinate entries in a hierarchical database, the path from the first item must go up to a node common to both entries, then back down to the second entry. The department information points to the information about each supervisor in the department. The supervisor points to each workstation supervised. Finally, the workstation points to information about the employees who work at that workstation.

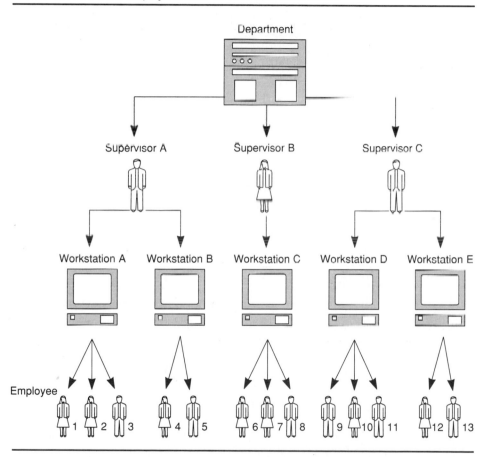

to workstations, and defining a third relationship as the composite of the two: supervisors and production workers. If a production worker's workstation is changed, the pointer also must be changed.

## Relational Databases — uses indexes

Of the three models, **relational databases** offer the greatest flexibility in accessing data because no predefined access paths exist. The data is stored as **tables** or **arrays** and is located by indexes. A table is analogous to a file; a row

**FIGURE 10.4**

In the network organization, each lower-level entry can be subordinate to more than one high-level entry. Here, the supervisor points to each workstation supervised but there is some overlapping. For example, supervisors A and B both may supervise workstation B. Pointers between workstations and those who use them are also more complex.

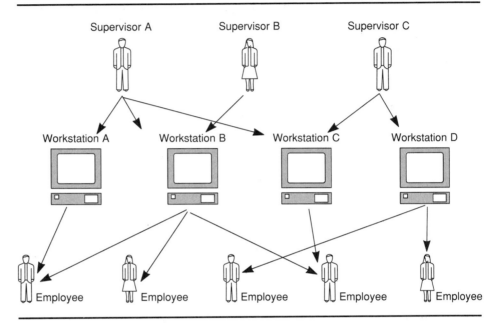

within the table to a record; and each entry in the column—called an **attribute**—is the individual data element.

A relational database stores and retrieves information in much the same way that we store and retrieve information from file cabinets. If you needed a copy of an invoice sent to the ZZZ Corporation, you would first decide in which file drawer the invoice was stored. Next, you would select the correct folder and from it pull the invoice you needed.

In a relational database, all related files are stored within the database. Each file is a collection of information on the same subject. The file consists of records, each of which includes all the information about that one subject (Figure 10.5).

## THE DATABASE ADMINISTRATOR

With all the potential options and users, someone must have both the technical knowledge and the managerial ability to coordinate database activities. The **database administrator (DBA)** is this person. The DBA designs the system,

**FIGURE 10.5**
In a relational database, each entry is found through an index. For example, an entry showing a customer's payment could be related to an entry concerning the sales representative who serviced that account. It might also be related to entries showing items sold.

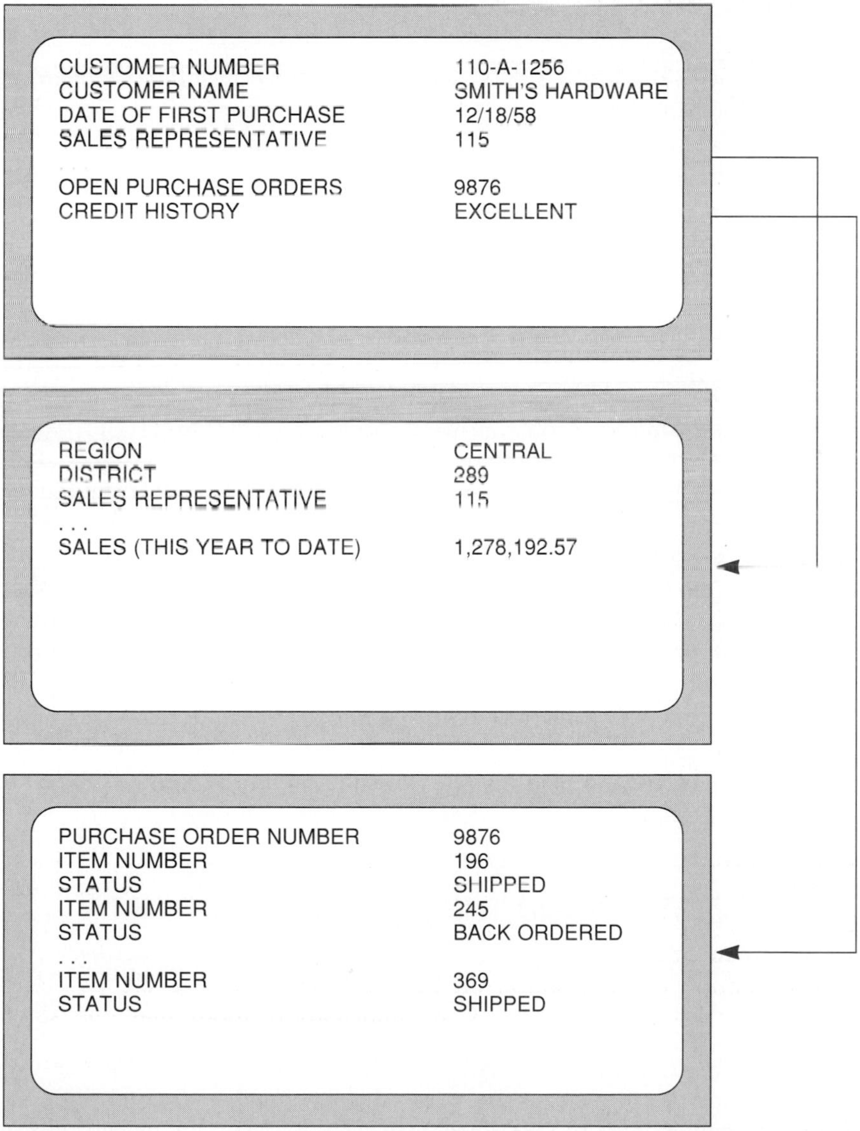

CUSTOMER NUMBER          110-A-1256
CUSTOMER NAME            SMITH'S HARDWARE
DATE OF FIRST PURCHASE   12/18/58
SALES REPRESENTATIVE     115

OPEN PURCHASE ORDERS     9876
CREDIT HISTORY           EXCELLENT

REGION                   CENTRAL
DISTRICT                 289
SALES REPRESENTATIVE     115
. . .
SALES (THIS YEAR TO DATE)   1,278,192.57

PURCHASE ORDER NUMBER    9876
ITEM NUMBER              196
STATUS                   SHIPPED
ITEM NUMBER              245
STATUS                   BACK ORDERED
. . .
ITEM NUMBER              369
STATUS                   SHIPPED

monitors and manages the database, maintains the system, sets standards for security, and resolves conflicts among users. The DBA may also provide educational and consulting services to the users.

## 10. PROBLEMS

Deciding what should go into a database file is not easy. Each department has different opinions on what is needed. In addition, departments might define the same field differently. For example, traffic might consider an inventory item on hand when the freight car arrives at the plant, whereas manufacturing might consider it available only when the freight car or truck is unloaded and the material is ready for use.

Although databases solve the problems of redundancy, wasted storage, and inaccuracies found in conventional files, they also create new problems. Among these are new problems of security and privacy of data. The programmer also must clearly understand the data needs of the group to be served by the database before creating it.

One of the most common problems in database design is change. The database often is designed before the data relationships are completely understood. Later, changes in the organization's understanding of the relationshps among data elements may adversely affect the original database design.

Another area of conflict relates to the proper use of data. For instance, many people supported government efforts to uncover welfare fraud by comparing the contents of several databases. Others were concerned and frightened by the implications of this program. Is it ethical to gather data for one purpose and then use it for another without notification of and/or permission from data subjects? What about data errors? What rights do the subjects have? Should they know what is on file? Have they the right to challenge the validity of data? Must subjects be notified before information is released? Many ethical questions must be resolved about the proper use of databases.

## DECENTRALIZATION AND THE ETHICAL USE OF DATA

Information can be either centralized—all in one central location under a central control—or decentralized—with each operating unit having its own information system. Even centrally located databases are used by many users, often from remote locations, and may be downloaded to remote locations for use there. With this decentralization come the advantages of local end-user control and faster access. Unfortunately, with decentralized databases, increased difficulty in maintaining security and data integrity also occur. If data may be accessed from more than one location, it is necessary to ensure that it is not changed from multiple locations at the same time; if passwords are used, it is essential that their secrecy be maintained; if accessed remotely, the system must be protected from unauthorized persons using repetitive, automated generation of passwords followed by attempts to sign-on using them. Computer crimes are difficult to detect, and many organizations may not even admit that they have occurred.

The database must be accessible by many users of differing abilities. It must be accessed from different locations. Although electronic protection schemes such as passwords and limits to remote locations increase security, they interfere with the ease of use for the legitimate users of the system.

What are some types of criminal or unethical use? Unfortunately, many activities are not even considered criminal by the user or may be so borderline that it is difficult to decide if the usage is improper. We recognize that breaking into a house is criminal. But what about breaking into a computer system? This means that the user is accessing the system without authority or reading unauthorized data.

Perhaps the user is permitted to read inventory data but not payroll. Reading payroll is a type of unlawful entry. Related crimes are those of industrial espionage whereby company formulas or customer lists are stolen through unauthorized access.

Another common problem is the unauthorized use of computer time. The use may be strictly for personal reasons—playing a game or writing a personal letter on the word processor at work—or it may be for profit, such as writing a program on your computer at work and then selling the program or the results.

Data and programs may be altered or stolen. The theft of company mailing lists and the altering of programs or data to increase a person's pay without authorization are examples.

Finally, computer facilities and data may be damaged. "Time bombs," which are really logic bombs, may be placed in a program by a hacker or a disgruntled employee, causing the program to fail or the data to be destroyed at some future time. A **hacker** is a person who uses his or her technical knowledge to make an unauthorized access to either a computer system or its data. Damage-causing program modifications that spread from program to program or from disk to disk are called **viruses.**

Providing easy access to authorized users while preventing unauthorized use is a problem that has yet to be solved.

## SUMMARY

A database is a collection of integrated data or of related files that are created and managed by a database management system. The database type of organization has several advantages, including reduced data redundancy, increased data integrity, more effective security, and easier sharing of data across functional areas.

A **database management system (DBMS)** is a series of programs that create, modify, and control access to the database. The DBMS is almost always a purchased package consisting of (1) a data dictionary, containing information about the database; (2) a query language, used to access the database; and (3) the access method programs, which permit the user to access the database.

A data dictionary contains a description of the data contained within the database. Query languages permit the user to retrieve information easily from the file. The query language can also be used to generate reports. The access method programs convert the logical request to get a record into the physical activities needed to retrieve the data.

Data security prevents unauthorized access to data. When data was stored on the older types of files, access to the data was controlled by monitoring who would access the entire file. A common method of limiting access is the use of passwords. Passwords may limit access to the system, as in sign-on passwords; they may also further limit access after the user is signed on.

The DBA or database administrator is the person who designs the system, monitors and manages the database, maintains the system, sets standards for security, and resolves conflicts among users. The DBA may also provide educational and consulting services to the users.

There are three common types of databases: hierarchical, network, and relational. Hierarchical and network models reflect how their data is logically related. Rapid access to the data is possible. Relational databases offer the greatest flexibility in accessing data because no predefined access paths exist. The data is stored as tables or arrays and is located by indexes.

Although databases solve the problems of redundancy, wasted storage, and inaccuracies found in conventional files, they also create new problems. Among these are new problems of security and privacy of data.

## VOCABULARY

## EXERCISES

1. What problems with conventional file organizations do databases attempt to solve?
2. What is a commercial database?
3. What is a database management system? Name at least three features usually found in one.
4. What is a data dictionary?
5. What is a query language?
6. Name the three most common types of database structure.
7. Which structure uses indexes to locate entries?
8. Which one allows only one parent record to each child record?
9. Which structure permits multiple parent entries for a single child entry?
10. Discuss the problems of data security and data privacy.
11. Why is choosing a type of database file structure difficult?
12. Discuss the ethics of data use.

## PROJECTS

1. Research one of the commercial databases, such as Dow Jones or Compu-Serve, and report on what services it provides.
2. Obtain a copy of the Privacy Act of 1974. After studying it, draw up what you believe would be an appropriate and workable law for private industry.
3. A person's medical history may affect his or her future medical problems. An insurance company would like to assign a fair-risk class to all those it insures; therefore, it would like to have a new client's medical history. How do you feel about the release of information? Should a person wishing to purchase insurance be required to release health information? What if the client was in good health? What if the person once had cancer but was now cured? What if the new client had been an alcoholic but was no longer drinking?

# 11

# Telecommunications

## CHAPTER OBJECTIVES

*After completing this chapter, you will be able to:*

1. Describe a telecommunications system and its hardware components.
2. Explain what is meant by *handshaking*.
3. Identify several types of communication links.
4. Define a network.
5. Describe several network configurations.
6. Discuss the advantages and disadvantages of distributed data processing.
7. Differentiate between distributed data processing and a distributed database.
8. Discuss the current issues in telecommunications: privacy, security, and integrity.
9. Discuss current trends in telecommunications.

## OVERVIEW

For centuries, people have tried to improve their methods of communication (see On the Job 1). Messengers, letters, telegraphs, and telephones have been used in an attempt to improve the usefulness of information by increasing the speed of its access.

Compare the value of knowing of the Alaskan gold strike immediately after gold was discovered to finding out months later. Imagine the value of being able to review a copy of an important contract within minutes rather than waiting days for its arrival by mail.

Since the development of the earliest computers, we have been trying to improve the speed at which information is communicated. Data first was batched together and carried to a central site for processing; later, it was entered at remote terminals and forwarded to the central computer. Still later, the data was entered on-line to the central computer and eventually was processed not only at the central site but also at various remote locations. Telecommunications involves the transmission of programs and data between terminals and the computer using communications lines.

## HARDWARE

Data communication systems transmit data over communications lines; that is, the central computer is linked to terminals via communications lines. From these remote locations, the terminals are able to enter transactions and to make queries.

The hardware components of a data communication system consist of a terminal, a modem, a communication channel, a second modem, perhaps a communications processor, and finally the computer (Figure 11.1). These components may be individual units or combined into one physical unit as in microcomputers. In addition, a communications program is also required. This is a software program that supports the transmission of data.

**FIGURE 11.1**

The digital signals generated by the terminal *(a)* are changed by a modem *(b)* into analog signals for transmission over telephone lines *(c)*. At the other end, the signal is translated back to digital form by a second modem for use by the computer. The signal is then transmitted to the computer *(d)*, perhaps through a front-end processor. When a message is returned to the terminal, the procedure is reversed.

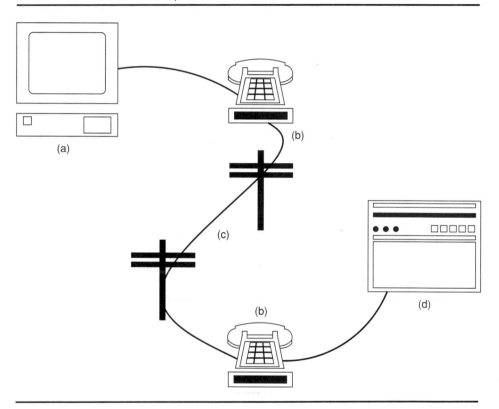

## Terminal

The terminal is used to send and receive information. As the terminal issues a request for service, it enters a **wait state,** waiting for the computer to notice that the terminal has a message waiting. The computer **polls** the various terminals, checking to see if a message is waiting. If one terminal has no message, the computer checks the next terminal; if a message is there, the computer services that terminal and transmits the message from the terminal to the computer. The **response time** is the period that elapses between when a message is sent and when a response is received.

It is not necessary to poll all terminals equally. The polling procedure may be adjusted so that more frequently used terminals are polled more often than less frequently used ones.

## ON THE JOB 1

### Partners in Satellite Communications: Public Service or Monopoly?

Wouldn't it be convenient if any person or vehicle carrying the appropriate communications device could communicate worldwide? The technology exists in theory, but problems with communications protocol as well as the cost of development have slowed down progress.

In 1987, the Federal Communications Commission (FCC) directed that all MSS (Mobile Satellite Service) vendors form a joint venture to develop a space-based communications service. To establish financial solvency, each vendor was required to deposit $5 million into a common escrow account. Eight companies joined to form the MSS Consortium.

The Consortium plans to construct a satellite, launch it, and operate the space-based services. The group anticipates launching the satellite in 1990. Those in favor of the group effort say that, due to the high costs involved, the expenses must be shared among vendors. Those opposed argue that a consortium eliminates competition and thereby creates a monopoly situation.

An alternative to polling the lines is **contention,** whereby the terminal checks the line to see if it is in use. If the line is free, the terminal begins to use the line, monopolizing it until the transmission is complete. If the line is busy, the terminal waits and retries it.

### Modem

Because most computers and terminals use **digital signals** (those recognized by either the presence or the absence of an electronic pulse), whereas voice-grade telephone lines use **analog signals** (those representing a range of frequencies), some translation is necessary for computers and terminals to use the lines for transmission (Figure 11.2). The **modem,** standing for *mo*dulator/*dem*odulator, **modulates** or takes the digital signal issued by the terminal and translates it into an analog signal for transmission. At the other end of the line, the signal is captured by another modem, which reverses the process, **demodulating** or translating the signal back from analog to digital. Special modems are also used to connect microcomputers to a local area network. Modems are of several types. The **acoustical coupler** on an acoustical modem links the computer to telephone lines when a telephone handset is inserted into the holder. It is the oldest type but may have problems with external noise.

With the common use of telephone jacks, a newer type of model has become popular. It consists of modem circuits plus a plug into which a telephone jack may be inserted.

**FIGURE 11.2**

Digital signals are represented by the presence or the absence of a pulse, whereas analog signals cover the whole range of frequencies.

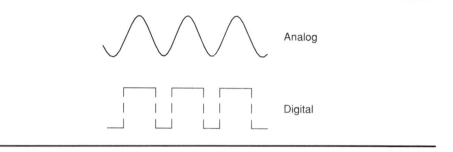

The acoustical coupler is an external device. Modems may also be internal, however. As modems continue to become smaller and smaller, a built-in modem on a chip will probably become a feature of all computers.

## Communication Channel *— path over which data is moved.*

*12.*

Almost any device capable of transmitting electronic information can be used as a communication channel. A **communication channel** is simply the pathway over which data is moved between devices. Links may be by telephone lines, coaxial cable (underground or undersea communication lines), optical fibers, or microwave radio signals. The link may also include satellites.

The capacity of a channel to transmit data is crucial. **Bandwidth** refers to the amount of data that can be transmitted in a unit of time. It is usually measured in bits per second, referred to as **baud.** One baud is synonymous with one-bit-per-second transmission. **Voice-band channels**—sometimes referred to as voice-grade channels—can transmit data up to 9600 baud. Communications between PCs or terminals and the host computer typically fall into this range, usually transmitting at 1200 or 2400 baud.

*9600 baud.*

The next range is referred to as **medium band channels,** typically transmitting at 9600 to 256,000 baud. Television signals travel in this band.

*high speeds*

**Broad bands** are capable of transmitting at very high speeds—in the millions of bits per second.

### Telephone Lines (twisted pair)

Many users use telephone lines for communications. Telephone lines are a physical medium that can also be used to transmit data. **Twisted pair** is made of pairs of insulated wires that are twisted around each other. This twisting minimizes interferences. Many pairs are enclosed in the same cable. Twisted-pair cables provide a lower transmission capacity than do other methods.

Thousands of microcomputer owners access public services such as Compu-Serve by dialing up the service computer on their home phone and hooking it via a telephone line to their microcomputer. Other users, such as sales representatives, also use public telephones to link their portables to the office computer.

Most businesses that use phone lines do not use their dial-up or **switched lines** but instead choose to use **dedicated (leased) lines.** In this case, the line is leased to the company for its exclusive use. The computer-to-computer or computer-to-terminal connection remains in place at all times. No dialing is required for contact to be made.

### Coaxial Cable

Other computer users employ **coaxial cables** made of insulated wire surrounded by a flexible metal sheathing. These cables, often used for undersea telephone lines, can also be employed for data communications and may be run underground, underwater, or within a building to connect a local area network. They have a greater bandwidth and transmission capacity than twisted pair telephone lines.

### Fiber Optics

**Fiber optics** is one of the newer communications media. During the 1984 Los Angeles Olympics, approximately one half of the population of the globe watched some part of the events as the result of data transmission through optical fibers. The low cost and small diameter of the fibers, which allow installation in congested areas, and the ability to handle high-speed transmissions make optical fibers a popular choice for both data communications and as an alternative for audio telephone communications. The optical fiber is made up of glass filaments (see Figure 11.3). Data is transmitted as pulses of light. In addition, optical fibers have a natural resistance to electromagnetic interference. Any tapping into the fibers seriously degrades the performance, making security breaches easy to detect.

### Microwave

**Microwave radio signals** are also used for data transmission. They are electromagnetic waves that vibrate at one billion cycles per second. Their main disadvantage is that they travel in a straight line rather than with the curve of the earth (Figure 11.4). Because they do not bend, they must be caught, amplified, and retransmitted within line of sight. This problem is largely alleviated through the use of satellites.

### Satellites

The newest method of relaying communication signals uses **satellites** set in orbit (Figure 11.5). From 22,000 miles above the earth, these satellites amplify electronic signals and transmit them to another station. The signal that travels from earth to the communications satellite and back is often referred to as a

**FIGURE 11.3**
Optical fibers, glass tubes even smaller than the human hair, transmit data in the form of pulses of light. (Frankevitch/The Stock Market)

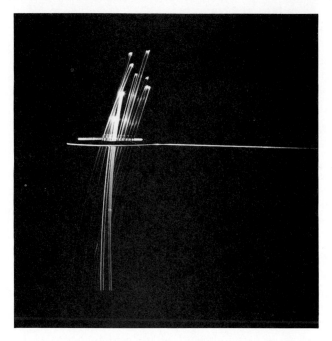

**satellite link.** A primary disadvantage of satellite communications is that security is difficult. To ensure the validity and security of data transmitted, that data is often encrypted. The use of secret codes attempts to prevent unauthorized individuals from sending as well as receiving messages.

Because each of the data transmission methods discussed may be performed by common carrier—a carrier offering communication services to the public—all fall under the jurisdiction of the FCC and are regulated by both the FCC and various state agencies.

### Computer and Front-End Processor

The host computer must accept the various types of transmission signals, as well as forward other signals to the terminals and computers communicating with it. This is in addition to processing applications programs occurring within the computer at the same time.

A **front-end processor,** located at the host, may be used to relieve the host of some of its communications tasks. The processor links the communications channels to the main computer. It handles inputting data from the various input devices so that the host computer can concentrate on processing tasks.

**FIGURE 11.4**

*(a)* Microwave radio signals, because they do not bend, must be retransmitted every 25 to 35 miles. *(b)* Relaying microwave radio signals via satellite largely eliminates the "line of sight" problem.

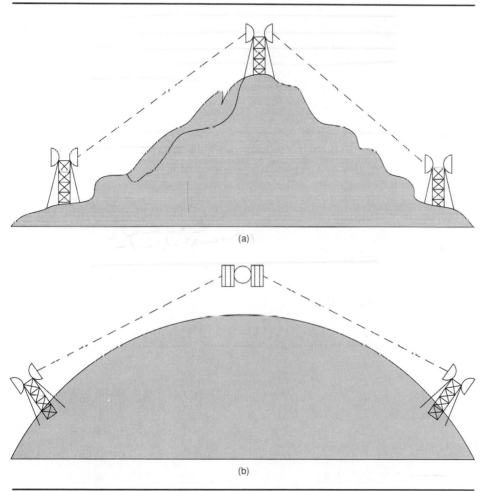

(a)

(b)

For example, a front-end processor might be used to check for valid user account numbers before users access the host computer.

## NETWORKS

Whenever two or more computers are connected by communications equipment, they are a **network.** The network is the communications path linking computers. One great advantage of networking is that it provides a method for instantaneous transmissions to many people at one time.

**FIGURE 11.5**
Technicians check the MARISAT-B spacecraft scheduled for launch from the Kennedy Space Center. It is the second spacecraft in the world's first maritime satellite communications system. (NASA)

Most networks use common carriers for communications, but a growing number do not. These local area networks (LANs) share data and resources among several computers or workstations within a local area such as an office building or factory. The computers, terminals, and other peripherals in a LAN are linked by cable in such a way that all can use the cable at the same time and they can communicate with each other rapidly over distances up to a mile.

With a LAN, many users can share resources. A file server links databases to the network, permitting multiple users to share access to the databases. Print servers link printers to the network, permitting multiple users to also share printers. A wide variety of other specialized devices can also be linked and shared.

LANs are often used to link microcomputers. The microcomputers may process their own data or may retrieve data that has been stored on a PC, usually high-performance, referred to as the **file server.** The printers may also be controlled through a PC referred to as the **print server.**

Three main network configurations exist, although most networks are a hybrid or mix of configurations. The three primary types are point-to-point, star, and ring.

## Point-to-Point Network

In a **point-to-point network,** two computers are directly linked to each other, permitting two-way communication (Figure 11.6). Communication is both fast and expensive.

## Star Network

In the **star**-shaped **network,** a central host is connected to any number of other systems. All communication among the other systems is through the host (Figure 11.7). This gives the host tight control over communications among branch nodes. Unfortunately, one drawback is that, if the host computer fails, the entire system will fail, affecting all users.

## Ring Network

In a **ring network,** all computers are considered equal to one another. No host controls communications. Each computer may communicate directly with each of the others (Figure 11.8). If one computer fails, the others will be unaffected since there are multiple access paths to each node.

**FIGURE 11.6**

In a point-to-point network, an exchange of information occurs between two computers.

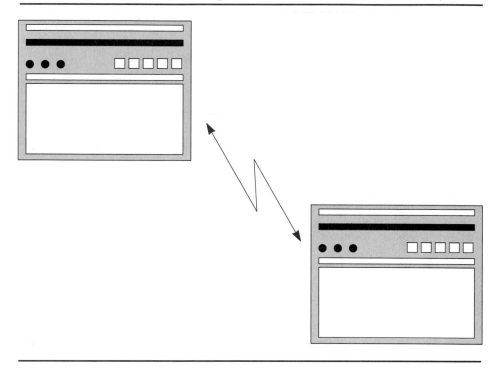

## Line Control

The rules or standards for the exchange of information among computers or between a computer and its terminals are referred to as **line protocol.** The protocol specifies how messages are to be sent. Certain prearranged signals have specific meanings to the computer. The manufacturer determines these signals and their meanings.

**Handshaking** is the initial exchange of signals that occurs when a device comes on-line. When this occurs, the two machines exchange signals to acknowledge each other's presence—an action similar to the handshake sometimes exchanged when two people meet. If the signals are understood correctly, a valid connection is established.

## Software

Communication between points on the network is controlled by software. These programs move, prioritize, and log messages. They also poll terminals, convert codes and protocols, and perform many other functions.

**FIGURE 11.7**
In a star network, one host exists with several smaller computers attached. This is most useful for a company with one central headquarters and dispersed branch offices.

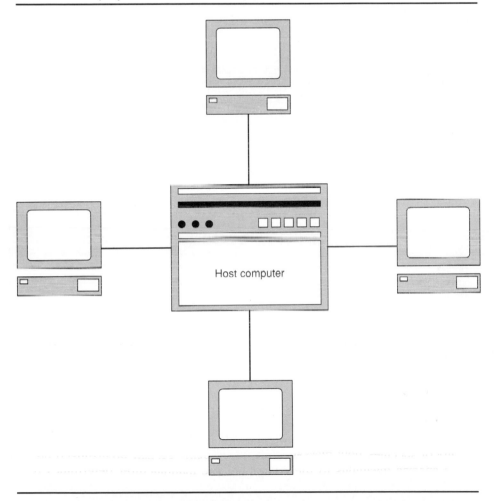

Host computer

The telecommunication software used by a mainframe is usually located in the front-end processor. Functions performed by this software may also be split between the front-end processor and the host.

Microcomputers also require communications software, and many different software packages are available. The telecommunications software must be compatible with the operating system and appropriate for the needs of the user.

Data communications may be bisynchronous or asynchronous. **Bisynchronous communication** means that the data is sent at fixed, known intervals. **Asynchronous communication** means that the data will be sent and received

**FIGURE 11.8**
The ring network has no central host. All computers may talk to all others. This system is most useful in a decentralized organization.

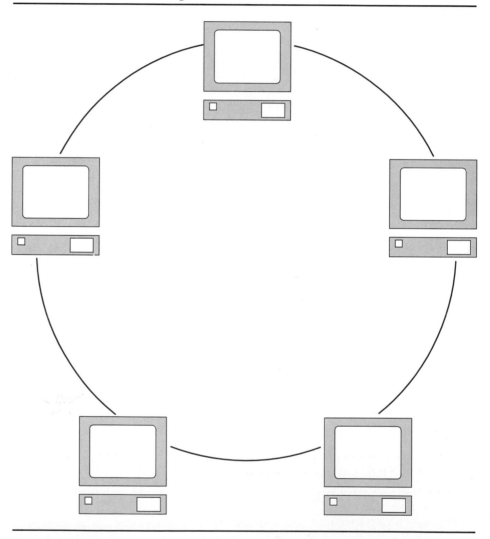

whenever the devices are ready. Both devices must use the same method of communications.

## DISTRIBUTED DATA PROCESSING

*data may be processed remotely*

13

Although the ability to speed up data processing by using telecommunications represents a significant advance, the change to distributed data processing offers even more progress. In **distributed data processing,** not only may the computer be accessed from remote locations, but the data may also be processed remotely.

A distributed data processing system consists of multiple computers linked together by a communications network. In the system, each computer handles its own local workload although the network permits sharing of the data and processing tasks. When data is processed where it is captured or used, the cost is lower and the response quicker. The use of a local computer offers easier access and the possibility of modifying the programs to meet unique local needs.

Unfortunately, remote sites often lack programming and systems expertise. The remote computer may be smaller than the host system, which may impose memory limitations. The very ease of making program modifications may reduce the consistency of the information obtained.

## SOME CHANGING APPLICATIONS

Technological advances, decreasing hardware costs, and telecommunications have led to significant changes in how office work is performed. As the speed and ease of communications have increased (see On the Job 2), several technologies have taken on a new importance. They include electronic mail, facsimile systems, and teleconferencing and telecommuting.

### Electronic Mail — communication between computers

15. **Electronic mail** or **messaging** is any communication between persons that is transmitted or received via computer. It includes messages and facsimile transmissions. (Facsimile transmissions involve sending photographs and other documents.) Electronic mail originated with time-sharing companies such as Telemail and Tymeshare's ONTYME. It was provided as an additional customer service. In addition to these public data networks, in-house systems permit terminal users to leave each other messages stored by the computer as though in an electronic mailbox.

The speed of transmittal is obviously one of the greatest advantages; also, no mail is lost. Text, graphs, and pictures may all be transmitted, and the receivers do not have to be available when the message is sent; they can collect their mail after returning to the office or when calling in to the company computer while on the road.

Electronic mail seems to encourage spontaneity, since the recipient does not have to be available when the mail is sent. This is both good and bad. Responses can be sent quickly, but in the case of an angry response, there is no cooling-off period. On the other hand, there also seems to be a more objective evaluation of the contents of the message; since the sender is not present, the message is more likely to be evaluated on its own merits.

## ON THE JOB 2

### Electronic Pen Pals

Highland Park and Gross Ile schools in Wayne County, Michigan, are involved in an internation project in which their students become electronic pen pals with students in Sheffield, England. Currently, there are 24 participants from the United States, Canada, Germany, Italy, Australia, and Japan. Two conferences have been set up using the University of Michigan's Confer II system. One conference is used by staff, the other by students.

Another characteristic is that electronic mail leaves an electronic trail. Although this is an advantage, it sometimes causes a problem. You probably remember the messages left by Lt. Col. Oliver North on the National Security Council's electronic mail system. Computers, unlike shredders, keep backup files.

A growing trend is storing the message in voice instead of textual form so that the message may be retrieved as a vocal rather than a written one.

### Facsimile Systems

**Facsimile (fax) systems** transmit copies of documents, whether textual or pictorial, electronically via a telecommunications link. This link is usually telephone lines or microwave via satellite. Unlike other methods of transmission, the facsimile system sends not only text but an exact replica of the document—drawings, signatures, and so forth.

Imagine your newspaper having only photographs that were taken locally or that were several days old. It would not be as interesting to read. For many years, wire services have been transmitting facsimiles of photographs to their member newspapers. Other companies are also using facsimile systems to transmit all types of documents rapidly to remote locations. In 1987, there were about 600,000 fax machines in use. It is estimated that this number was almost 1.5 million by the end of 1989. Plug-in fax boards are now available for many PCs, putting fax ability within the price range of the small office. It is difficult to overestimate the usefulness of fax. When an authorized original is not required, no other method of rapid delivery can perform as well.

### Teleconferencing and Telecommuting

**Teleconferencing** is a type of meeting in which the participants use electronic or image-producing equipment rather than meeting face to face. **Telecommuting** is working from home or from some other remote workplace using computer hookups for communications. The use of both is growing.

The most simple form of teleconferencing uses only the telephone. The participants meet via conference call. This type of meeting is adequate when no visuals are needed or when any necessary visuals are already at all locations. Almost all telephone systems today permit conference calls.

A more complex system allows the use of telephones with visual display. The visual display component is the computer terminal. An image is displayed on terminal screens at both ends of the conversation. The users may interact while the screen is displayed. One user may even call attention to something by highlighting an area on the opposite screen.

A third type of teleconference uses full-motion video. Video monitors permit the participants to see and hear everything that is occurring at all locations (Figure 11.9). All types of teleconferencing allow those involved to participate without the lost time involved in travel and the expense of the trip. Teleconferencing is costly, but when the costs of travel and lost time are considered, it often becomes very cost-effective. It also permits participation by those who might not otherwise be able to do so.

Consider the logistical problems involved in scheduling a conference of doctors and other health professionals from around the world who are involved in spinal cord injury rehabilitation. To correspond via letter would be too slow. A one-day meeting would involve a minimum of one day away from other

**FIGURE 11.9**
Full-motion video teleconferencing permits the participants to appear to be face to face.
(Frank Siteman/Stock Boston)

activities and a maximum of perhaps a week for those traveling halfway around the world.

Consider also a company doing business across the United States. A meeting involving all salespeople would pull the sales force off the road and away from their real function: selling. If the meeting were held in the middle of the country, those traveling from the east and west coasts would lose at least several days. The travel costs—lodging, transportation, food—would be significant. With full-motion video, teleconferencing has become a very useful alternative.

There are disadvantages to teleconferencing, however. Although convenient, it is not as social. Whether from habit or fact, most people believe that things can be accomplished in a face-to-face meeting that would be impossible to achieve from a remote location. The social aspect of business, missing in both teleconferencing and telecommuting, is something we are reluctant to give up.

## CURRENT ISSUES

The ease with which we can access data through telecommunications systems also increases the danger of improper use of the data. Current issues include privacy, security, and ethics.

### Privacy

National and state tax information is stored on computers. The FBI, CIA, and various state and local police agencies use computers to store information. Sensitive medical information is also stored on large databases. What information should be stored, and how accurately is it maintained?

Also, how do we ensure that those accessing this information have the right to do so? The increasing ease of using computers and telecommunications is making it simpler for both those who are and those who are not authorized to access information.

Since 1970, laws have been passed in an attempt to protect our privacy (see Figure 11.10). The **Freedom of Information Act of 1970** permits individuals to gain access to data about themselves that is maintained by federal agencies. The **Privacy Act of 1974** further protects an individual's privacy by guaranteeing that:

1. Persons can know what information the government keeps about them.
2. The person can change that information when it is incorrect.
3. Information collected for one purpose cannot be used for another purpose without the individual's consent.

Although these laws affect only federal information, other laws have been passed regulating access to some data kept in the private sector.

**FIGURE 11.10**

These are just a few of the recent federal laws concerning privacy.

| Year | Title | Description |
|------|-------|-------------|
| 1970 | Freedom of Information Act | Allows an individual to find out what personal data has been collected by federal agencies and to secure copies of that data to see that it is correct. |
| 1970 | Fair Credit Reporting Act | Allows individuals to inspect their credit record and to challenge the information in it. If any information is challenged, the credit agency is legally required to investigate its accuracy. |
| 1974 | Privacy Act | Established laws to prevent federal government abuses against the privacy of an individual. |
| 1974 | Education Privacy Act | Restricts access to computer records of grades and behavior evaluations in both public and private schools. |
| 1976 | Copyright Act | Protects creative and intellectual property including plays, books, songs, and computer programs. |
| 1978 | Rights to Financial Privacy | Restricts government access to customer files in financial institutions and permits citizens the right to examine data about themselves in those files. |
| 1980 | Electronic Funds Transfer Act | Requires institutions that offer EFT (electronic funds transfer) check service to tell their customers about third-party access to the customer's account. |
| 1986 | Electronic Communications Privacy Act | Makes it illegal to intercept data communications. |
| 1986 | Computer Fraud and Abuse Act | Provides for federal jurisdiction over interstate computer crimes in the private sector. |

Many violations of privacy may not be considered crimes. Is it wrong for a programmer to access the employee master file to find out the address of a fellow employee to send a get-well card? What if that fellow employee just happens to be single and attractive and is not ill at all? When does curiosity become criminal?

## Security

In an attempt to make computers more accessible to the public, we have opened the door to violations of both security and privacy. With only a home computer, a modem, a telephone, and some programming experience, a person may obtain illegal access to another computer system.

Security measures taken to make access more difficult include the use of user codes, identification numbers, and passwords. Access can be limited by location, with only certain user codes authorized at certain sites. Passwords may be changed frequently, data may be encoded, and individual data items may be protected from those not having a second password or sufficient security clearance.

In the past, computer security was usually based on what you knew (such as a password) or what you had with you (such as a key, card, or token). These methods do not work too well, since what you have or know can be transferred to someone else. A newer method of security is based on who you are—**biometric security.**

Biometric security devices identify you by digitally measuring your physical or behavioral characteristics such as fingerprints, voice inflection, or the pattern of blood vessels across your retina. For example, the retina of your eye may be scanned by a low-intensity light source. The print of the blood vessels in this area, referred to as your eye signature, is then stored in a microprocessor. Since this eye signature is as unique to you as your fingerprint, it can be matched to a current scan of the same section of your eye for identification purposes. Biometric security devices are almost failsafe.

## Ethics

Ethics in the use of stored data is a more nebulous subject than either privacy or security. For example, many articles discuss the ethics of making illegal copies of software. Because electronic information is easy to obtain and reproduce, and because it is also volatile, it is easy and tempting to make unauthorized copies. Much is written about how to better regulate the reproduction of software and how to eliminate the making of illegal copies.

Data processors want the ability to make a backup copy in case the original is destroyed. Authors want to receive just profits from their labor. How can both be satisfied? How can backup copies be permitted while copying by unauthorized persons is prohibited? Several methods are employed to permit only one backup copy or to permit a copy only by someone holding the "key." The conflict still has to be better resolved.

The illegal or unauthorized copying of software is referred to as software piracy. Software is protected by our copyright laws in the same way that books are. When you buy a book, you purchase the right to use the book—to read it, shelve it, draw in the margins, or destroy it. You do not buy the right to call the text of the book your own; ownership of the text of the book remains with the author or publisher. In the same way, when software is purchased, the purchaser really buys only the disk it is on and obtains a license to use the software stored on it; the software itself is not owned. The license to use the software may cover a single computer or it may be a site license, which is a contract that permits the purchaser to make an unlimited number of copies but limits the site(s) or location(s) where the software may be used.

**Shareware** is distributed free. It may be freely copied and tried out; in fact, copying and distribution are usually encouraged. If the user likes the software and decides to keep it to use regularly, he or she is expected to pay a fee to the publisher. Only those who have paid this fee are entitled to receive documentation and updates.

Software is often copy-protected by the addition of special codes that either prevent copying or limit the number of copies that can be made. Unfortunately, these codes are not very effective. Ways to circumvent them develop as quickly as the coding schemes do.

The unauthorized use of computer time is another problem. Is it proper for a student to use a university computer for other than the assigned programs? Is it right to write extra programs for practice? What about running games on university or work time? What about writing a brief program for one's own use? What about writing a program, running it, and then selling the results?

## TRENDS

Although today, data is communicated over many media, optical fibers will be the medium of the future. Use of satellites will also continue to grow, with many large firms providing private carrier service. Already, Comsat, IBM, and Aetna have joined to support Satellite Business Systems.

The use of modems will decline as more transmissions become digital and do not have to be converted to send over telephone lines. AT&T has announced a plan to convert their telephone system from an analog system to a digital one by 1995. Once the conversion is complete, the lines will carry both voice and data in digital form.

The continuing decline in hardware prices should result in more and more inexpensive equipment, making sophisticated telecommunications and networking more practical for the small business.

One of the greatest problems in networks today is the problem of **incompatibility:** one device is unable to communicate with another because they lack a common protocol. Many people anticipate that this problem will soon be alleviated.

## SUMMARY

Telecommunication systems, consisting of a terminal, modem, communication channel, second modem, and perhaps a front-end communications processor, are revolutionizing how data is processed. Many types of communications links are used: telephone lines, coaxial cable, fiber optics, microwave, and satellites.

Whenever two or more computers are connected by a communications link, they are considered a network. Most are hybrid, but the classic network configurations are point-to-point, star, and ring.

Current communications applications include electronic mail, facsimile transmission, and various types of teleconferencing.

The ease of computer use and the ability to access the computer over communications channels have created new problems in privacy, security, and ethics.

## ▨ VOCABULARY

## ▨ EXERCISES

1. What is shareware?
2. What is a digital signal?
3. What is an analog signal?
4. Why do signals have to be translated from digital to analog?
5. What is the difference between a leased and a switched line?
6. What are the advantages to using optical fibers?
7. Why must microwave signals be retransmitted?

8. Why are satellites so useful in signal transmission?

9. What is the difference between LANs and other networks?

10. Compare point-to-point, star, and ring networks. Are most networks one of these types?

11. What is a modem? How are modems changing?

12. What is meant by voice band? Broad band? What band rates are used today?

13. What is meant by distributed data processing?

14. The ease of transmitting data has led to problems in security, privacy, and data integrity. Discuss these issues.

15. What is electronic mail? Discuss the advantages and disadvantages of it.

16. What is the difference between teleconferencing and telecommuting?

## PROJECTS

1. Imagine that you are the manager of a central data processing department. Each of the departments in the plant has recently been given one or more remote terminals. What problems can you foresee?

2. Research and present your findings on the current activities of INTELSAT.

3. Research and present a report on current regulations affecting common carriers.

4. You are the sales manager for a New England shoe company. The spring sales meeting is now six months away. You have always met at a conference center in the Berkshires, but this year you have read a lot about teleconferencing and wonder if it might be a good method for your company. What questions would you have to answer before you could decide?

# 12

# Trends

## CHAPTER OBJECTIVES

*After completing this chapter, you will be able to:*

1. Define the term *robot*.
2. Describe how robots are currently being used and discuss projections for future use.
3. Discuss artificial intelligence and what is meant by artificial intelligence in robots.
4. Discuss Japan's 10-year plan and its results so far.
5. Discuss the problems that exist in developing artificial intelligence.
6. Explain what is meant by expert systems and how they are used.
7. Discuss CAD/CAM.
8. Discuss computer graphics.
9. Define the term *natural language* and discuss some of the difficulties encountered in developing one.

## OVERVIEW

We've come a long way. From the time of Babbage's theories to Japan's 10-year plan for developing artificial intelligence, equipment has been conceived, designed, and developed to meet the information needs of society. Yet with all the developments of the past few years, we've only started. For the most part, we communicate with machines that depend on a constant power source, and we use languages native to neither the machines nor ourselves. The development of natural languages, artificial intelligence, and nonvolatile memory (memory whose contents are not lost if power to the system is lost) will improve the situation. Other major computer applications will include **robotics** and expert systems as well as neural networks and object-oriented programming.

## ROBOTICS

In the United States, we have long been familiar with the terms *white-collar* and *blue-collar* workers. Now we have a new group entering our work force, the *steel-collar* workers or **robots** (Figure 12.1). The creation and use of these robots is referred to as **robotics.**

Unimation, the largest U.S. manufacturer of robots, was founded in 1959. By 1980, there were approximately 1,450 robots in the United States. Development of the microprocessor permitted increased processing power in a smaller-sized machine. This and the continued inflation of wages have led to greater acceptance of the industrial robot. Growth is expected to be about 35 percent annually; by 1990, more than 20,000 robots will be in the work force.

When most of us hear the word *robot,* we mentally conjure up the picture of a large, metallic humanoid. We see it walking and talking—a sort of industrialized R2D2. Most industrial robots, however, are really robotic arms rather than whole bodies. They are generally used for performing repetitive jobs such as spot welding, or hazardous or unpleasant tasks such as working in spray-painting booths or handling molten metal (see Figure 12.2 and On the Job 1). They are used extensively in manufacturing applications. Other robot tasks include machine loading and unloading, assembly-line activities, and inspections.

## ON THE JOB 1

### Robot Guards

Imagine a 4-foot-tall, 400-pound prison guard who willingly goes on "suicide" missions during prison riots, sending information to the outside as long as he survives. Imagine a guard who can withstand bullets and the blast of fire hoses, a guard who is never sleepy or bored.

The guard is Denny, a robot developed by Denning Mobile Robotics, Inc., of Woburn, Massachusetts. This company has recently signed a five-year contract to produce up to 1,000 robots for Southern Steel Company, the largest manufacturer of prison security systems in the United States.

Denny feels his way along the hallways at 3 miles per hour. Using sensors, he hunts for intruders, relaying information about their presence to a staffed central control room. "You have been detected" is an important part of his limited vocabulary. When battered, he will attempt to escape by turning and running; when his batteries run low, he will return to his recharging station.

**FIGURE 12.1**

Much of industrial assembly work is done by robots. (Chuck O'Rear/Woodfin Camp & Associates)

**FIGURE 12.2**
Robots are often used in jobs that are unappealing or hazardous to most people. (Richard Pasley/Stock Boston)

The early robots differed from machines in that they could be programmed to perform various functions rather than a single function or one of a series of alternative functions. They had a manual dexterity that enabled them to perform a variety of movements, but they lacked any sensory ability. More modern robots have sensory ability: a sense of touch, limited vision, and at times even a sense of smell.

Although even a special-purpose robot may be programmed to perform various tasks, general-purpose robots are always designed to perform a wide variety of tasks. Commands are usually entered through a control panel, and their "brains" are microchip processors (Figure 12.3). Advances in robotics include designing robots with artificial intelligence so that they are more able to respond to unstructured situations.

## THE INTELLIGENT MACHINE

When you sit down and use a computer, you quickly realize that it is not very intelligent. It does respond to what you tell it—you type RUN and it runs a program—but it seems to lack any real comprehension of what you are telling it. If instead of keying in RUN, you had keyed in "Please run the program that updates the inventory file," it would have stared blankly back at you, probably displaying its opinion: "SYNTAX ERROR."

The computer obviously is responding to specific commands without any real understanding of what the intent of the command is. But what if the computer could really understand what you intend? What if it could "think"?

**FIGURE 12.3**
General-purpose robots resemble our image of robots more than do the industrial robotic arms. (Bob Daemmrich/Stock Boston)

## Artificial Intelligence (AI)

Artificial intelligence, also called AI, is the ability of a computer to mimic human thought—to behave in such a way that, if a person performed the same task, we would describe that person as thinking or showing intelligence.

For over 30 years, computer scientists have been carrying out research on how to make a computer think. Early experiments centered on computerized chess games. Because chess is a complex game requiring intelligence, a computer would demonstrate intelligence if it could learn to play. Computers wrote and played chess programs successfully, but these games were based on all possible moves being considered and the most appropriate chosen. Is this really intelligence? The computer selected from available choices. It did not learn from its experience (**heuristic learning**) but began each game with the same knowledge base.

To define computer intelligence, we must define human intelligence. Human intelligence involves learning from experience. It does not take long for a child to learn that a stove should not be touched when Mother says "hot!" or for an adult to learn that questions to the boss are better asked after morning coffee. To develop computer intelligence first requires that we know something about how humans think, reason, learn, and communicate.

To say that a computer is demonstrating intelligence is to say that it is capable of reasoning. It can learn from its experiences and plan its future activities based on its acquired knowledge. We would call it intelligent if its response to a given situation could not be distinguished from a human response. This does not mean that its response is the *same* as that of a person but that its response is indistinguishable from a human's. A well-known test, the **Turing test,** was developed by a British mathematician, Alan Turing, as a method of identifying intelligence in machines. The test required that a person be seated in front of two terminals, one operated by a computer and one by a human—both hidden behind a curtain. The person was to participate in a conversation with both, using the terminals to communicate. If the person was unable to decide which terminal was operated by the human and which by the computer, the computer passed the test and was considered intelligent.

Whatever "common sense" is, we would expect the intelligent computer to show it. We would also expect it to be able to make some value judgments—not just select what will work but select the "best" choice from the possibilities based on more than quantitative judgments.

Finally, we would like the computer to understand language—not the stylized languages of computer programming today but the natural languages we speak.

With these qualities, the computer would be able to respond to human speech and its own environment, and to demonstrate creativity.

## AI and Japan's 10-Year Plan

In 1980, Japan developed its 10-year project on artificial intelligence, administered by the Institute for New Generation Computer Technology (**ICOT**), which is sponsored by Japan's Ministry of International Trade and Industry. Its purpose is to perform basic technological research and development. The project is divided into three stages: a three-year initial stage (1982 to 1984), a four-year intermediate stage (1985 to 1988), and a three-year final stage (1989 to 1991). Results successfully obtained in the first segment included the development of **ESP,** a sequential logic programming language designed for future software development. The intermediate stage included the development of the basic computer architecture necessary to create the knowledge- and inference-based subsystem that will be the heart of the system.

The research done by ICOT is open to experts in other nations. Results have been presented at the International Conference on Fifth-Generation Computer Systems, held in Tokyo in late 1984. Representatives of over 60 countries were in attendance. In March of 1988, ICOT unveiled a small trial model of a fifth-generation computer that consisted of 64 linked CPUs (see the section on Neural Networks, later in this chapter).

Approximately $242 million is being put into the final 3-year stage of the 10-year plan in hopes of developing a prototype computer linking 1,000 CPUs, operating 500 times faster than existing computers, and able to perform inference and dialogue in natural languages.

## Expert Systems

**Expert systems,** one phase of artificial intelligence, are informational systems that combine facts with the way experts use those facts for decision making. They consist of a knowledge base derived from the expert(s). By inputting a series of facts supplied by the user and inferences supplied by the program, the system develops decisions.

One expert system, PROSPECTOR, is used by geologists in exploring for minerals. As all expert systems do, it has taken the rules (including some informal "rules of thumb") of expert geologists and built these rules into a computer program that attempts to duplicate the expert's decision-making process. Other expert systems perform such tasks as medical diagnosis and locomotive maintenance.

Again, these systems today consist of only a series of rules and the associated decision making. The decisions are not "intuitive"; the systems do not "understand" the data they work with, nor do they learn from their experience. They do bring to the problem the ability to consider rapidly many rules in arriving at the solution. They do not have off days, and they are never away on vacation or at a conference when the decision must be made. They make available the knowledge of experts without the user's needing to interact directly with those experts. This not only makes accessing the knowledge easier, but it also frees the experts for other tasks not yet capable of being handled by the system. However, expert systems do not really demonstrate much intelligence as we defined it earlier.

Since expert systems require input and guidance from the user during execution, they have become quite user-friendly. Query languages are used for inquiry, with true natural languages the goal. Icons identify the various system functions, and function keys perform them. Windows are common, permitting the user to integrate two or more programs or program functions concurrently. Languages used for developing expert systems include APL, LISP, SIMSCRIPT, MUMPS, and PROLOG.

## Natural Language

In Chapter 3, we saw that some computers are capable of voice recognition. They can recognize and respond properly to human speech. What, then, is the problem with using natural language?

In voice recognition, the computer works with a limited vocabulary. Certain sounds (words) have certain meanings, and the speech is highly stylized. A forklift driver might say "15 cartons of X2MCV" as the freight cars are being unloaded, and this shipment might be added to the inventory. The driver couldn't say, "I got another pallet of those hand-mixer motors" and have the inventory updated.

The development of computers that recognize natural language requires that we understand how *we* recognize language and then teach the computer to recognize it in the same way. Again, because we are intelligent beings, we always make inferences. We also respond to certain physical rules about our language without being aware of them. For example, when the letter *s* is added to an English noun, it makes the noun plural; the *gadget* arrived; the *gadgets* arrived. But when the *s* is added to a verb, the verb is usually made singular: they *run;* she *runs.* Although we rarely think about these rules, we have been successfully obeying them for years.

Another problem in the development of natural languages is our idioms—expressions that cannot generally be understood from the meaning of the individual words; for example, "The cat took cold from being left out." We also have homonyms, words spelled and pronounced alike but with different meanings: "The secretarial pool was not busy that day, so they swam in the pool and then challenged their supervisor to a game of pool."

With the development of natural languages, almost anyone will be able to work with computers without the artificial barriers of programming languages. The whole nature of computer use will change.

## GRAPHICS

Graphics is the processing of picture images. Business graphics generate graphs from data without humans doing the drawing (see Chapter 6). More interesting are the artistic creations of computer graphics (see On the Job 2). Here, images

**FIGURE 12.4**
The use of computer graphics in artwork is becoming common. (Masahiro Sano/The Stock Market)

are drawn using mice, light pens, or graphics tablets. They may also be generated mathematically. Once created and stored in the computer, they can be altered by changing colors, increased and decreased in size, and have their angle of sight altered. They can also be duplicated (Figure 12.4).

## CAD/CAM

**CAD** refers to computer-aided design. It is used to design a multitude of industrial and consumer products. A CAD system may be a specialized workstation; it may also be a high-performance PC (Figure 12.5). The drawings are entered in a multitude of ways including scanning. **CADD** systems are CAD systems that have special features for drafting. These features include the ability to add text as well as size annotations. **CAM** refers to computer-aided manufacturing. It includes automated process control, robotics, and material requirements

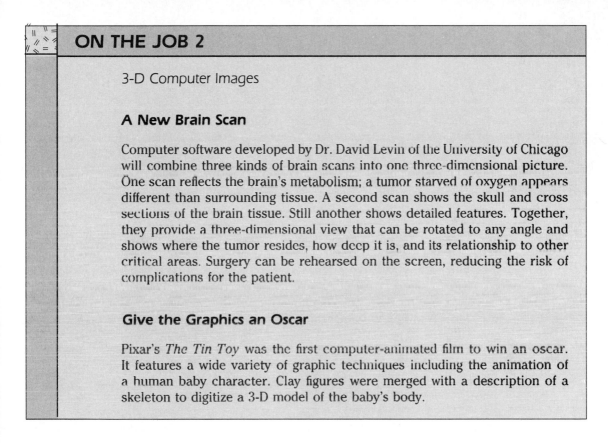

planning (Figure 12.6). **CAD/CAM** integrates computer-aided manufacturing with computer-aided design.

## NEURAL NETWORKS

In the past, most computers have been built to handle algorithmic problem solving; they follow a list of steps to achieve their goal. **Neural networks** are different. Their architecture is modeled on how our brain works (see On the Job 3).

We recognize patterns and adapt behavior accordingly. For example, imagine that you have three classes today. All of them will be covering new material— material that you have not yet read. The first professor has given three pop quizzes this semester, each one as you finished reading a chapter; the second professor has given only two, but both were before the chapter was discussed; the third professor is morally opposed to pop quizzes. You have time to study for only one class. Which will you prepare for? You choose to study for the

## ON THE JOB 3

Neural Network Chip

California Institute of Technology researchers have developed the CCD–ND/ 256, a neural network computer chip with 256 processors and 65,536 interconnections. Unlike traditional processors, in which electrons travel along miniaturized metal wires engraved in silicon, these chips have packets of electrons injected directly into the silicon. Charge-coupled devices, incorporated into the chip, send packets from one "neuron" to another enabling every one of the 256 processors to exchange data with every other processor.

second class; your brain recognized a pattern and adapted its behavior accordingly.

Neural networks are "trained"; they are given a set of examples of input and the resulting output. From these, they can develop their own problem-solving algorithms by recognizing patterns much as human experts do. Neural

**FIGURE 12.5**
CAD software is available for generic use. It is also available for highly specialized use such as the design of printed circuit boards. (Hank Morgan/Rainbow)

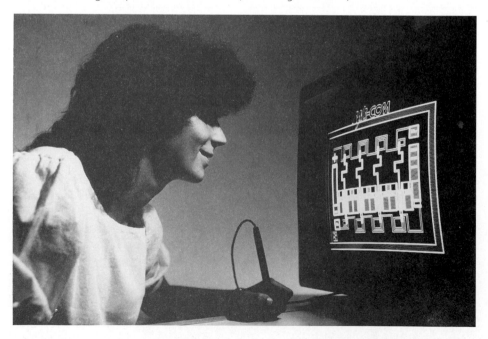

**FIGURE 12.6**
CAM systems are used for process control and material requirements planning, among other purposes. (Mark Weidman)

networks are ideally suited to scanning masses of data and discerning trends (for example, in quality-control applications).

Although neural network research is about 30 years old, there has recently been a renewed interest in its potential, largely as a result of the higher density and lower cost of microchips.

## PROGRAMMING CHANGES

Compared with the rapid advances in hardware development, programming productivity has increased at a minimal rate. In 1985, 14 major aerospace and electronics companies joined together to form the Software Productivity Consortium, located in Reston, Virginia, to explore ways of increasing productivity. Two changes to programming that have the potential to markedly improve programming speed are object-oriented programming and reusable code.

### Object-Oriented Programming

Object-oriented programming wraps the data with the instructions for using it, as discussed in Chapter 4. For example, in a word processing program, you need both the instructions (the program) and the data (the file you are processing). Potentially, object-oriented programming languages can both improve programmer productivity and cut application time. Some object-oriented languages include SMALLTALK-80, OBJECTIVE-C, and Apple's OBJECT PASCAL.

### Reusable Software

Change is costly. For some systems, approximately 80 percent of the system's total life-cycle costs come from modifications made after the original design. If it were possible to build systems more rapidly and modify them quickly to meet the users' needs, much of this cost could be eliminated. Because much coding is redundant, reusable modules could be linked together as necessary to create all-new or significantly revised programs.

The use of **reusable code** is essential to **automatic program generators.** These automatic program generators enable a programmer to quickly and easily generate a program from a screen layout or other abbreviated instructions.

## COMPUTER VIRUSES

One unfortunate trend we have seen lately is a nationwide epidemic of computer viruses. These viruses are annoying or destructive programs often written by hackers. The programs may lie dormant for extended periods of time and be

## ON THE JOB 4

Newspaper Attacked

In early May 1988, the *Providence Journal-Bulletin* was invaded by a computer virus. This virus was discovered when one reporter saw a "disk error" message on her screen when she attempted to print out a copy of an article she had been working on. Damage was limited to the loss of one floppy disk containing several months of work. It underscored the danger to newspapers of computer malfunctions, as newspapers are becoming increasingly dependent on personal computers and their networks to write and edit articles.

passed from system to system without anyone's awareness, contaminating any computers, files, and disks with which they come in contact. Eventually, the virus program will be activated. Once active, it may freeze the system, leave messages to operators, reformat hard disks, and/or destroy data (see On the Job 4).

Solution to the problem lies in locating the viruses while they are still dormant, eliminating their spread through better security, and effectively prosecuting the originators.

## SUMMARY

Current computer research centers on intelligence: what it is and how to make a computer demonstrate it.

Robots are reprogrammable, mechanical devices—often the mechanical arms used in industrial applications. Modern robots have some sensory capability—touch, vision, and smell—as well as the mechanical dexterity of the early robots.

Artificial intelligence is the ability of a computer to mimic human thought. To build a "thinking" computer, we must first understand how we ourselves think. Among the current applications of artificial intelligence research are expert systems and natural language processing.

Interest in neural networks has recently been renewed. Their architecture is based on how our brain works; they can develop their own problem-solving algorithms by recognizing patterns much as humans do. This makes them ideally suited to scanning masses of data to discern trends.

CAD refers to computer-aided design. It is used to design a multitude of industrial and consumer products. CADD systems are CAD systems that have special features for drafting. CAM refers to computer-aided manufacturing. CAD/CAM integrates computer-aided manufacturing with computer-aided design.

Programming improvements include the introduction of object-oriented programming languages and the development of reusable software.

A disturbing development is the spread of computer viruses and the resultant destruction of data and contamination of disks.

## VOCABULARY

| | |
|---|---|
| Automatic program generators    254 | Heuristic learning    247 |
| CAD    250 | ICOT    247 |
| CAD/CAM    251 | Neural networks    251 |
| CADD    250 | Reusable code    254 |
| CAM    250 | Robot    243 |
| ESP    248 | Robotics    243 |
| Expert systems    248 | Turing test    247 |

## EXERCISES

1. How is a robot different from a purely mechanical device?
2. How are robots being used in industry?
3. What is artificial intelligence?
4. What is CAD/CAM?
5. Why is it so difficult to design a "thinking" machine?
6. What is an expert system?
7. Describe some of the uses of computer graphics.
8. What is a natural language?
9. What are some of the difficulties in developing natural language comprehension?
10. What is meant by object-oriented programming? What are its advantages?
11. How are neural networks "trained"?
12. What is a computer virus?

## PROJECTS

1. Research and report on ICOT's current activities and the progress of Japan's 10-year plan.
2. Do some research on the artificial intelligence labs at Yale and Stanford Universities, and report on them.

3. CADUCEUS and MYCIN are two expert systems. Research and report on what they are designed to do and who uses them.

4. "Ship two pallets of those wrenches to Jones' company" is a statement that you might hear at work. Why would this be more difficult for the computer to understand than for you?

5. Research and report on computer viruses: how they are spreading and the "vaccines" that are being developed to stop them.

# BASIC

## INTRODUCTION

Programming languages instruct the computer; they tell the computer what to do, what data to do it to, and what to do with the answers obtained.

The most widely used language on microcomputers today is BASIC. BASIC, Beginner's All-Purpose Symbolic Instruction Code, was developed in the mid-1960s at Dartmouth for use by students and other beginning programmers. It is one of the most widely available computer languages, used on both micros and mainframes. It is also designed to be interactive; that is, the user can enter information into a program from the terminal while the program is running.

For several weeks now you have been reading about computers and perhaps have run some programs on one. Now it is time to put away your reading and try to create a few computer programs yourself. Unlike many computer languages, BASIC is not a standardized language. This appendix uses a subset of IBM's BASIC.

Many BASIC programs are now compiled rather than interpreted. However, either a compiler or an interpreter may be used; so, for convenience, this appendix uses the word *translator* to refer to both.

Before you start, make sure that you can turn on the microcomputer you will be using. Once you turn it on and off, be sure that you can load the BASIC translator, if that is necessary. With these tasks behind you, now look at BASIC and try a few programs.

## ERROR CORRECTION

As you begin to learn BASIC, you will want to try to run some programs. Some errors will occur as you key statements in, so we begin here by learning how to correct these errors. Because the method of making changes is system dependent, your instructor will point out any modifications to these procedures that are necessary to make corrections on your system.

If the program is located in the internal storage of your computer, you may list it, enter new lines, and modify existing ones. Once the program has been keyed in and saved on disk or tape, it may be necessary to recall the program, make the changes, and replace the older version with the corrected one.

Once a statement has been entered into your program, it can be changed by reentering the entire line preceded by the same line number. It does not matter in what order the corrections are made; the replacement will be by line number. Ask your instructor how to enter changes on a line that has been keyed in and appears on your screen but that has not yet been entered; such changes are generally very easy to make but also very system dependent.

If the line is to be deleted rather than replaced, you need only enter the line number and press the RETURN key. This replaces the existing line with a blank line that is not kept as part of the program.

To add an omitted statement, simply enter a line number whose value is between the two line numbers between which you wish the omitted line to appear. Additions of lines, as with changes to lines, take place by line number; it is not necessary to key a new line in the program listing at the point where the line is to be inserted.

## SYSTEM COMMANDS

Before going on to the BASIC statements, we will look at some of the system commands.

Once the program is written, we may need to list, store, retrieve, and execute it. To do this, we need a way to communicate with the computer. System commands provide that way. The system commands are system dependent; any differences between this section and the commands used by your system will be explained by your instructor.

### NEW

The NEW command clears the contents or primary storage and prepares it to receive a new BASIC program.

### LIST AND LLIST

The LIST command causes the BASIC program now stored in primary storage to be displayed on the terminal. For many systems, the program can be listed on the printer by using the LLIST command; for others, the LIST command is used and the peripheral device assignment is changed through job control language, a language that directs the operating system how to run an applications program.

### RUN

The RUN statement causes the program currently stored in primary storage to be executed.

## SAVE

The SAVE command is used to copy the program currently residing in main memory onto a disk or tape for external storage.

## LOAD

The LOAD command copies a program stored on disk or tape back into primary storage for execution or maintenance.

## USE OF THE COMMANDS

Now that you have seen the system commands, you may be wondering how to use them. Your system may use different commands; however, if you are using an IBM DOS system or one that is compatible, the following may help you.

If you are preparing to enter a new BASIC program, you will key in the word NEW and press the RETURN (ENTER) key. This will clear memory.

After you have keyed in several instructions, you may want to display what you have entered. Use LIST in one of the forms that follows:

LIST                will list the entire program.

LIST 100-500        will list lines 100 through 500, inclusive.

LIST 225            will list only line 225.

If you do not have a full-screen editor, you may delete lines by keying in the line number and pressing ENTER; you may modify one line by entering that line again.

Once the program is keyed in, you will want to save it on your disk.

SAVE MYPROG         will save the program on the default drive under the name
                    MYPROG.

SAVE B:MYPROG       will save the program on the specified drive (in this case,
                    drive T3).

To recall the program (copy it back into memory), you will use the LOAD command.

LOAD MYPROG         will look for the program on the default drive.

LOAT A:MYPROG       will search for your program on drive A.

When the program is in memory, you can execute it by keying in the command RUN and pressing ENTER.

Many of these commands can also be performed by using function keys. Your instructor will tell you which to use.

# DATA REPRESENTATION

Fields used in a BASIC program may be either variables or constants. **Constants** are fields whose values do not change during the running of the program, whereas **variables** have changing values. For example, if you were calculating a payroll, the number of hours an employee worked would be a variable because each person's hours might vary. The FICA limit would be a constant; it would remain the same throughout the running of the program regardless of whose pay was being calculated.

Fields may also be either string or numeric. **Numeric fields,** as the name implies, contain numbers. **String fields** are alphanumeric; they can contain numbers, letters, and special symbols.

### Numeric Variables

**Numeric variables** have numeric values that change during the running of the program. The name of the field always refers to the current value of the field. Again using a payroll example, if the field containing the hours worked was named HR, whenever HR was used it would refer to the hours worked on the record being processed at that time.

In BASIC, the names of numeric fields must begin with a letter. Although most BASIC translators allow field names to be many characters in length, for many translators only the first two characters are significant and must be unique.

### String Variables

**String variables** have values that will change during the execution of the program. String variable names must end with a dollar sign, $. The first character must be a letter. For many translators, only the first two characters are significant.

See Appendix B for a detailed discussion of data representation.

# RESERVED WORDS

BASIC has only a few **reserved words.** These reserved words are used by BASIC for its own purposes and thus cannot be used as field names. These reserved words include PRINT, LET, and all the other BASIC statements. Because these words are recognized by BASIC as operations, they may not be used by the programmer as data names.

## LINE NUMBERS

BASIC requires that every statement appears on a separate line and that each line have its own number. Most programmers do not use consecutive numbers for these lines; they increment the statement number by 10 or by 100. This permits additional lines to be inserted between two existing ones if the program needs to be changed without requiring you to renumber the entire program.

## SPACES

Spaces within BASIC statements are included for readability. Although some BASIC translators have spacing requirements, programmers are usually allowed to use the spacing they prefer. A+B is the same as A + B.

## LINE FORMAT

BASIC statements begin with a number, and the number is followed by the operation to be performed. The operation, in turn, is followed by the operands or fields on which the operation is to be performed.

## INPUT/OUTPUT AND MISCELLANEOUS STATEMENTS

We will begin to learn BASIC by introducing the REM statement and the INPUT/OUTPUT statements: INPUT, PRINT, READ, and DATA.

### REM Statement

The REM (remark) statement is used to include comments in a BASIC program. This line is ignored by the translator but is printed whenever the program is listed.

```
10 REM

20 REM S. HABA

30 REM 12/10/90

40 REM INTRODUCTION TO MICROCOMPUTERS

50 REM THIS PROGRAM IS USED TO PRINT EACH

60 REM SALESPERSON'S NAME AND AMOUNT OF SALES.
```

The use of REM Statements documents the program as it is written, making it much easier to read and to debug. Comments can be added to the program being created to explain how the program works.

## INPUT Statement

One way of entering data is to use the INPUT statement. You may use it to read data stored externally on a file or to read data keyed in from the terminal while the program is running.

If data is to be entered from the terminal keyboard while the program is running, the program will halt each time the INPUT statement is encountered; a question mark will appear on the screen, and the user may enter the data.

```
100 INPUT N$,S
```

would cause the program to halt so that the user could enter the values for a string variable named N$ and a numerical variable named S. This has some obvious problems: how is the user to know why the program is halting and what is to be entered?

The solution is to use **prompts**—messages to the operator that prompt the correct response. The INPUT statement may contain prompts enclosed within quotation marks.

```
100 INPUT "ENTER SALESPERSON'S NAME AND SALES";N$,S1
```

will display the message ENTER SALESPERSON'S NAME AND SALES on the screen. It will accept the first value entered by the operator and store it in the field called N$; it will also accept the second value entered by the operator and store it in a numeric field called S1.

One value must be entered for each variable name in the list. They must be entered in the same order in which the variables are listed, the values separated by commas. The values entered must also agree in type with the variable names; that is, string variable names must receive alphanumeric values and numeric variable names must receive numeric values.

## PRINT and LPRINT Statements

The PRINT statement is used to display information on the screen. For some systems, the LPRINT is used to write output to the printer; for other systems the PRINT statement is used and the output device is changed by the job control language.

```
100 INPUT "ENTER SALESPERSON'S NAME AND SALES";N$,S1

200 PRINT "THE SALESPERSON'S NAME IS ",N$

300 PRINT "HE SOLD ", S1 , "DOLLARS WORTH LAST WEEK."
```

Statement 200 would cause the salesperson's name entered in statement 100 to be printed. Statement 300 would display the amount of sales entered in line 100.

The list of fields to be printed may be separated by either commas or semicolons. With semicolons, the fields are separated by a small distance, usually

**FIGURE A.1**

A simple program can be written using only an INPUT and a PRINT statement.

```
100 INPUT "ENTER SALESPERSON'S NAME AND SALES";N$,S1
200 PRINT "THE SALESPERSON'S NAME IS ",N$
300 PRINT "HE SOLD ", S1, "DOLLARS WORTH LAST WEEK."
```

If the name Robert Cohen ($10,000) were entered, the output would be:

```
THE SALESPERSON'S NAME IS      ROBERT  COHEN
HE SOLD                10000   DOLLARS WORTH LAST WEEK.
```

one space. Use of the comma results in a larger space; the field to be printed is spaced to the beginning of the next zone. The number of spaces in a zone or zones in a print line is system dependent.

Figures A.1 and A.2 illustrate the program so far and the output from running it. In Figure A.1, the fields are controlled by commas. Figure A.2 illustrates the running of the program when the spacing is controlled by semicolons.

Arithmetic expressions may also be printed. Suppose you have a variable called AGE and the value 29 had been stored in this field.

```
200 PRINT AGE-5
```

would cause 24 to print. This is because AGE was 29; so $29 - 5$ is 24.

## READ Statement

The READ statement obtains values from internally stored data. It is used with the DATA statement discussed next. The values defined in a DATA statement are placed within the variables listed after the READ statement. For example:

```
100 READ N$
```

would cause the value read next from a DATA statement to be stored in the field called N$.

## DATA Statement

Data may be stored within a program in one or more DATA statements.

```
200 DATA "LINDA CHAN",752
```

would store two values for later reading by the program. The alphanumeric value is enclosed in quotation marks and must be read into a string variable

## FIGURE A.2

Changing from commas to semicolons in the PRINT statement causes a change in the output. Note the difference between the output in this figure and the output in Figure A.1.

```
100 INPUT "ENTER SALESPERSON'S NAME AND SALES";N$,S1
200 PRINT "THE SALESPERSON'S NAME IS ";N$
300 PRINT "HE SOLD ";S1; "DOLLARS WORTH LAST WEEK."


THE SALESPERSON'S NAME IS ROBERT COHEN
HE SOLD  10000 DOLLARS WORTH LAST WEEK.
```

## FIGURE A.3

Data may also be entered by including one or more DATA statements in the program itself. A READ statement reads the values found in DATA statements.

```
50 REM SAME LISTING BUT USING A DATA STATEMENT
100 READ N$,S1
150 REM LINE 100 READS THE DATA FOUND IN LINE 500
200 REM THE FIRST FIELD READ IS STORED IN N$; THE SECOND, IN S1
250 PRINT "THE SALESPERSON'S NAME IS ";N$
300 PRINT "HE SOLD ";S1; "DOLLARS WORTH LAST WEEK"
500 DATA "ROBERT COHEN",10000
```

In this example, statement 500 is read by statement 100:

```
THE SALESPERSON'S NAME IS ROBERT COHEN
HE SOLD  10000 DOLLARS WORTH LAST WEEK
```

name. The numeric value is not enclosed within quotation marks and must be read into a numeric variable name (Figure A.3). Although DATA statements are usually found at the beginning or the end of a program, they may be located anywhere within the program and are read sequentially. The values stored in the DATA statement are separated by commas.

A READ statement always reads the next unused value in a DATA statement. READ and DATA statements do not have to be matched one READ to one DATA statement (Figure A.4).

## LET Statement

Another way to change the value of a field is to use the LET statement.

```
n LET variable = expression
```

**FIGURE A.4**
This program can have *(a)* two READ statements or *(b)* two DATA statements. The output will be the same *(c)*.

```
50 REM SAME LISTING BUT USING A DATA STATEMENT
100 READ N$
125 READ S1
150 REM LINE 100 READS THE DATA FOUND IN LINE 500
200 REM THE FIRST FIELD READ IS STORED IN N$; THE SECOND, IN S1
250 PRINT "THE SALESPERSON'S NAME IS ";N$
300 PRINT "HE SOLD ";S1; "DOLLARS WORTH LAST WEEK"
500 DATA "ROBERT COHEN",10000
```
(a)

```
50 REM SAME LISTING BUT USING A DATA STATEMENT
100 READ N$,S1
150 REM LINE 100 READS THE DATA FOUND IN LINE 500
200 REM THE FIRST FIELD READ IS STORED IN N$; THE SECOND, IN S1
250 PRINT "THE SALESPERSON'S NAME IS ";N$
300 PRINT "HE SOLD ";S1; "DOLLARS WORTH LAST WEEK"
500 DATA "ROBERT COHEN"
550 DATA 10000
```
(b)

```
THE SALESPERSON'S NAME IS ROBERT COHEN
HE SOLD  10000 DOLLARS WORTH LAST WEEK
```
(c)

changes the value found in the variable by evaluating the arithmetical expression and placing the result in the variable. (The n before the LET stands for the statement line number.) For example:

```
200 LET A = A + 1
```

would increase the value of A by 1. If B equals 6 and C equals 3,

```
200 LET A = B/C
```

will result in A equaling 6/3 or 2. If you were writing a program to calculate a salesperson's commission, you could use the LET statement to perform the calculations (Figure A.5). The word LET may also be omitted.

## END Statement

The END statement is the last logical statement within a program. It consists of a statement number and the word END. Encountering this statement terminates the program.

**FIGURE A.5**

If the salesperson is to receive 3 percent of sales as commission, you will need to calculate 3 percent of $10,000. Note how the LET statement is used. In this program, C1 represents the commission.

```
100 READ N$,S1
150 LET C1 = .03 * S1
175 REM C1 IS THE COMMISSION
176 REM S1 IS THE AMOUNT OF SALES
250 PRINT "THE SALESPERSON'S NAME IS ";N$
300 PRINT "HE SOLD ";S1; "DOLLARS WORTH LAST WEEK."
400 PRINT "HIS COMMISSION IS $";C1
500 DATA "ROBERT COHEN"
550 DATA 10000


THE SALESPERSON'S NAME IS ROBERT COHEN
HE SOLD  10000 DOLLARS WORTH LAST WEEK.
HIS COMMISSION IS $ 300
```

## BRANCHING

All the programs illustrated so far received one record, processed it, and stopped. The real power of data processing, however, comes from the ability to perform the same sequence of activities over and over again. Branching and looping enable this to occur.

In branching, one alters the normal flow of instructions and proceeds to a location in a program other than the next sequential instruction. Looping is the repetitive execution of a series of instructions. The BASIC statements used to loop include: GOTO, IF/THEN/ELSE, and FOR/NEXT.

### GOTO Statement

The GOTO statement permits you to alter the sequence of instructions to be executed.

```
200 GOTO 500
```

would cause an unconditional branch to statement 500 (Figure A.6). The GOTO used alone is not especially useful unless it is coupled with a decision-making statement such as IF/THEN. With the development of structured programming, the GOTO has been largely replaced by the GOSUB statement, which is discussed later.

**FIGURE A.6**

Using this GOTO enables us to read several salespersons' records. But how would we know when to stop?

```
10 REM C1 IS THE COMMISSION
20 REM S1 IS THE AMOUNT OF SALES
30 REM N$ IS THE SALESPERSON'S NAME
100 READ N$,S1
200 LET C1 = .02 * S1
300 PRINT "THE SALESPERSON'S NAME IS ";N$
400 PRINT S1 "DOLLARS WORTH WERE SOLD LAST WEEK"
500 PRINT "THE COMMISSION IS $";C1
600 GOTO 100
700 DATA "ROBERT COHEN",10000
800 DATA "SARA ANDERSON",11980


THE SALESPERSON'S NAME IS ROBERT COHEN
 10000 DOLLARS WORTH WERE SOLD LAST WEEK
THE COMMISSION IS $ 200
THE SALESPERSON'S NAME IS SARA ANDERSON
 11980 DOLLARS WORTH WERE SOLD LAST WEEK
THE COMMISSION IS $ 239.6


OUT OF DATA IN 100
```

## IF/THEN/ELSE STATEMENT

The IF/THEN/ELSE statement permits the programmer to have two different things occur, depending on such factors as the data found or the number of times something has been processed.

```
500 IF L > 500 THEN A = 6 ELSE A = 5
```

would compare the contents of L to 500. If L contained a number greater than 500, A would equal 6; if not, A would equal 5.

Such a statement would be very useful in our program if we wanted to pay two different commission rates depending on the amount sold (Figure A.7). Multiple actions may be performed with the same IF/THEN/ELSE statement. If multiple statements are entered on the same line, they should be separated by colons.

```
200 IF L = 5 THEN A = 5: GOTO 500 ELSE A = 6: GOTO 900
```

For good structured programming practice, these statements are indented for readability:

```
300   IF L = 5   THEN

                 A = 5

                 GOTO 500

      ELSE

                 A = 6

                 GOTO 900
```

Nonnumeric data is also frequently used in comparisons. For example, the following program receives input from the keyboard and checks to verify that the user has a parking permit. If so, the next parking space number (beginning with 200) is issued. The program ends when someone keys in "END" as their name.

```
10    LET A = 200

20    PRINT "PLEASE KEY IN YOUR NAME"

30    INPUT N$

40    IF N$ = "END" GOTO 80

50    PRINT N$; "DO YOU HAVE A PARKING PERMIT? YES OR NO"

60    INPUT A$

70    IF A$ = "YES" THEN

                    PRINT "NEXT AVAILABLE PARKING SPACE IS ";A

                    LET A = A + 1

                    GOTO 20

            ELSE

                    GOTO 20

80    END
```

## FOR/NEXT Statement

The FOR/NEXT statement lets the programmer perform a loop, or repetition of a series of program instructions, a given number of times. All lines between the FOR statement and the NEXT statement are repeated for each of the values indicated. For example,

```
10 FOR A = 1 to 3

20 PRINT A

30 NEXT A

40 END
```

**FIGURE A.7**

The IF/THEN statement makes it possible to do one of two different things based on some condition. Here, the IF/THEN is used both to end the program and to use two different commission rates based on the amount of sales.

```
100 READ N$,S1
200 IF S1 > 9000 THEN  C1 = .025 * S1
    ELSE              C1 = .02 * S1
300 PRINT "THE SALESPERSON'S NAME IS ";N$
400 PRINT "HE SOLD ";S1; "DOLLARS WORTH LAST WEEK"
500 PRINT "HIS COMMISSION IS $";C1
600 DATA "ROBERT COHEN",10000


THE SALESPERSON'S NAME IS ROBERT COHEN
HE SOLD  10000 DOLLARS WORTH LAST WEEK
HIS COMMISSION IS $ 250
```

**FIGURE A.8**

Here, five mailing labels are being printed for one customer using a FOR/NEXT loop.

```
100 READ N$,A$,C$
200 FOR A = 1 TO 5
300 PRINT " "
400 PRINT N$
500 PRINT A$
600 PRINT C$
700 PRINT " "
800 NEXT A
900 END
1000 DATA "JOHN WILLIAMS","17 HEBRON WAY","AFTON, VA 19854"

JOHN WILLIAMS
17 HEBRON WAY
AFTON, VA 19854

JOHN WILLIAMS
17 HEBRON WAY
AFTON, VA 19854

JOHN WILLIAMS
17 HEBRON WAY
AFTON, VA 19854

JOHN WILLIAMS
17 HEBRON WAY
AFTON, VA 19854

JOHN WILLIAMS
17 HEBRON WAY
AFTON, VA 19854
```

would cause A to be printed three times, once when A = 1, once when A = 2, and once when A = 3.

The FOR/NEXT statement is also useful in performing any activity that has to be repeated a given number of times. In Figure A.8, several mailing labels are being produced for each person.

## SUBROUTINES AND THE GOSUB STATEMENT

A **subroutine** is a complete routine performed within the program. For example, in a payroll program, a subroutine might be written to perform each state's tax calculations. A program directs that the subroutine be performed; at the end of the subroutine, control is returned to the next line of the program. The GOSUB statement is used to perform subroutines.

The ability to perform an activity or routine from anywhere in a program and then to return is tremendously useful. It permits the programmer to take full advantage of the structured programming techniques described earlier. With the introduction of the GOSUB and related subroutines, you will be able to build structured programs that will be easier to debug and maintain.

The first line of the subroutine may be any valid BASIC statement but the last line must be a RETURN statement. The GOSUB statement is found in the main body of the program, directing that the subroutine be performed.

```
530 GOSUB 750
```

would direct that the subroutine found at statement 750 be performed. Figure A.9 shows how a subroutine can be used to print mailing labels.

## GOOD STYLE AND STRUCTURE

This appendix merely introduces BASIC; it makes no attempt to expose you to the full power and usefulness of the language—especially to arrays and files. Even with this limited exposure, however, you can still develop good style and structure in your programs.

Programs are written for others to use. Moreover, they are frequently modified, either by the original programmer or by someone else. If a few weeks later you, the original programmer, cannot follow the program's logic, how could anyone else? Here are some suggestions to make your programs easier to understand, modify, and debug.

1. Use the REM statement often. Use it anywhere you want to make a comment. You'll need more comments than you think. The routine that is clear to you today will be mystifying next week. Use REMs to record your name, class section number, date of coding and/or modifications, meanings of variable names, and a description of what the various parts of the program do.

**FIGURE A.9**
Mailing labels could also be printed using a GOSUB.

```
100 REM THIS PROGRAM PRINTS ONE LABEL FOR EACH CUSTOMER USING THE
    GOSUB STATEMENT
200 READ N$,A$,S$
300 IF N$ = "END" GOTO 1000
350 GOSUB 500
400 GOTO 200
499 REM THIS IS A SUBROUTINE THAT PRODUCES A LABEL
500 PRINT " "
600 PRINT N$
700 PRINT A$
800 PRINT S$
900 PRINT " "
950 RETURN
1000 END
1100 DATA "JOHN ITO","HEBRON WAY","AFTON VA 19844"
1200 DATA "MARY HERNANDEZ","EAST OAK STREET","CHAPEL HILL NC 02355"
1300 DATA "ROBIN GRAVES","MAIN STREET","SWAMPSCOTT MA 01977"
...
2700 DATA "END"," "," "

JOHN ITO
HEBRON WAY
AFTON VA 19844

MARY HERNANDEZ
EAST OAK STREET
CHAPEL HILL NC 02355

ROBIN GRAVES
MAIN STREET
SWAMPSCOTT MA 01977
```

2. Set your remarks off by using a blank REM statement before and after each group of REMs.

3. Use parentheses in formulas even when they are not required. Although normal algebraic rules are followed, they can be forgotten. With parentheses, there is no doubt about your intentions.

```
250 R = A + B / C
```

means the same as

```
250 R = A + (B / C)
```

but the latter's meaning is more clear.

4. If you need to divide in a program, make sure that you code your program so that you cannot divide by zero. A division by zero will cause a run-time error.

5.  When you originally enter a program, have your lines increment by at least 10. This will make it easier to insert additional statements between existing lines. You can automatically number lines by using the AUTO statement:

    AUTO 100,10

    will cause the numbering to begin with line 100 and continue in increments of 10.

6.  If you need more room between statements for a long insertion, you can renumber existing statements with the RENUM command:

    RENUM 100,50

    will begin at current statement 100 and renumber all following statements in increments of 50. This statement will renumber only the statements themselves, not any branch-reference line numbers. (That is, GOTO 3100 remains GOTO 3100 even though statement 3100 is now numbered 4500.) If you do use the RENUM command, verify all referenced line numbers.

7.  When first testing a program, make sure you save it before you test it. You might get into an infinite loop.

8.  Whenever possible, use subroutines. Testing, debugging, and modifications will be easier.

---

## SUMMARY

BASIC was developed at Dartmouth for student use. It is the most widely used computer language today. Data may be represented as either string (alphanumeric) or numeric fields. String constants are enclosed in quotation marks; numeric constants are not.

Two ways to enter data are with the INPUT statement, which allows the data to be entered at run time, and the READ statement, which reads data made available in DATA statements.

Results are displayed using the PRINT statement. Writers may use as many or as few REM statements as they wish to make the program more clear to the reader. These are not interpreted.

The LET statement enables the user to place a value in a field. The END statement is the last logical statement within a program. System commands are used to inform the system of what is supposed to be done. They are independent of the language used.

Two other statements are the GOTO, which permits the user to alter the sequence of instructions to be executed, and the GOSUB, used to perform subroutines.

## ▦ VOCABULARY

Constants   261

Numeric field   261

Numeric variable   261

Prompt   263

Reserve word   261

String variable   261

String field   261

Subroutine   271

Variables   261

## ▦ EXERCISES

1. Type in the following program:

   ```
   100 LET A = 1000

   200 LET B = 12

   300 LET C = 36

   400 PRINT A / B; "FEET"

   500 PRINT A / B; "YARDS"
   ```

   When the program is keyed in correctly, run it.

2. Insert REM statements to clarify what this program does (it converts the value in A to feet and then to yards).

3. Renumber the program, incrementing by 50.

4. Modify the program so that you can enter several different values for A by using one or more DATA statements. Make sure that your loop will end.

5. Modify the program again so that data may be entered from the keyboard and the answer displayed on the screen.

6. Write a program that will calculate everyone's course grade. Unless told otherwise, assume that you take three tests worth 20 percent each and a final worth 40 percent. Unless told otherwise, you may enter the data any way you prefer for this and subsequent exercises.

7. Write a program that will calculate the cost of four tires if each tire costs P dollars, federal excise tax is T percent and sales tax is S percent. For example, the cost P might be $67, the federal excise tax 8%, and the sales tax 4%.

8. Write a program that will convert any Celsius temperature to the corresponding Fahrenheit one. The formula is:

$$\text{Fahrenheit} = 9/5 \text{ Celsius} + 32$$

9. Write a program that will permit you to enter a list of numbers at the keyboard, average them, and then display the result.

10. Modify the program in Exercise 9 so that it not only calculates the mean but also displays the highest and lowest numbers in the group.

# Data Representation

## NUMBERING SYSTEMS

Computers use the binary numbering system for storage and calculations. We usually use the decimal numbering system for our calculations. How do these systems correspond?

Basic mathematical laws are in operation regardless of which numbering system you use. One of the easiest ways to learn binary is to review what you know about decimal. The arithmetical laws will remain true regardless of which base you are working with.

### Decimal and Binary Numbers

**Decimal** is referred to as base 10; 10 digits are in the decimal numbering system: 0 through 9. **Binary,** in a computer, is one of two states: positive/negative, on/off, and so on. These two states are represented by the two digits 0 and 1; it is referred to as base 2.

The 10 digits in the decimal system each have two values. They have one value based on the digit itself: 1 has a value different from 3, which has a value different from 7. The digit also has a positional value: 37 is not equal to 73. The only difference is in the position of the numbers; the digits used are exactly the same. In binary, the digits also have a positional value; 1101 is not the same as 1110.

In decimal, that positional value is a progressive power of the base. When you were very young, you learned to refer to these positional values as the units or ones position, the tens position, or the hundreds position. These are really powers of the base 10: the ones position is 10 to the zero power, or 1; the tens position is 10 to the first power, or 10; the hundreds position is 10 squared, or 100 (Figure B.1). The real value of any decimal number is the actual value of the digit times the progressive power of the base (Figure B.2). Binary numbers work in exactly the same way: the digit 1 or 0 has its actual value, and each position in the number is worth a progressive power of the base 2 (Figure B.3).

**FIGURE B.1**

In the decimal system, the positional value is always a progressive power of the base 10.

| $10^3$ | $10^2$ | $10^1$ | $10^0$ | Power of the base |
|---|---|---|---|---|
| 1000s | 100s | 10s | 1s | Positional value |
| n | n | n | n | The number |

**FIGURE B.2**

The actual value of any number is the value of the digit times the positional value.

| $10^2$ | $10^1$ | $10^0$ | Power of the base |
|---|---|---|---|
| 100 | 10 | 1 | Positional value |
| 3 | 4 | 2 | The number |

or

$$3 \times 100 = 300$$
$$4 \times 10 = 40$$
$$2 \times 1 = 2$$
$$\overline{\phantom{00000}342}$$

**FIGURE B.3**

The positional values of a binary number are progressive powers of the base 2.

| $2^3$ | $2^2$ | $2^1$ | $2^0$ | Power of the base |
|---|---|---|---|---|
| 8 | 4 | 2 | 1 | Positional value |
| n | n | n | n | The number |

The real value of any binary number is the actual value of the digit times the progressive power of the base. To convert from binary to decimal, you multiply each digit by that progressive power of the base and then sum the results (Figure B.4).

To convert from decimal to binary, you divide the decimal number by the base 2, recording the remainders until a quotient of zero is obtained. The remainders are then listed, with the last remainder as the high-order (leftmost) digit and the first remainder as the low-order (rightmost) digit (Figure B.5). This successive-remainders division algorithm may be used to convert a number stored in demical to any base equivalent by changing the divisor. It is difficult for people to work with long strings of zeros and ones without making transposition errors. Binary numbers, whether addresses or data stored in memory, are most often represented in octal or hexadecimal to people using the computer.

**FIGURE B.4**
The decimal value of any binary number is the sum of each digit times its positional value.

| $2^3$ | $2^2$ | $2^1$ | $2^0$ | Power of the base |
|---|---|---|---|---|
| 8 | 4 | 2 | 1 | Positional value |
| 1 | 0 | 1 | 1 | Binary number |

or

| 1 | × | 8 | = | 8 | |
|---|---|---|---|---|---|
| 0 | × | 4 | = | 0 | |
| 1 | × | 2 | = | 2 | |
| 1 | × | 1 | = | 1 | |
| | | | | 11 | Value |

**FIGURE B.5**
Conversion to decimal from binary is accomplished by dividing the decimal number by the base 2, saving the remainders, and then listing these remainders from the last obtained (high-order) to the first obtained (low-order).

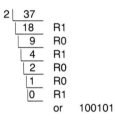

| 2 | 37 | |
|---|---|---|
| | 18 | R1 |
| | 9 | R0 |
| | 4 | R1 |
| | 2 | R0 |
| | 1 | R0 |
| | 0 | R1 |
| | or | 100101 |

**FIGURE B.6**
The value of the rightmost position in the number is 1. The leftmost, or high-order, position in the same number has a positional value of 64.

| $8^2$ | $8^1$ | $8^0$ | Power of the base |
|---|---|---|---|
| 64 | 8 | 1 | Positional value |
| n | n | n | The number |

## Octal Numbers

**Octal** is base 8; eight digits, 0 to 7, are in the octal numbering system. Each position in an octal numbering system is worth a progressive power of 8 (Figure B.6). Octal numbers may be converted to their decimal equivalent by multiplying each digit by the power of the base for that position and summing the results.

A decimal number may also be converted to octal by using the division algorithm (Figure B.7).

Octal is used to represent long strings of binary digits because any three binary digits can be represented by one octal digit (Figure B.8). To convert any binary number to octal, you need only divide the binary number from right to left into groups of three bits and then convert each group into its octal equivalent (Figure B.9). To convert any octal number back to binary, the reverse is done. Each octal character is converted to its three-bit binary equivalent.

**FIGURE B.7**
(a) The decimal value of octal 174 is found by multiplying each digit by its positional value and summing the results. (b) To find the octal equivalent of a decimal number, divide the decimal number by the base 8. Next, list the remainders from the last obtained (high-order) to the first obtained (low order).

(a) 174 in octal – ?

| $8^2$ | $8^1$ | $8^0$ | Progressive power |
|----|----|----|----|
| 64 | 8 | 1 | Positional value |
| 1 | 7 | 4 | The number |

or

$1 \times 64 = 64$
$7 \times 8 = 56$
$4 \times 1 = 4$
                124  Value

(b) 8 | 100
        12   R4
         1   R4
         0   R1 or 144

**FIGURE B.8**
These are the octal digits. Decimal 8 would be represented in octal by 10, decimal 9 by 11, and so on.

| Decimal | Octal | Binary |
|---------|-------|--------|
| 0 | 0 | 000 |
| 1 | 1 | 001 |
| 2 | 2 | 010 |
| 3 | 3 | 011 |
| 4 | 4 | 100 |
| 5 | 5 | 101 |
| 6 | 6 | 110 |
| 7 | 7 | 111 |

**FIGURE B.9**

Any three binary digits can be represented by one octal digit. (a) To convert from binary to octal, divide the binary number from right to left in groups of three and represent each group by the equivalent octal digit. (b) To convert octal to binary, convert each binary digit to the three equivalent binary digits.

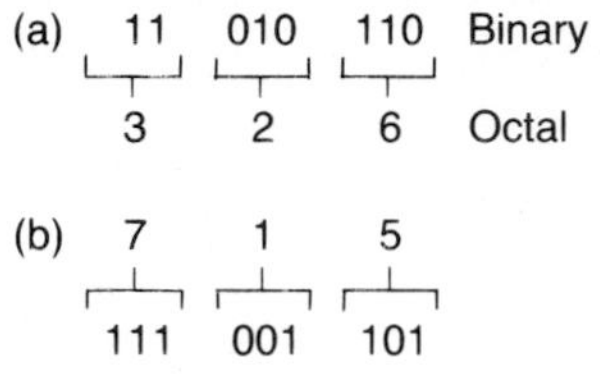

| | | | | |
|---|---|---|---|---|
| (a) | 11 | 010 | 110 | Binary |
| | 3 | 2 | 6 | Octal |
| (b) | 7 | 1 | 5 | |
| | 111 | 001 | 101 | |

**FIGURE B.10**

Hexadecimal compared to decimal and binary numbering systems.

| Decimal | Hexadecimal | Binary |
|---------|-------------|--------|
| 00 | 0 | 0000 |
| 01 | 1 | 0001 |
| 02 | 2 | 0010 |
| 03 | 3 | 0011 |
| 04 | 4 | 0100 |
| 05 | 5 | 0101 |
| 06 | 6 | 0110 |
| 07 | 7 | 0111 |
| 08 | 8 | 1000 |
| 09 | 9 | 1001 |
| 10 | A | 1010 |
| 11 | B | 1011 |
| 12 | C | 1100 |
| 13 | D | 1101 |
| 14 | E | 1110 |
| 15 | F | 1111 |

## Hexadecimal Numbers

**Hexadecimal,** or base 16, is also used to represent binary data and addresses. Hexadecimal, however, presents a new problem. You need 16 digits, and you are accustomed to using only 10. The hexadecimal numbering system uses the 10 digits with which you are familiar plus the first six letters of the alphabet (Figure B.10).

The decimal equivalent of any hexadecimal number can be obtained by multiplying the value of the digits by the power of 16 for each location and summing the results. The conversion from decimal to hexadecimal is again done by the division algorithm (Figure B.11). Each octal character represented three binary digits; each hexadecimal character represents four binary digits. To convert from binary to hexadecimal, divide the binary number from right to left into groups of four bits and convert each group to its hexadecimal equivalent. To convert from hexadecimal to binary, convert each hexadecimal digit to its equivalent four binary digits (Figure B.12).

**FIGURE B.11**

Conversion from decimal to hexadecimal.

To find the decimal equivalent of any hex number, multiply each hex digit by its positional value (a progressive power of the base 16). Then sum the results:

| $16^2$ | $16^1$ | $16^0$ | Progressive power of the base |
|------|------|------|-----------------------------|
| 256 | 16 | 1 | Positional values |
| 3 | A | 9 | The hex number |
| 3 | $\times$ | 256 | = | 768 |
| A(10) | $\times$ | 16 | = | 160 |
| 9 | $\times$ | 1 | = | 9 |

The decimal equivalent    937

Conversion of a decimal number to its hex value can be done by dividing the decimal number by 16, recording the quotient repeatedly until the quotient becomes 0, each time recording the remainder, and finally listing the remainders from the last obtained (high-order digit) to the first obtained (low-order digit).
   To convert 1098 from decimal to hex:

```
16 | 1098
      68     R 10 or A
       4     R 4
       0     R 4 or 44A
```

**FIGURE B.12**

*(a)* To convert from hex to binary, convert each hex digit to its four-position binary equivalent.
*(b)* To convert a binary number to hex, divide the binary number from right to left into groups of four bits each. Next, convert each group into its one-position hexadecimal equivalent.

```
(a)   C      7      A
     ┌─┴─┐  ┌─┴─┐  ┌─┴─┐
     1100   0111   1010

(b)  1     0110   1010
     └┬┘   └─┬─┘  └─┬─┘
      1      6      A
```

## CODING SCHEMES

Letters, numbers, special symbols—in a computer, they are all stored as a string of binary digits. Which configuration of binary digits represents which character is determined by the code used to store the data. Several coding schemes are used, but the two most common ones are EBCDIC and ASCII.

### EBCDIC

**EBCDIC,** the Extended Binary Coded Decimal Interchange Code, is an 8-bit code. The eight bits, called a *byte,* are made up of a zone portion and a digit portion (Figure B.13). The **zone portion,** the four high-order bits in a byte, indicates whether the character is a number, a letter (and, if a letter, in which group of letters: A–I, J–R, or S–Z), or a special symbol. The **digit portion,** the four low-order bits, indicates which number, which letter of the group, or which special symbol. For example, let's compare the number 2 and the letters A and N. All numbers stored in display format have a zone portion of 1111 in binary or F in hexadecimal. The digit portion of the number indicates the number. For the number 2, this would be represented as a binary 2, or 0010. The number 2 would be represented as 1111 0010 in EBCDIC. The number 3 would still have a zone portion of 1111, but the digit portion would be a binary 3, or 0011 (Figure B.14).

The 26 letters of our alphabet are divided into three groups: A–I, J–R, and S–Z. The first group of nine letters is represented by 1100 or a hexadecimal C in the zone portion. The digit portion indicates the letter within the group. For the letter A, the zone portion would be 1100 and the digit portion 0001 or a binary 1 because A is the first letter within the group. The letter B would have the same zone portion, whereas the digit portion would be a binary 2 or 0010 (Figure B.15).

The second group of nine letters, J to R, has a 1101 or hexadecimal D in the zone portion. Which letter in the group is stored is again represented by the digit portion. For example, the letter N, the fifth letter of this group, is stored as 1101 0101.

The last group of letters, S to Z, is represented by a zone of 1110 or hexadecimal E. This group contains only eight letters; the digit portion contains 2 through

**FIGURE B.13**

EBCDIC uses eight bits to form a character. The eight bits are divided into two parts: a high-order four-bit zone portion and a low-order four-bit digit portion.

| Zone portion | Digit portion | |
|---|---|---|
| ZZZZ | DDDD | |
| 1100 | 0101 | Represents the letter E |

9. Therefore, S would be stored as 1110 0010 (Figure B.16). For a table of the EBCDIC code, see Figure B.17. Note that this table does not show the lowercase letters, which are represented differently than the uppercase letters in both EBCDIC and ASCII.

## ASCII

**ASCII,** or American Standard Code for Information Interchange, is a 7-bit code. The first bit for data representation is always 0; therefore, it is not shown. The American National Standards Institute sponsored this code's development.

**FIGURE B.14**

The digits 0 through 9 are represented in EBCDIC by a zone portion of all ones. The digit portion represents the number itself: 1 is 0001, 2 is 0010, and so on.

| Digit | EBCDIC in binary | | Hex equivalent |
|-------|------|------|----------------|
| | Zone | Digit | |
| 0 | 1111 | 0000 | F0 |
| 1 | 1111 | 0001 | F1 |
| 2 | 1111 | 0010 | F2 |
| 3 | 1111 | 0011 | F3 |
| 4 | 1111 | 0100 | F4 |
| 5 | 1111 | 0101 | F5 |
| 6 | 1111 | 0110 | F6 |
| 7 | 1111 | 0111 | F7 |
| 8 | 1111 | 1000 | F8 |
| 9 | 1111 | 1001 | F9 |

**FIGURE B.15**

The letters A through I have a zone portion of 1100. The digit portion indicates the letter. A, the first letter of the group, has a digit portion of 1, B has a digit portion of 2, and so on.

| Character | EBCDIC in binary | | Hex equivalent |
|-----------|------|------|----------------|
| | Zone | Digit | |
| A | 1100 | 0001 | C1 |
| B | 1100 | 0010 | C2 |
| C | 1100 | 0011 | C3 |
| D | 1100 | 0100 | C4 |
| E | 1100 | 0101 | C5 |
| F | 1100 | 0110 | C6 |
| G | 1100 | 0111 | C7 |
| H | 1100 | 1000 | C8 |
| I | 1100 | 1001 | C9 |

**FIGURE B.16**

*(a)* The letters J through R are represented by a zone portion of 1101 and a digit portion of 0001 to 1001, indicating the position of the letter within the group: J is 1, K is 2, and so on. *(b)* The letters S through Z are represented by a zone of 1110 and the digits 0010 to 1001. Note that in this group only, the digit portion begins with 2.

**(a)**

| Digit | EBCDIC in binary | | Hex equivalent |
|:---:|:---:|:---:|:---:|
| | **Zone** | **Digit** | |
| J | 1101 | 0001 | D1 |
| K | 1101 | 0010 | D2 |
| L | 1101 | 0011 | D3 |
| M | 1101 | 0100 | D4 |
| N | 1101 | 0101 | D5 |
| O | 1101 | 0110 | D6 |
| P | 1101 | 0111 | D7 |
| Q | 1101 | 1000 | D8 |
| R | 1101 | 1001 | D9 |

**(b)**

| Digit | EBCDIC in binary | | Hex equivalent |
|:---:|:---:|:---:|:---:|
| | **Zone** | **Digit** | |
| S | 1110 | 0010 | E2 |
| T | 1110 | 0011 | E3 |
| U | 1110 | 0100 | E4 |
| V | 1110 | 0101 | E5 |
| W | 1110 | 0110 | E6 |
| X | 1110 | 0111 | E7 |
| Y | 1110 | 1000 | E8 |
| Z | 1110 | 1001 | E9 |

The byte is divided into a zone portion and a digit portion. Numbers contain a 011 in the zone portion. The digit portion again indicates the number. For example, the number 3 is represented by 011 0011.

The letters of the alphabet are divided into two groups. The letters A to O are represented by a 100 in the zone portion, with the digit portion representing the letter. The second group, P to Z, contains 101 in the zone portion.

For a table of the ASCII code, see Figure B.18. Note that the lowercase letters are again omitted.

## PACKED EBCDIC NUMBERS

Recall that the zone portion of each EBCDIC digit in display format is a 1111 or hexadecimal F. It is essential to know whether a number is positive or negative. This is indicated in EBCDIC by what appears in the zone portion of the rightmost (low-order) digit. A positive number is indicated by a 1100 in

**FIGURE B.17**
The EBCDIC code.

| Digit | EBCDIC in binary | | Hex equivalent |
| | Zone | Digit | |
|---|---|---|---|
| 0 | 1111 | 0000 | F0 |
| 1 | 1111 | 0001 | F1 |
| 2 | 1111 | 0010 | F2 |
| 3 | 1111 | 0011 | F3 |
| 4 | 1111 | 0100 | F4 |
| 5 | 1111 | 0101 | F5 |
| 6 | 1111 | 0110 | F6 |
| 7 | 1111 | 0111 | F7 |
| 8 | 1111 | 1000 | F8 |
| 9 | 1111 | 1001 | F9 |
| A | 1100 | 0001 | C1 |
| B | 1100 | 0010 | C2 |
| C | 1100 | 0011 | C3 |
| D | 1100 | 0100 | C4 |
| E | 1100 | 0101 | C5 |
| F | 1100 | 0110 | C6 |
| G | 1100 | 0111 | C7 |
| H | 1100 | 1000 | C8 |
| I | 1100 | 1001 | C9 |
| J | 1101 | 0001 | D1 |
| K | 1101 | 0010 | D2 |
| L | 1101 | 0011 | D3 |
| M | 1101 | 0100 | D4 |
| N | 1101 | 0101 | D5 |
| O | 1101 | 0110 | D6 |
| P | 1101 | 0111 | D7 |
| Q | 1101 | 1000 | D8 |
| R | 1101 | 1001 | D9 |
| S | 1110 | 0010 | E2 |
| T | 1110 | 0011 | E3 |
| U | 1110 | 0100 | E4 |
| V | 1110 | 0101 | E5 |
| W | 1110 | 0110 | E6 |
| X | 1110 | 0111 | E7 |
| Y | 1110 | 1000 | E8 |
| Z | 1110 | 1001 | E9 |

the zone portion of the low-order digit, and a negative number is indicated by a 1101 or hexadecimal D in the zone portion of the low-order digit. For example:

| Decimal | Hexadecimal | Binary |
|---|---|---|
| 123 | F1 F2 F3 | 1111 0001 1111 0010 1111 0011 |
| +123 | F1 F2 C3 | 1111 0001 1111 0010 1100 0011 |
| −123 | F1 F2 D3 | 1111 0001 1111 0010 1101 0011 |

**FIGURE B.18**
The seven-bit ASCII code.

| Character | ASCII | In binary |
|:---:|:---:|:---:|
| 0 | 011 | 0000 |
| 1 | 011 | 0001 |
| 2 | 011 | 0010 |
| 3 | 011 | 0011 |
| 4 | 011 | 0100 |
| 5 | 011 | 0101 |
| 6 | 011 | 0110 |
| 7 | 011 | 0111 |
| 8 | 011 | 1000 |
| 9 | 011 | 1001 |
| A | 100 | 0001 |
| B | 100 | 0010 |
| C | 100 | 0011 |
| D | 100 | 0100 |
| E | 100 | 0101 |
| F | 100 | 0110 |
| G | 100 | 0111 |
| H | 100 | 1000 |
| I | 100 | 1001 |
| J | 100 | 1010 |
| K | 100 | 1011 |
| L | 100 | 1100 |
| M | 100 | 1101 |
| N | 100 | 1110 |
| O | 100 | 1111 |
| P | 101 | 0000 |
| Q | 101 | 0001 |
| R | 101 | 0010 |
| S | 101 | 0011 |
| T | 101 | 0100 |
| U | 101 | 0101 |
| V | 101 | 0110 |
| W | 101 | 0111 |
| X | 101 | 1000 |
| Y | 101 | 1001 |
| Z | 101 | 1010 |

Since a number has only one sign, the individual digits of an EBCDIC number are frequently stored in what is referred to as **packed format** in order to save space. Packing also expedites mathematical calculations.

With packing, the zone portion is removed from all digits but the low-order one (as illustrated in Figure B.19). Note that, although the low-order digit retains

**FIGURE B.19**
Seven unpacked numbers take seven bytes. Packed, they take only four bytes.

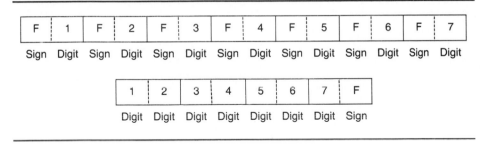

**FIGURE B.20**
By omitting each zone except for that in the low-order byte, we can store a five-digit number in three bytes.

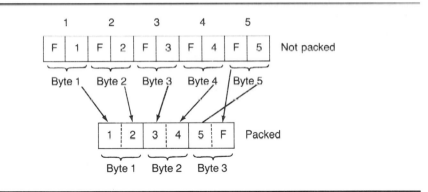

its sign, the sign is moved so that it follows the digit rather than preceding it as it did before packing.

Let's look at the number 12345. If it were stored in display format, it would take five bytes. If packed, it can be stored in three bytes (Figure B.20). There is a simple formula that you can use to calculate the new number of bytes required when a number is packed: the number of bytes needed to store a packed number in EBCDIC is equal to one more than the number of characters in the number divided by 2 (Figure B.21).

Packed numbers can also be signed and, in fact, usually are. Figure B.22 compares unsigned, positive, and negative numbers, showing how they would be stored in both display and packed format.

**FIGURE B.21**
Calculating the number of bytes needed for a packed number. The remainder from calculating *(a)* is dropped. The high-order position in *(b)* is padded with a zero.

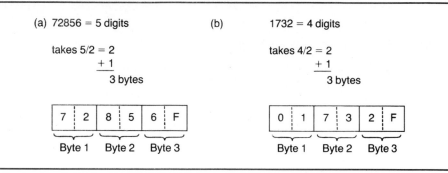

| | (a) 72856 = 5 digits | (b) | | 1732 = 4 digits |
|---|---|---|---|---|

takes 5/2 = 2
+ 1
―――――
3 bytes

takes 4/2 = 2
+ 1
―――――
3 bytes

| 7 | 2 | 8 | 5 | 6 | F |
|---|---|---|---|---|---|

Byte 1   Byte 2   Byte 3

| 0 | 1 | 7 | 3 | 2 | F |
|---|---|---|---|---|---|

Byte 1   Byte 2   Byte 3

**FIGURE B.22**
In EBCDIC, a zone of 1100 or C indicates that the field is positive; a zone of 1101 or D indicates that the field is negative.

|  |  | EBCDIC |  |
|---|---|---|---|
| Decimal | | Not packed | Packed |
| 1  2  3 | | F 1 F 2 F 3 | 1 2 3 F |
| + 1  2  3 | | F 1 F 2 C 3 | 1 2 3 C |
| − 1  2  3 | | F 1 F 2 D 3 | 1 2 3 D |

## VOCABULARY

ASCII    283
Binary   276
Decimal  276
Digit portion   280
EBCDIC   282

Hexadecimal   280
Octal   278
Packed format   286
Zone portion   282

## EXERCISES

1. What is the value of each position in a four-digit number if that number is in decimal? Hexadecimal? Octal? Binary?

2. Convert the following binary numbers to decimal.
   a. 100101.
   b. 111001.
   c. 010101.
   d. 100111.
3. Convert the following octal numbers to decimal.
   a. 137.
   b. 6422.
   c. 2630.
   d. 14751.
4. Convert the following hexadecimal numbers to decimal.
   a. AF12.
   b. 39C7.
   c. D08.
   e. A45B6.
5. Convert the following decimal numbers to binary, octal, and then hexadecimal.
   a. 1,296.
   b. 5,000.
   c. 17,842.
   d. 36.
6. Convert the following octal numbers to binary. Check by converting both the original octal number and the converted binary number to decimal.
   a. 644.
   b. 121.
   c. 731.
7. Convert the following hexadecimal numbers to binary.
   a. 1AEF.
   b. 12C.
   c. BD.
8. Convert the following binary numbers to hexadecimal.
   a. 10011110.
   b. 11010011.
   c. 101000.
9. Write your first name as it would be expressed in the ASCII code and then as it would be expressed in EBCDIC.
10. Translate into English the following quotation from the EBCDIC code as expressed in hexadecimal.
    C1D5C4 C9 C1D4 D9C9C7C8E3
    C1D5C4 E8D6E4 C1D9C5 D9C9C7C8E3
    C1D5C4 C1D3D3 C9E2 D9C9C7C8E3 C1E2 D9C9D7D8E3 C3C1D5 C2C5
11. In the following quotation from *The Pirates of Penzance,* two words are written in ASCII. Translate them to complete the quotation:
    Things are seldom what they 1010011 1000101 1000101 1001101, 1010011 1001011 1001001 1001101 milk masquerades as cream.

# Glossary

**abacus**    A counting device consisting of parallel rods with beads that slide up and down.

**access**    To store or retrieve data.

**access method programs**    The programs used to retrieve data from an input device and store it in main memory or to retrieve data in main memory and to write or display it on an output device.

**acoustical coupler**    Links a computer to telephone lines when the telephone handset is inserted into its holder.

**Ada, Augusta, Countess of Lovelace**    Mathematician and associate of Babbage who is often given credit for being the first programmer.

**address**    A label or number that identifies a particular register or an exact location in main memory or on a storage device.

**alphanumeric field**    Field that can contain letters, numbers, and/or special symbols.

**ad hoc**    For a special purpose.

**AI**    See artificial intelligence.

**ALU**    See arithmetic logic unit.

**American Standard Code for Information Interchange**    See ASCII.

**analog computers**    Equipment that represents numerical quantities by continuous physical variables such as length, flow, pressure, or voltage.

**analog signals**    A signal or message transmitted in an analog form—that is, by continuous variables.

**analytical engine**    A device proposed by Babbage that would be able to receive instructions input from punched cards. These instructions would then be stored internally in the computer's memory. Once the calculations were complete, the engine would print out the results.

**application programs**    A program designed to solve a particular problem for an in-house system, such as setting up inventory or payroll procedures.

**application software**    See application programs.

**arithmetic logic unit (ALU)**    That portion of the central processing unit that performs arithmetic and logical operations.

**array**    A collection of similar data items arranged for easy retrieval. A table has both arguments (fields to match to) and functions (fields to be retrieved); an array has only functions.

**artificial intelligence (AI)**    The part of computer science concerned with developing and using a computer that can perform human thought processes such as learning, reasoning, and self-correction.

**ASCII**    The acronym for American Standard Code for Information Interchange, a 7-bit (plus parity bit) code developed by the American National Standards Institute to achieve comparability among various types of information processing and communications equipment.

**assembler**    A program that translates an assembly language program into the equivalent machine language code.

**assembly language**    A low-level programming language that uses mnemonic instructions instead of binary numbers to represent the corresponding machine language instruction.

**asynchronous communication**    The transmission of a single character at a time. Each character is preceded and followed by one or more bits that signal the start and stop of the character.

**Atanasoff, John**    Codeveloper of the ABC computer.

**attributes**    Characteristics of a person or thing.

**audit trail**    A trail of what and how transactions were processed that is available for use in an audit, an official examination of accounting records.

**automatic program generators**    Enable a programmer to quickly and easily generate a program from a screen layout or other abbreviated instructions.

**auxiliary storage**    Storage located outside the processor, most often in the form of tape or disk.

**Babbage, Charles**    An English mathematician credited with designing the first computer.

**bandwidth**    The transmission capacity of a computer or communications channel.

**bar code**    A code that consists of a number of ink lines of varying widths imprinted on a label and read with a scanning device, often called the universal product code.

**BASIC**    Acronym for Beginners All-Purpose Symbolic Instruction Code, a language developed at Dartmouth that is easy to learn and use.

**batch processing**    Information processing in which the data is gathered or "batched" for processing at one time rather than processed as the activity occurs.

**baud**    A measure of how much data can be transmitted in a unit of time; 1 baud = 1 bit per second.

**Berry, Clifford**    Codeveloper of the ABC computer.

**binary code**    The base 2 numbering system; only the digits 0 and 1 are used.

**binary digit (bit)**    The smallest unit of storage in the computer. It is referred to as a *bit*, the contraction of Binary Digit. Groups of bits form other units of storage such as bytes or words.

**biometric security**    A system that identifies the user by digitally measuring physical or behavioral characteristics such as fingerprints or patterns of blood vessels.

**bisynchronous communication**    Each data character is transmitted as one continuous stream since sending and receiving devices are synchronized before transmission starts.

**bit**    See binary digit.

**block**    A unit of storage consisting of one or more logical records that are treated as a unit for reading or writing.

**blocking**    The process of grouping a specified number of logical records into a physical record called a *block*.

**boot**    The starting of a computer. The bootstrap routine locates the operating system, loads it, then passes control to it.

**bpi**    Bit per inch; the number of bits stored in a linear inch.

**branch**    An instrument that transfers control to an instruction other than the next sequential one. Branch instructions give the programmer the ability to perform alternate instructions under different conditions.

**broad band channel**    Channel that is capable of transmitting at very high speeds—millions of bits per second.

**buffer**    A storage area used to facilitate the transfer of data between an input/output device and main memory.

**bulletin board** Computer systems that function as centralized information and message sources.

**bus lines** A circuit for the transfer of data or electrical signals between two devices.

**byte** A group of consecutive bits that form a unit of storage in a computer. A byte frequently equals one alphanumeric character and usually comprises eight bits, although it may contain more or less depending on the computer.

**C** A programming language designed for use on microcomputers. It combines low-level language control with high-level coding ease.

**cache memory** A special section of high-speed memory used to improve computer performance.

**CAD** Computer-aided design.

**CAD/CAM** Computer-aided design integrated with computer-aided manufacturing.

**CADD** Computer-aided design systems with special features for drafting.

**CAI** See computer-aided instruction.

**CAM** Computer-aided manufacturing including numerical and process control, material requirements planning, and robotics.

**CASE (computer-aided software engineering) packages** Software packages used as an aid in developing information systems. They include features that aid in analysis, design, programming, and documentation.

**cathode ray tube (CRT)** A televisionlike tube used for viewing data in computer systems.

**CD–ROM** A computer storage disk in the form of a compact disk. It is read only.

**cell** On a spreadsheet, a unit of storage that holds one unit of information.

**cell pointer** An indicator pointing to the cell to be referenced next.

**central processing unit (CPU)** The part of the computer that fetches, decodes, and executes instructions. It consists of the arithmetic/logic unit and the control unit.

**centralized database** A database that is held in a single, centralized location.

**CGA** Color graphics adapter, a video display board from the PC that generates low-resolution text and graphics.

**character** A letter, number, or special symbol.

**child entry** A subordinate node in a database.

**chip** An integrated circuit on a silicon chip.

**clone** An identical or close and comparable computer or software package.

**coaxial cable** A cable consisting of an insulated tube through which an insulated conductor runs. It is used for the transmission of data in a communications system as well as telephone, telegraph, and television signals.

**COBOL** Acronym for COmmon Business Oriented Language, a high-level programming language designed to perform business-oriented functions.

**code** (1) A set of rules defining the way in which bits can be arranged to represent the character set such as ASCII or EBCDIC code. (2) To write a program. (3) The instructions that make up a program.

**commercial database** Provides organizations and individuals with data such as demographics, current news, and so on for a fee.

**communications channel** A pathway over which data is transferred between remote devices.

**communications program** The software that transmits data to and receives data from terminals or between computers.

**compiler** A program that translates a source program written in a high-level language into equivalent machine language instructions.

**computer** An electronic device for performing high-speed arithmetic and logical operations. It consists of an arithmetic/logic unit, a control unit, input/output devices, and memory.

**computer-aided instruction (CAI)** The use of a computer to provide instruction and exercises. Drills, tutorials, and so on are programmed so that the student can interact with the instructional programs by using a terminal. Level of performance is monitored by the CAI program, enabling each student to perform at his or her level.

**computer system** Consists of hardware and software.

**computer viruses** See viruses.

**constant** A value that remains unchanged during the execution of a program.

**consultant** A person who gives expert professional advice to others for a fee.

**contention** The condition occurring when two or more devices request the same resource. It is resolved by several methods, among them assignment on a "first come, first served" basis or assignment of different priorities to different programs or devices.

**control unit** The part of the central processing unit that receives an instruction from a program in main memory, decodes the instruction, and sends signals to the units in the computer that will execute the instruction. It controls the execution of the entire computer.

**courseware** The course materials available in computer-aided instruction.

**CPU** See central processing unit.

**CRT** See cathode ray tube.

**cursor** A visual position indicator on a display terminal. It is most often a short, highlighted line or square at the place where a character is to be entered or changed.

**custom program** See custom software.

**custom software** A program or group of programs written to meet the specific needs of a particular customer or user.

**cyberphobia** Fear of computers.

**cylinder** The group of tracks that are written one above another in a disk pack. All data written on a cylinder can be accessed from one position of the access arm.

**daisy wheel** A print device that contains images of the characters each on the end of a spoke surrounding a hub. The wheel is rotated until the required character is under the print hammer.

**DASD** See direct storage access device.

**data** The characters input to a computer system and processed by it.

**data cell** See cell.

**data dictionary** Computer program that contains information about the contents of each data store and data element in the system.

**data element** A field within the database.

**data flow** The path taken by data through a system.

**data flow diagram (DFD)** Layered approach to showing the flow of data through a system. DFDs use four symbols: process, external entity, data flows, and data stores.

**data integrity** The preservation of data from accidental change; the assurance that a data item contains the same value at any location stored.

**data redundancy** Data being kept in multiple locations.

**data security** Used to prevent unauthorized access to data.

**data store** Files, reference books, logs, and so on in which information is retained.

**database** A collection of interrelated files that are created and managed by a database management system.

**database administrator (DBA)**    An individual who is responsible for the design, creation, and maintenance of the database.

**database management system (DBMS)**    A series of programs that control the security as well as the storage and retrieval of data in the database.

**DBA**    See database administrator.

**DBMS**    See database management system.

**decentralized databases**    Databases that are held and used in several locations often with communications between computers and various databases.

**decision block**    A diamond-shaped symbol on a flowchart used to represent decisions.

**decision diamond**    See decision block.

**decision support system (DSS)**    An on-line system used to aid in the decision-making process in business.

**dedicated (leased) lines**    Also called private lines, they are communications lines that are used exclusively for one purpose.

**demodulate**    The process of converting analog data to digital data.

**desktop publishing**    The production by computer of high-quality printed output (both text and graphics) that is camera ready.

**destructive write-to**    The act of writing to memory destroys the prior contents of memory.

**DFD**    See data flow diagram.

**diagnostic**    An error message printed in a program listing from a compiler or an assembler.

**difference engine**    A device designed by Babbage and intended to be used to calculate mathematical tables.

**digit portion**    In the EBCDIC code, the four low-order bits used to represent the digit or particular letter within the group.

**digital computer**    A device that makes calculations using data represented as a series of discrete digits.

**digital signal**    A signal characterized by discontinuous characters that represent a specific pattern of binary digits.

**direct access storage device (DASD)**    Any storage device that permits data stored on it to be accessed directly; that is, preceding data does not have to be read. Two common types are magnetic disk and magnetic tape.

**direct file**    (1) Any file whose record key points directly to the location of the record on the file. (2) Any file whose records are stored in a random order on a direct access storage device.

**disk**    See magnetic disk.

**diskette**    See floppy disk.

**disk pack**    A group of magnetic disks stacked to form one physical storage unit.

**distributed data processing**    The processing and/or storage of data at multiple locations within an organization. These locations are usually connected by communications lines.

**documentation**    A collection of written descriptions and procedures that provides information about a program or system and guidance in how to use it.

**dot matrix**    Using patterns of tiny dots to form characters and graphic images.

**download**    To transfer data from a larger computer system to a microcomputer or one of its storage devices.

**drill (in CIA)**    An exercise that teaches by repetitive practice.

**drum plotter**    A plotter in which the paper is wrapped around a movable drum over which a pen can be moved from side to side.

**DSS**    See decision support system.

**dumb terminal**    A terminal that can input and output data but that cannot be programmed to perform any other functions.

**EBCDIC**    An acronym for Extended Binary Coded Decimal Interchange Code, an 8-bit (plus parity) code used to represent the character set.

**Eckert, Jr., J. Presper**   Codeveloper of the ENIAC.

**EDVAC**   See Electronic Discrete Variable Automatic Computer.

**EGA**   Enhanced graphics adapter, a video display board for PCs that produces medium-resolution color text and graphics.

**electromechanical**   A device having both mechanical and electronic parts.

**Electronic Discrete Variable Automatic Computer (EDVAC)**   The first computer to use the stored program concept.

**electronic mail or messaging**   A system in which messages, memos, or other text are entered at a terminal and transmitted from there to another terminal where the receiver can display them at his or her convenience.

**Electronic Numerical Integrator And Calculator (ENIAC)**   Developed in 1946 by Mauchly and Eckard. Memory was made up of vacuum tubes.

**electronic spreadsheet**   A software program that simulates paper spreadsheets, using a matrix of rows and columns.

**electrostatic printer**   A printer using special paper. The image is controlled by charging the paper as it passes a line of electrodes. The image is displayed when toner is picked up by the charged areas.

**electrothermal printer**   A printer using special paper. The image is created by applying heat to the paper.

**ENIAC**   See Electronic Numerical Integrator And Calculator.

**ESP**   A computer language used for AI applications.

**execution time (E-time)**   (1) In a machine cycle, the time required to execute an instruction and place the results back in main memory. (2) The time during which a program is being executed.

**expansion slot**   A receptacle in the computer into which printer or other circuit boards may be plugged.

**expert system**   A computerized system based on the collected knowledge of experts in a field. It is used to assist in decision making.

**external entity**   People and organizations outside of the system.

**facsimile system (fax)**   A system that transmits images over communications lines and, using special equipment, reproduces the image on paper after transmittal.

**family of computers**   A group of computers designed by their manufacturer to be upwardly compatible.

**FAX**   See facsimile system.

**fiber optics**   The technology of transmitting data by using flexible strands of glass or plastic through which light or laser beams are passed.

**field**   A group of characters that form a unit of information such as age, telephone number, or job classification.

**fifth-generation computer**   A computer having a very large scale integration microprocessor that can handle verbal input and output as well as demonstrate artificial intelligence.

**file**   A collection of logically related records.

**file server**   In a LAN, a computer that is used to store the files and programs shared by users on the network.

**first-generation computer**   A computer using vacuum tubes for memory, capable of using stored programs, and using magnetic tapes for auxiliary storage.

**fixed-length record**   File records each containing the same number of bytes.

**flatbed plotter**   A plotter in which the paper is held stationary over a flat surface; the pen moves over the paper.

**floppy disk**   A disk, usually $3\frac{1}{2}$, $5\frac{1}{4}$, or 8 inches, made of a flexible piece of mylar and coated with a magnetic material.

**flowchart**   A graphic representation, using the standard flowcharting symbols, of the logic in a program or system.

**flowcharting template**    A plastic or metal guide that can be used to trace shapes representing programming or systems activities or devices.

**font**    Printing type of one type and style.

**formula**    A mathematical expression made up of numbers, symbols, and letters. For example, A = 2C + 7.

**FORTRAN**    Acronym for FORmula TRANslator, a high-level programming language designed primarily for scientific and mathematical programs.

**fourth-generation computer**    A physically smaller version (a microcomputer) of the third-generation computer, which uses a microprocessor.

**4GLS**    Fourth-generation programming language, characterized by being very high level, nonprocedural languages.

**Freedom of Information Act of 1970**    Permits individuals to gain access to data about themselves that is maintained by federal agencies.

**front-end processor**    A smaller computer used in timesharing systems to control the remote terminals and to convert data transmitted between the host computer and the terminals into the appropriate code and format.

**Gantt chart**    Chart that enables one to measure the actual time spent on a project against the estimated time. It does not indicate the interrelationship of tasks.

**gigabyte (G)**    One billion bytes.

**glare shields**    A mesh screen that is placed over the display screen in order to reduce glare.

**graph**    A pictorial representation of information.

**graphics**    Pictorial representations such as charts, graphs, and two- or three-dimensional images.

**hacker**    A person who has extensive knowledge of computer systems. The term *hacker* often is used to refer to the person who uses that extensive technology to gain unauthorized access to computer systems and data.

**handshaking**    The exchange of control characters between an input/output device and an input/output interface to indicate that data has been sent, data has been accepted, or that the device is ready to receive data.

**hard copy**    Printed output.

**hard disk**    A disk whose base—made of aluminum or other rigid material—is coated with a magnetic material.

**hardware**    The physical components of a computer system.

**hashing**    Applying a mathematical calculation to the keys of a record and using the resulting value to point to the location in memory where a record will be stored; see also randomizing.

**heuristic learning**    Learning from experience or using a trial-and-error method by applying rules of thumb and evaluating progress.

**hexadecimal code**    The base 16 numbering system

**hierarchical database**    Forms a treelike structure with each entry having only one parent entry although it may have many subordinate child entries.

**hierarchy chart**    See tree diagram.

**high-level languages**    A programming language using Englishlike words that is not dependent on the machine language or the computer. It must be translated into machine language before the computer can execute the program.

**Hollerith, Herman**    Developer of the tabulating machine.

**IBG**    See interblock gap.

**IC**    See either information center or integrated circuit.

**icon**    A meaningful picture representing an item or activity.

**icon-driven program**    A program using pictorial representation of choices on the screen of a computer. An activity or device is chosen by selecting the picture—or icon—that represents it.

**ICOT**    The Institute for New Generation Computer Technology, whose purpose is to perform basic technological research and development.

**impact printer**    A printer that uses a striking motion to transfer the character image onto paper.

**incompatibility**    The inability to perform together.

**indexed file**    A file on which the record is located by searching an index for the record's unique key to determine the record's location.

**information**    Data that has been processed and is in a meaningful form.

**information center (IC)**    A facility that helps users interact with computers.

**inkjet printer**    A printer that uses an ink spray to create characters.

**input**    Data or programs entered into a computer for processing.

**input/output block**    A flowcharting symbol used to represent any input or output activity such as reading or writing.

**input-output device**    A peripheral device, such as a printer or disk drive, which is used to hold data when not in the CPU.

**input, processing, and output chart**    See IPO chart.

**instruction time (I-time)**    That part of a machine cycle in which an instruction is fetched from main memory and decoded.

**integrated circuit (IC)**    A silicon chip containing interconnected electrical components that form an electronic circuit.

**integrated package**    See integrated software.

**integrated software**    Software designed to perform multiple functions that can all access the same data.

**intelligent terminal**    A terminal that can perform some processing of data before transmitting it to the computer.

**interactive language**    A language in which each statement is immediately translated into machine language, allowing the programmer to correct errors as they occur.

**interactive video system**    A system consisting of a videodisk or CD–ROM that is controlled by a computer. They are used both for entertainment and for interactive education.

**interblock gap (IBG)**    The space that separates blocks on a secondary storage device.

**internal storage**    Same as main memory, the computer's internal working storage.

**interpreter**    A program that translates each statement in the source program into machine language and then executes it before translating the next statement.

**interrecord gap (IRG)**    The space that separates records on a secondary storage device.

**IPO (input, processing, and output) chart**    It describes in detail the input to a module, the processing of that module, and the output from the module.

**IRG**    See interrecord gap.

**iteration structure**    A structure in which a series of instructions is repeated; also referred to as a loop.

**JCL**    See job control language.

**job control language (JCL)**    A language unique to the computer system that identifies for the operating system the resource requirements, accounting information, security, priority, and so on, of the program being run.

**key field**    A field within a record that is used to uniquely identify that record. Examples include employee number, social security number, and inventory number.

**kilobyte (k)** One thousand bytes (approximately).

**LAN** See local area network.

**large scale integration (LSI)** The technology that permits one chip to contain hundreds of thousands of logic gates.

**laser printer** A printer using the method of copy machines to print a page at a time.

**LCD (liquid crystal display)** A display technology used in laptop computers.

**LED (light-emitting diode)** A display technology using a type of semiconductor diode that emits light when charged with electricity.

**Leibniz, Gottfried** A mathematician and philosopher who developed a calculator that enabled the user to add, subtract, multiply, divide, and extract square roots.

**light pen** A stylus attached to some CRTs that can be used to move, delete, or create new images on the screen.

**line protocol** The set of rules governing communications between two or more devices in a communications system.

**local area network (LAN)** A network within a small area not using common carriers for a communications link.

**logic error** An error in the design of a program or system.

**logic flow** The order in which statements within a program are executed.

**loop** See iteration structure.

**low-level language** A programming language, using symbolic code. It is based on the machine language of a particular computer that is translated by an assembler into machine language before execution.

**LSI** See large scale integration.

**machine cycle** The time it takes to perform one operation such as executing one instruction or reading or writing one record.

**machine language** The programming language that consists of a set of machine codes that can be directly executed by a computer.

**machine-readable format** The recording of data in such a way that it can be read or sensed by a computer.

**Macintosh OS** The operation system used by the Macintosh computer.

**magnetic disk** An oxide-coated platter capable of recording data in the form of magnetic spots.

**magnetic ink character recognition (MICR) encoding** Characters written in magnetic ink, such as on checks and deposit slips.

**magnetic strip** A short length of magnetic tape that is attached to items such as credit cards or badges. It is read by a special reader.

**magnetic tape** Mylar tape coated with a magnetic film that can be magnetized to store data. The data can be accessed only in sequence.

**main memory** Storage, located within the computer, that is used to hold both data and instructions. It permits random access and can be both written to and read from.

**mainframe** One of the large computers typically having word lengths of 32 bits or greater and memory of several million bytes and operating faster that minicomputers and microcomputers.

**maintenance** The testing and cleaning of the hardware, the routine updating and reorganization of files, and the updating of application programs.

**main storage** See main memory.

**management information system (MIS)** A computer-based system that provides the user with information to support routine decision making.

**Mark I** An electromechanical calculating machine built at Harvard in 1944.

**mark sensing** The reading by an optical mark reader of pencil marks on a form.

**mass storage device**    An external storage device capable of storing very large amounts of data.

**Mauchly, John W.**    Codeveloper of the EDVAC.

**medium band**    An electromagnetic wave that vibrates between 300,000 and 3 million cycles per second.

**megabyte (MB)**    One million bytes (approximately).

**megahertz (MHz)**    One million cycles per second.

**menu**    A list of program functions on a screen from which a person can select the function to be performed.

**microcomputer**    A small, low-cost computer containing a microprocessor.

**microfiche**    A sheet of microfilm on which hundreds of pages of copy can be stored. A special machine is required to read it.

**microfilm**    Film on which documents are photographed in a reduced size for convenient storage.

**microprocessor**    A chip that contains the arithmetic/logic unit, a scratchpad memory, and the control unit. It is the central processing unit of a microcomputer.

**microsecond**    One millionth of a second.

**Microsoft Works**    An integrated software package from Microsoft Corporation.

**microwave radio signal**    A high-end ratio wave frequency transmitted through open space. A microwave signal travels in a straight line.

**millisecond**    One thousandth of a second.

**minicomputer**    A medium-sized computer that resembles mainframes in appearance and ability to handle multiprocessing but that is slower, has a smaller memory, and typically supports fewer peripheral devices.

**MIPS**    One million instructions per second.

**MIS**    See management information systems.

**modem**    Acronym for modulator/demodulator, a device that converts between digital and analog signals.

**modular programming**    The breaking down of a program into separate sections called modules, each of which can be programmed as a single unit.

**modulate**    To take a digital signal and translate it into an analog signal.

**mouse**    A small, hand-held device that is moved over a surface, causing the cursor to move to a corresponding point on the CRT.

**MS–DOS**    The operating system from Microsoft Corporation used on the IBM and IBM-compatible personal computers.

**multiprocessing**    The simultaneous processing processors, either in the same computer or in two or more computers that are linked together.

**multiprogramming**    The concurrent execution of two or more programs by one computer. Each program executes for a period of time, and, when an interrupt occurs, waits until its turn comes again.

**multitasking**    The concurrent execution of a number of tasks by the same computer in the same partition. The related tasks solve a problem that cannot be handled by a single program.

**nanosecond**    One billionth of a second.

**natural language**    A human, spoken language.

**nested structure**    The embedding of a block of instructions or data within another block of instructions or data, most often in the form of embedded IF statements.

**network**    A system of terminals, computer(s), and related devices connected by communications channels.

**network database**    A type of database in which relationships between nodes are indicated by pointers, and a node may be subordinate to more than one other node.

**neural networks** Computer architecture modeled on how our brains work.

**NLQ** Near letter quality, a description of print quality.

**node** (1) In a data structure, an item of data that provides a link to other items of data. (2) In a network, a device that links two or more other units to the network.

**nondestructive read-out** The act of reading data stored within the computer memory does not alter or destroy the contents of that memory.

**numeric field** A field consisting only of the digits 0–9 and, optionally, a decimal point and sign (positive, negative).

**numeric variable** A numeric field whose value changes during the execution of a program.

**object module** A program in machine language that is output from a compiler or assembler.

**object-oriented programming (OOP)** A type of program or programming language in which the data is wrapped with the instructions for using it.

**OCR** See optical character recognition.

**octal code** The base 8 number system, which uses the digits 0 to 7.

**off-line** A system or peripheral equipment that is not under the control of the central processing unit.

**on-line** A system or peripheral equipment that is under the control of the central processing unit.

**operating system** A collection of programs that control the operation of the computer.

**optical character recognition (OCR)** The process of reading characters that have been printed, typed, or handprinted using a special print font. Reading is done by optical scanner.

**optical disk** A disk coated with a heat-sensitive material on which data is densely recorded using a laser beam. Reading is also done by a laser.

**optical recognition** The ability to recognize or read marks or characters produced by ordinary pencil, ink, or print.

**OS/2** A single user, multitasking operating system that runs on the 80286- and 80386-based IBM PCs and compatible machines.

**OS–MVS** An IBM mainframe operating system.

**output** The results of computer processing. Output is printed, displayed, or stored after processing.

**output device** A device that produces only output, such as a printer.

**packed format** See packed numbers.

**packed numbers** Two numbers or a number plus a sign that are combined in one byte to reduce storage space.

**page (in virtual storage)** A portion of a program or data. In paging, pages are transferred between external storage and main memory as they are needed.

**parallel port** Allows the user to hook up a printer.

**parent entry** A node in a database that has one or more nodes subordinate to it.

**Pascal** The programming language named for Blaise Pascal, a French mathematician.

**Pascal, Blaise** French mathematician who developed the Pascaline calculator in the mid-1600s.

**Pascaline** A calculator, developed in the 1600s and consisting of eight movable dials, that was capable of both addition and subtraction.

**password** A code used to identify an authorized user.

**payback analysis**    Looks at the development and operating costs of a project to determine what they are and when they will occur.

**PC–DOS**    Another name for the MS–DOS operating system used on the IBM PCs and their clones.

**performance measurement programs**    Records performance activity and provides information on system and peripheral device use.

**peripheral device**    Any device such as a disk drive or printer that is used for input/output operations.

**personal computer**    A computer designed for the individual user.

**PERT (program evaluation and review technique) chart**    A chart that enables one to measure the actual time spent on a project against the estimated time. PERT charts indicate the interrelationship of tasks and the critical path(s) through them.

**physical records**    See block.

**physical request**    The physical actions required to read a record from or write a record to an auxiliary storage device.

**picosecond**    One trillionth of a second.

**pixel**    An acronym for picture element, one of the tiny elements that form a digitized picture on the screen.

**plotter**    An output device that produces charts, maps, graphs, and so on, as output.

**pointer**    An address stored in a record or an index that specifies the storage location of another record on the file.

**point-of-sale terminal (POS)**    A terminal, connected to a computer, that collects and stores data at the same time the sale is made.

**point-to-point network**    A network in which there is a direct connection between the computer and each terminal.

**poll**    Continuous interrogation of attached devices by the computer to which they are attached to determine if a device wishes to transmit.

**POS**    See point-of-sale terminal.

**preliminary feasibility study**    The first step in the SDLC. It determines the urgency of the problem, cost/benefit of solution, and the advisability of proceeding with the project.

**present value analysis**    Converts costs and benefits to today's dollars.

**primary storage**    See main memory.

**print server**    A computer within a network that is used to control one or more printers.

**printer**    An output device that prints computer output on paper.

**Privacy Act of 1974**    Guarantees that people can know what information the government keeps about them, can change that information when it is incorrect, and that information collected for one purpose cannot be used for another purpose without the individual's consent.

**process**    Any action taken by the computer that causes the manipulation of data.

**process block**    A flowcharting symbol used to indicate such processes as moves and arithmetic activities. Not used for comparisons and input/output activities.

**program**    A logically arranged set of instructions that direct the activities of a computer.

**prompt**    A message or symbol shown on the display screen informing the user that information may now be entered and may even suggest what to enter next.

**proprietary software**    Computer programs owned by a person or company and may be purchased or used only with permission of the owner.

**prototyping**    Using an experimental, working model of a system to illustrate the proposed system for users.

**pseudocode**    A nonexecutable, language-independent instruction used as an aid in program development and documentation.

**purchased software packages**    Computer programs that are bought by the user from a vendor.

**query language**    A high-level programming language that provides easy retrieval of information from a file.

**RAM**    See random access memory.

**random access memory (RAM)**    A type of memory that can be accessed directly. It can be both read from and written to.

**randomizing**    The production of an unpredictable number dependent only on chance.

**range**    A group of values (maximum to minimum) or a group of cells (within a spreadsheet).

**reader/sorter**    A device capable of both reading records and sorting them—for example, the device used to sort MICR encoded documents and to store the information on a secondary storage device.

**read-only memory (ROM)**    Memory that can be read from but not written to.

**read/write head**    An electromagnetic device used to transfer data between main memory and a storage device.

**real-time processing**    See transaction-oriented processing.

**record**    A group of logically related fields treated as a unit.

**register**    A special-purpose storage location in the central processing unit used to hold data and addresses currently being used.

**relational database**    A database in which the data is presented as tables.

**relative file organization**    A file in which the record keys can be manipulated to produce the physical location of the data.

**reserved word**    A word that has a predefined meaning in a programming language and that is used in that language only for that specified purpose.

**resolution**    The degree of sharpness of a printed or displayed image.

**response time**    The time that elapses between the entry of a command on a terminal and the receipt of the computer's response.

**return-on-investment analysis**    Calculates the savings potential of a project and relates this potential to the original cost in an attempt to measure the realtionship between the original costs and the potential benefits.

**reusable code**    A computer code that is saved and utilized in the creation of many programs, often by using automatic program generators.

**ring network configuration**    A network in which the terminals and computers are linked together in a circular pattern. Each unit is connected only to the two units on each side of it.

**robot**    A stand-alone computer system that performs both physical and computational activities.

**robotics**    The design, production, and use of robots.

**ROM**    See read-only memory.

**rotational delay**    The time that elapses while the surface of a direct access storage device revolves to the desired position under the read/write head.

**RPG**    Stands for Report Program Generator, a high-level programming language designed to quickly produce simple business reports. Current versions are RPG II and RPG III.

**satellite**    A human-made object orbiting the earth or other celestial body.

**satellite link**    A signal traveling from earth to a communications satellite and back again.

**scrolling**    To move forward or backward through a number of lines in a file being displayed on a CRT screen.

**SDLC**    See systems development life cycle.

**second-generation computer**    A computer characterized by solid state transistor circuitry, assembly languages, and the use of disks as well as tape for storage.

**secondary storage devices**    External storage such as disk or tape.

**sector**    A wedge-shaped portion of a direct access storage device that can hold a specific number of characters. Each sector is numbered and can be addressed by that number.

**seek time**    The time it takes to position the read/write head over the desired cylinder on a direct access storage device.

**selection structure**    A logical structure in which a decision is made leading to the choice of one of two actions.

**sequence structure**    A logical structure in which instructions are executed one after another.

**sequential file**    A file in which the records must be accessed in sequence.

**serial port**    Allows the user to hook up a modem, mouse, or printer.

**shareware**    Software that is distributed free. If the user likes it and decides to keep it to use regularly, he or she is expected to pay a fee to the publisher. In return for this fee, the user receives documentation.

**simulation**    The representation of complex problems by building mathematical models that describe them and then evaluating alternative courses of action by manipulating the models and analyzing the results.

**smart card**    A credit card with a built-in computer. When inserted into a special reader, it can exchange information with a computer system. Since it has its own microprocessor, it can also be programmed.

**software**    The programs that direct computer operations.

**soroban**    A Japanese calculating device similar to the Chinese abacus.

**source module (source code)**    A program written in a source language before it is processed by the assembler, compiler, or interpreter.

**spooling**    The temporary storing of computer input or output before it is executed or printed.

**spreadsheet**    A program that stores data in columns and rows on a CRT screen and permits manipulation of and calculation with the data.

**star network**    A network in which all communication takes place through a central computer.

**string fields**    Alphanumeric fields. They can contain letters, numbers, and special symbols.

**string variables**    String fields whose values change during the execution of a program.

**structure chart**    See hierarchy chart.

**structured coding**    A type of coding that conforms to structured programming techniques, such as all procedures having only one entry and one exit point (decisions have two exits) and all coding containing only legal structures (sequence, selection, and iteration).

**structured programming**    The whole package of structured techniques including structured coding, structured walkthroughs, and top-down design.

**structured systems design**    An approach to systems design in which each system is broken down into its primary functions. In turn, each function is broken into its subfunctions, until the system is described in minute detail.

**structured systems development**    Methodology of systems development that includes structured systems design.

**subroutine**    A sequence of instructions that perform a specific task. The task can be performed repeatedly within one program or performed as needed by many programs.

**subschema** An individual user's view of the database. It may be of the entire database or only a part.

**supercomputer** An extremely fast computer that can perform billions of additions per second.

**supermicros** High-powered microcomputers capable of typical mini and mainframe activities such as multiprogramming.

**switched lines** A communications link established by dialing.

**symbolic code** A programming code that uses mnemonic names for instructions and symbolic names for storage locations. Symbolic code is closely related to machine code.

**syntax error** An error caused by violating the structure rules of a particular programming language.

**system** A group of interrelated elements that work together to perform a specific task.

**system software** The programs used to control the computer and to run the application programs.

**systems analyst** The person who develops a system by developing solutions and evaluating alternatives, managing the systems development project, and/or implementing the new system.

**systems analysis** The study of a project to see how it can best be accomplished.

**systems development life cycle (SDLC)** Formal systems development methodology in which the development process is partitioned into formal stages, each of which must be performed and approved before the subsequent stage.

**systems flowchart** A graphical representation of the way data from source documents is processed until it is available to the end-users.

**table** A collection of related data organized into arguments and functions to enable the data to be quickly accessed.

**tape** See magnetic tape.

**telecommuting** Substituting computers and telecommunications for physical presence at the normal work site.

**teleconferencing** Holding conferences by using telecommunications equipment.

**template** See flowcharting template.

**terminal** A device connected to a computer by any type of communications line and used to send data to and receive data from the computer.

**test data** A small sample of data used to test a program or system to see if there are any logic errors.

**third-generation computer** A computer characterized by integrated circuitry and high-level programming languages.

**throughput** The amount of processing that can occur in a given amount of time.

**time-sharing** Computer operation in which each program receives a given slice of time; the programs are operated in turn.

**track** One of the concentric circles used to record data on the surface of a disk.

**trail (as in audit trail)** See audit trail.

**transaction-oriented processing** Processing each transaction as it occurs.

**transfer rate** The rate at which data is transferred between a secondary storage device and main memory.

**transfer time** The time it takes for data to be transferred between a secondary storage device and main memory.

**transistor** A semiconductor device used as an electrical switch in digital computers.

**tree diagram** A chart designed to show the logic structure of a program—that is, what modules are included in a program and how they are related.

**Turing test** A method of identifying intelligence in machines; named after Alan Turing, a British mathematician.

**turnaround**    The amount of time it takes to receive output after the program or inquiry is submitted.

**tutorials (in CAI)**    Intensive individualized instruction in a subject using computer-aided instruction techniques.

**twisted pair**    A pair of small insulated wires twisted around each other to minimize interference from other wires in the cable. They are commonly used in telephone cables.

**unit record equipment**    Any of the equipment that performs operations on punched cards: sorters, keypunches, collators, and so on.

**UNIVAC I**    The first commercially available computer.

**universal product code (UPC)**    A standard bar code printed on retail merchandise and containing vendor identification number and product number.

**UNIX**    A multiuser, multitasking operating system developed at AT&T's Bell Labs.

**UPC**    See universal product code.

**utility program**    A program that performs a task that is required by many of the programs using the system: copying, sorting, and so on.

**vacuum tubes**    An electrical component that was used as off and on switches in first-generation computers.

**variable**    A field whose value changes during the execution of the program.

**variable-length records**    Records whose length may differ within the same file.

**VDT**    See visual display terminal.

**very large scale integration (VLSI)**    The integration on a chip containing 100,000 or more gates. These chips are used for microprocessors.

**video graphics array (VGA)**    A display system used on the PS/2 and added to some PCs.

It has a higher resolution than either CGA or EGA.

**video monitor**    Another term for the video display terminal. See also visual display terminal.

**virtual memory**    The technique of segmenting a program, allocating the active segments to reside in main memory, and holding the inactive segments until needed on a direct access storage device. The technique permits more programs to be run concurrently than the size of main memory alone would permit.

**virus**    Annoying or destructive computer programs that may lie dormant for extended periods of time but that, once activated, may freeze the system, destroy data, and so on.

**visual display terminal (VDT)**    A terminal that has a screen for the viewing of data.

**voice band channel**    A channel that transmits at a rate of up to 9600 baud.

**voice output**    Produced either by digitizing words, syllables, or sounds or by voice synthesis.

**voice recognition**    The storing of speech patterns by the computer and the subsequent interpretation of spoken input by matching it to those patterns at a later time.

**voice synthesis**    The generation of speech by a computer.

**von Neumann, John**    Father of the stored program concept.

**VLSI**    See very large scale integration.

**wait state**    The interruption of the execution of a program, usually to permit the execution of an input/output operation.

**wand reader**    A hand-held electronic device that can optically read data.

**window**    A portion of a file or picture displayed on a CRT.

**word processing**    A system used to enter, edit, store, retrieve, and print text. A word processing system frequently also includes a spelling checker, a grammar checker, and a thesaurus.

**word wrap (wrap around)**     The automatic division of a line into two or more lines because of space limitations. In a word processor, this division normally occurs only between words.

**WORM**     A write-once, read-many optical disk device.

**wrap around**     See word wrap.

**zone portion**     (1) On a punched card, the top three rows. (2) In the EBCDIC code, the four high-order bits in a byte.

# Index

# Study Guide

# 1 Introduction

## DISCUSSION QUESTIONS

Find, list, and describe five uses of computers on your campus.

1.

2.

3.

**4.**

**5.**

## MULTIPLE-CHOICE QUESTIONS

For each numbered item, fill in the letter of the matching definition.

_____  1.  Fear of computers is known as:
    a.  Acrophobia.          c.  Cyberphobia.
    b.  Kleptomania.       d.  Claustrophobia.

_____  2.  Which of these is not usually a part of a computer system?
    a.  Central processing unit.   d.  Terminal.
    b.  Software.          e.  All are parts of a computer
    c.  Printer.             system.

_____  3.  Which one of these individuals is not associated with the development of computers?
    a.  Charles Babbage.    d.  Howard Aikens.
    b.  Harold Wilson.      e.  John Atanasoff.
    c.  Herman Hollerith.

_____  4.  The first computers used:
    a.  Transistors.        d.  Integrated circuits.
    b.  Electromechanical devices. e.  Bionic memory elements.
    c.  Vacuum tubes.

_____  5.  The first commercial computer was the:
    a.  EDVAC.         d.  BISMAC.
    b.  ENIAC.         e.  UNIVAC.
    c.  ABC.

## TRUE/FALSE QUESTIONS

Answer the following questions with true (T) or false (F).

_____  1.  The first commercial computer was the UNIVAC I.

_____  2.  The first generation of computers used VLSI chips.

_____  3.  Time-sharing means that you can use the system only at specified times.

_____  4.  Herman Hollerith developed the early unit record systems.

_____  5.  ENIAC programs were hard-wired into the machine.

_____  6.  EDVAC programs were read in and then stored in the computer's memory.

_____  7.  ENIAC was programmed in FORTRAN.

_____  8.  Magnetic tapes and disks are used to store information.

_____  9.  Machine language is the most commonly used high-level language.

_____ 10.  The computer field has reached a plateau in development. Those choosing careers in it find it is now a static and unchanging profession.

## MATCHING QUESTIONS

For each numbered item, fill in the letter of the matching definition.

_____  1.  ABC.

_____  2.  Machine language.

_____  3.  UNIVAC I.

_____  4.  VLSI.

_____  5.  Tabulating Machine Company.

_____  6.  Printers, tape drives, VDTs.

_____  7.  Cyberphobia.

_____  8.  Time-sharing.

_____  9.  ENIAC.

_____ 10.  Artificial intelligence.

a.  Techniques in software that, among other things, allow computers to act in more human and responsible ways.

b.  Atanasoff-Berry contribution to computer development.

c.  First commercial computer.

d.  Programming directly in instructions that the machine uses.

e.  Fear of computers.

f.  First vacuum tube computer.

g.  Use of one computer by many users, where each uses a slice of time.

h.  Company that later became IBM.

i.  Very large scale integration.

j.  Peripheral devices.

## SHORT ANSWER QUESTIONS

1. A computer system consists of _____ and

   _____ .

2. A computer system takes _____ and manipulates it to

   produce _____ .

3. A set of unprocessed facts is known as _____ .

4. _____ developed a very early mechanical computer.

5. The punched card system was developed by _____ .

6. The predecessor to IBM was the _____ Company.

7. The Automatic Sequence Controlled Calculator was known as

   _____ .

8. Final credit was given for the invention of the computer to

   _____ .

9. The idea of a stored program computer is credited to

   _____ .

10. The acronym EDVAC stands for _____ .

## APPLICATION

Find someone who uses a microcomputer in a small business. Describe how this microcomputer has changed the way that they conduct their business. Are they pleased with the results? Why or why not?

# 6 Microcomputer Applications

## DISCUSSION QUESTIONS

1. What is meant by an applications package?

2. What common business applications could be solved by using a spreadsheet?

3. What kinds of problems might be better solved by using a database instead of a spreadsheet?

4.  What tasks that you perform might be made easier by the use of a spread-sheet?

5.  Why are graphics a useful adjunct to a spreadsheet system?

## MULTIPLE–CHOICE QUESTIONS

For each numbered item, fill in the letter of the matching definition.

_____  1.  Which of the following is not a basic application on a microcom-puter?
   a.  Word processing.          d.  Graphics.
   b.  Operating system de-      e.  Databases.
       velopment.
   c.  Electronic spread-
       sheets.

_____  2.  Which one of the following is not usually an allowed content of a cell in an electronic spreadsheet?
   a.  A label.                  c.  A graphic symbol.
   b.  A formula.                d.  Numerical data.

_____  3.  Which is a form of graph usually not available as part of a graphics support system?
   a.  Arithmetic probability    d.  Line graph.
       distribution.            e.  XY (scatter) graph.
   b.  Pie chart.
   c.  Bar chart.

_____ **4.** Which one of these terms does not apply to word processing?

    a.  Justification.               d.  Formulas.

    b.  Spelling checker.        e.  Scrolling.

    c.  Word wrap.

_____ **5.** Which of these does not appear to be a current trend in using microcomputers?

    a.  Productivity enhance-    d.  Use of CRTs.
        ment.                    e.  Telecommunications.

    b.  Office automation.

    c.  Portability and stand-
        ardization.

## TRUE/FALSE QUESTIONS

Answer the following questions with true (T) or false (F).

_____ **1.** The shift from single-purpose to integrated software is taking place rapidly.

_____ **2.** A current trend in microcomputers should be toward standardization.

_____ **3.** Word processing systems cannot handle mass mailings and form letters.

_____ **4.** A word processor does not allow you to rearrange material without retyping it.

_____ **5.** The margins cannot be adjusted easily with a word processor.

_____ **6.** Word processors often include a spelling checker.

_____ **7.** The use of titles on the axes of a graph clarifies the meaning of the graph.

_____ **8.** Word wrap in a word processor eliminates the needs to return the carriage at the end of each line.

_____ **9.** Spreadsheets are used to do what-if calculations.

_____ **10.** Spreadsheets do not allow for graphical output.

## MATCHING QUESTIONS

For each numbered item, fill in the letter of the matching definition.

_____ **1.** Lotus 1-2-3.           **a.** Allows text to move up and down
_____ **2.** Integrated package.          the CRT.
_____ **3.** Cell pointer.           **b.** A popular spreadsheet.
_____ **4.** Window.           **c.** Useful in the preparation of form letters.

_____ **5.** Formulas.

_____ **6.** XY (scatter) chart.

_____ **7.** Late 1800s.

_____ **8.** Word wrap.

_____ **9.** Scrolling.

_____ **10.** Word processors.

**d.** Moved from cell to cell in a spreadsheet.

**e.** Feature that allows us to be unconcerned about splitting words.

**f.** What is used to manipulate data on a spreadsheet.

**g.** A package that is a collection of programs.

**h.** When typewriters were first used in the business community.

**i.** A type of graph.

**j.** Used to view a small portion of the spreadsheet.

## SHORT ANSWER QUESTIONS

1. To aid in the visual presentation of material, we

   use _____ .

2. A major trend in microcomputers should be toward

   _____ and _____ .

3. Microcomputers are a significant tool in _____ .

4. Word processors allow you to both _____ and

   _____ text.

5. Word processors can be used to prepare form letters

   for _____ .

6. We move text up and down the CRT display by _____ .

7. When the words line up vertically at the left and right margins, this is

   known as _____ .

8. A cell in a spreadsheet holds _____ ,

   _____ , or _____ .

9. We move from cell to cell in a spreadsheet by moving

   the _____ .

10. We look at a small portion of the entire spreadsheet through

    a _____ .

## CASE STUDY

Amalgamated Products has a problem in developing the budgets for each department. At the end of each year, department managers look at their costs for
the last six months. Estimates are made for the expenditures for January through
June. The next budget year begins on the first of July. The budgets for each
department contain the usual items such as labor charges, overtime, supplies,
and the like. The budget presents total costs and projections for expenditures
broken down by month. These costs may not be equal each month due to
such things as scheduled maintenance, vacations during the summer, inventory,
or plant shutdowns.

After each department manager has developed his or her budget, the budgets
are submitted to the plant supervisor, who develops a consolidated budget
for the entire organization. The entire budget-building process takes about
four to six weeks, including about six days of each manager's time. If a change
is suggested by the plant supervisor, one or more departmental budgets must
then be completely recalculated. The manual process takes up too much time
with the recalculations and what if questions that are constantly introduced.
Based on your understanding of spreadsheets, respond to the following questions:

1. Show a diagram of possible row and column headings on a spreadsheet
   for the budget system of an individual department.

2. How might we generate a consolidated budget without recopying information
   from each of the departmental budgets?

3. Different departments have different line items in their budget. How does this affect the final decisions?

4. We want to show expenditures versus time for a management presentation. How do we handle this?

5. Each manager has his or her own microcomputer. What impact does this have on our problem?

# 12 Trends

## DISCUSSION QUESTIONS

1. Name and describe four business situations where decision support systems that do what-if analysis might be useful.

2. What do you think is the future for robots in industry? Do you believe that there will be sociological or economic problems with the increased use of robots? Why or why not?

3. Is there really such a thing as artificial intelligence? Can human behavior be completely simulated? Defend your position.

4. Isaac Asimov wrote an interesting science fiction book called *I, Robot* (Garden City, N.Y: Doubleday, 1950). If you are familiar with the book, do you feel that Asimov correctly presents the concepts of a robot? Are there any flaws in his presentation? What do you think of his "Laws of Robotics." If you are not familiar with this book, describe how robots are characterized in any other well-known piece of science fiction. Are they presented accurately?

## MULTIPLE–CHOICE QUESTIONS

For each numbered item, fill in the letter of the matching description.

_____  1.  The computer processing of picture images is called:
   a.  Graphics.
   b.  Fax.
   c.  Telecommunications.
   d.  DSS.
   e.  CAD/CAM.

_____  2.  Which is not associated with robotics?
   a.  Sensory ability.
   b.  Spreadsheets.
   c.  Sense of touch.
   d.  Limited vision.
   e.  Manual dexterity.

_____  3.  Which of the following tasks are not commonly done with robots?
   a.  Spot welding.
   b.  Spray painting.
   c.  Machine loading and unloading.
   d.  Walking the family dog.
   e.  Delivery of parts in a factory.

_____  4.  Which of the following is not associated with artificial intelligence?
   a.  Turing test.
   b.  Learning.
   c.  Third-generation computing.
   d.  Selecting a best choice of action.
   e.  ICOT.

_____  5.  Which of these is not associated with expert systems?
   a.  Rules.
   b.  Knowledge base.
   c.  Rules of thumb.
   d.  Experts.
   e.  Intuition.

## TRUE/FALSE QUESTIONS

Answer the following questions with a true (T) or false (F).

_____ 1. CAD refers to computer-aided design systems with special features for drafting.

_____ 2. Neural networks are modeled on how our brains work.

_____ 3. Object-oriented programming wraps the data with the JCL it needs.

_____ 4. Computer viruses may lie dormant for extended periods of time.

_____ 5. The use of reusable code is essential to automatic program generation.

_____ 6. Robots can have a limited sense of vision.

_____ 7. We can identify intelligence in machines with the Turing test.

_____ 8. Expert systems consist of a knowledge base derived from an expert or experts.

_____ 9. Voice recognition systems have a wide vocabulary.

_____ 10. Idioms present little problem for computers in comprehending natural languages.

## MATCHING QUESTIONS

For each numbered item, fill in the letter of the matching description.

_____ 1. Turing test.

_____ 2. ICOT.

_____ 3. ESP.

_____ 4. Expert systems.

_____ 5. Idioms.

_____ 6. Graphics.

_____ 7. CAM.

_____ 8. CADD.

_____ 9. Neural networks.

_____ 10. Reusable code.

a. Administrator of Japan's 10-year plan.

b. Modeled on how our brains work.

c. A programming language designed for use in AI applications.

d. Used in automatic program generators to create new programs.

e. The processing of picture images.

f. Expressions that generally cannot be understood from the meaning of the individual words.

g. Has special features for drafting.

h. Developed as a means of identifying intelligence in machines.

i. Includes automated process control and MRP.

j. Combine facts with the way those facts are used for decision making.

## SHORT ANSWER QUESTIONS

1.  The recognition of _____ in natural languages is a problem.

2.  When we combine facts with the way that experts use those facts for decision making, we are talking about _____ .

3.  The ICOT project in Japan will run for _____ years.

4.  A test to determine intelligence in machines was suggested by _____ .

5.  Modern robots have a sense of _____ , _____ , and _____ .

6.  Typical robot activities include _____ , _____ , _____ , and _____ .

7.  _____ can be linked together to create new programs.

8.  In 1985, a group of aerospace and electronic companies joined together to explore ways of _____ .

9.  CADD differs from CAD in that _____ .

10. In _____ , images are drawn mathematically or by using mice, light pens, or specialized tablets.

# CASE STUDY

Amalgamated Products, the company discussed in cases for Chapters 6, 7, 8, 10, and 11 is having a problem in their warehouse. They are constantly running over budget. Turnover is high among the employees; the most common two reasons given is the repetitiveness of the job and the need to transfer from the warehouse in order to become more promotable. Because many potential employees see little chance for advancement in the warehouse, they usually prefer to accept other position openings within the company. Unfortunately, warehouse positions do require the ability to perform repetitive tasks accurately, the ability to count and monitor the inventory, and the ability to swiftly and accurately deliver parts as they are needed throughout the entire plant. It takes time to become familiar with the plant layout, plant needs, and also the parts inventory itself. With the high turnover, employees usually bid out of warehouse positions by the time they become experienced.

The warehouse supervisor has suggested that costs would decrease and accuracy improve if the warehouse were automated so that stock were picked and delivered by robotic devices. Stock could be picked from the shelves by robotic arms and delivered by robotic carts.

Management has looked into the costs and has determined that it might be a feasible solution. Based on what you know about robots, answer the following questions.

1. If the warehouse were automated, how would it affect the number of people employed? Why?

2. What would be the effect, if any, on the job skills required to work in the warehouse?

3. What would be the reaction of other company employees to the change? Why? Would their opinions change over time? Why? Do you think it is an appropriate solution?

# Appendix A
# BASIC

## DISCUSSION QUESTIONS

1. What is the history and purpose of BASIC?

2. What are system commands? Name three that you can use on your system.

3. What is a string field?

4. What is the purpose of a branch?

5.   What is the REM statement? Why is it useful?

## MULTIPLE–CHOICE QUESTIONS

For each numbered item, fill in the letter of the matching description.

_____   1.   The BASIC statement that permits the programmer to read data stored externally is:
         a.   REM.                    c.   INPUT.
         b.   READ.                   d.   DATA.

_____   2.   The BASIC statement that permits the programmer to read data stored internally is:
         a.   READ.                   c.   INPUT.
         b.   REM.                    d.   DATA.

_____   3.   The statement that permits the programmer to change the value of a field is:
         a.   REM.                    c.   ALTER.
         b.   LET.                    d.   CHANGE.

_____   4.   The statement that permits the programmer to perform a subroutine once is:
         a.   PERFORM.                c.   GOTO.
         b.   GOSUB.                  d.   FOR/NEXT.

_____   5.   The statement that permits the programmer to perform a subroutine a given number of times is the:
         a.   PERFORM.                c.   GOTO.
         b.   GOSUB.                  d.   FOR/NEXT.

## TRUE/FALSE QUESTIONS

Answer the following questions with true (T) or false (F).

_____   1.   String fields contain only numbers.
_____   2.   If you are preparing to enter a new BASIC program, you will key in the word BEGIN.
_____   3.   To recall a program stored on disk or tape (copy it back into memory), you use the LOAD command.

4. In BASIC, the names of numeric fields must begin with a letter.
5. All versions of BASIC are the same.
6. In looping, one alters the normal flow of instructions and proceeds to a location in a program other than the next sequential instruction.
7. Branching is the repetitive execution of a series of instructions.
8. BASIC statements used to loop include GOTO, IF/THEN/ELSE, and GOSUB.
9. A subroutine is a complete routine performed within the program
10. Since REM statements are not compiled, it is a waste of time to use more of them than absolutely necessary.

## MATCHING QUESTIONS

For each numbered item, fill in the letter of the matching description.

_____ 1. LOAD.
_____ 2. LLIST.
_____ 3. RUN.
_____ 4. String variable name.
_____ 5. Numeric variable name.
_____ 6. REM.
_____ 7. IF/THEN/ELSE.
_____ 8. GOSUB.
_____ 9. AUTO.
_____ 10. PRINT.

a. Must begin with a letter and end with a $.

b. Used to output information to either the printer or CRT based on the device specified in the command.

c. Copies a program stored on disk or tape back into primary storage for execution.

d. Must begin with a letter and not end with a $.

e. Directs that a subroutine be performed.

f. Allows for branching based on the value of some field.

g. On many systems, causes the program to be listed on the printer without specifying any device.

h. Causes the program currently stored in primary storage to be executed.

i. Causes automatic line numbering.

j. Used to insert comments.

## SHORT ANSWER QUESTIONS

1. _____ are fields whose values change during the execution of the program.

2. _____ are fields whose values do not change during the execution of the program.

3. _____ are alphanumeric: they can contain numbers, letters, and special symbols.

4. _____ are used to communicate with the system; they are system dependent.

5. Once a statement has been entered into your program, it can be changed by _____ .

6. LIST 100–600 will _____ .

7. 100 INPUT C$;S will cause the program

   to _____  _____ .

8. Messages to the operator that provide information about the anticipated response are called _____ .

9. The format of a basic statement consists of _____ ,

   followed by the _____ , followed by

   the _____ .

10. A complete routine performed within the program is called

    a _____ .

## APPLICATION

1.  Write a simple program to ask for the values of three numbers. The first number represents the principal, the second, a rate of interest, and the third, a period of time. Have the program calculate interest based on the three values. If interest = rate × time, then display the interest, principal, rate, and time on the screen.

2.  Modify the program to send output to the printer.

3.  Modify the program to use READ and DATA statements so that the input information is part of the program.

# Appendix B
# Data Representation

## DISCUSSION QUESTIONS

1. How is the octal equivalent of a decimal number found?

2. How do you convert from binary to hexadecimal?

3. How do you find the decimal equivalent of any hex number?

**4.** Convert D7A to binary.

**5.** Convert 1090 in decimal to its hex equivalent.

## MULTIPLE–CHOICE QUESTIONS

For each numbered item, fill in the letter of the matching description.

_____    **1.** Base 2 is referred to as:
    a.  Binary.          c.  Octal.
    b.  Hexadecimal.     d.  Decimal.

_____    **2.** Base 8 is referred to as:
    a.  Binary.          c.  Octal.
    b.  Hexadecimal.     d.  Decimal.

_____    **3.** Base 10 is referred to as:
    a.  Binary.          c.  Octal.
    b.  Hexadecimal.     d.  Decimal.

_____    **4.** Base 16 is referred to as:
    a.  Binary.          c.  Octal.
    b.  Hexadecimal.     d.  Decimal.

_____    **5.** EBCDIC characters consists of:
    a.  A zone and a digit por-    c.  A sign and a digit portion.
        tion.             d.  Two digit portions.
    b.  A zone and a sign por-
        tion.

_____ **6.** Packing enables how many characters to be stored in all but the last byte?

    a.  1.                             c.  2.

    b.  3.                             d.  4.

_____ **7.** 968 in decimal is the equivalent of what number in binary?

    a.  1111010000.           c.  1110111011.

    b.  1111001000.           d.  1101010001.

_____ **8.** 10110111 in binary is the equivalent of what number in decimal?

    a.  187.                         c.  257.

    b.  157.                         d.  183.

_____ **9.** 734 in octal is the same as what number in decimal?

    a.  1,336.                c.  537.

    b.  1,335.                d.  672.

_____ **10.** FA1C in hexadecimal is the same as what number in binary?

    a.  1111101000011100.    c.  111110110100101.

    b.  1111010111010011.    d.  111010000010111.

## TRUE/FALSE QUESTIONS

Answer the following questions with true (T) or false (F).

_____ **1.** In binary, the numeric characters are 0, 1, and 2.

_____ **2.** In all numbering systems, the positional value of a digit is a progressive power of the base.

_____ **3.** Any four binary digits can be represented by one octal digit.

_____ **4.** Each hexadecimal character represents four binary digits.

_____ **5.** To convert a hexadecimal number to a decimal one, you may multiply each digit by its positional value and sum the results.

_____ **6.** The positional values of the first three hex positions are 0, 16, 256, from right to left.

_____ **7.** The positional values of the first three octal characters are 1, 8, 64, from right to left.

_____ **8.** EBCDIC is a 7-bit code.

_____ **9.** A byte is made up of eight bits.

_____ **10.** The two most popular coding schemes are EBCDIC and ASCII.

## MATCHING QUESTIONS

For each numbered item, fill in the letter of the matching description.

_____ **1.** 4043.

_____ **2.** 3D.

_____ **3.** 111001011.

_____ **4.** 101010100.

_____ **5.** 111110000.

_____ **6.** 12.

_____ **7.** 1100001111.

_____ **8.** 45.

_____ **9.** B7.

_____ **10.** 110101111.

**a.** 10 in decimal is what number in octal?

**b.** 713 in octal is what number in binary?

**c.** 1AF in hex is what number in binary?

**d.** FCB in hex is what number in decimal?

**e.** 101101 in binary is what number in decimal?

**f.** 111101 in binary is what number in hex?

**g.** 783 in decimal is what number in binary?

**h.** 524 in octal is what number in binary?

**i.** 10110111 in binary is what number in hex?

**j.** 760 in octal is what number in binary?

## SHORT ANSWER QUESTIONS

1. Each octal number represents _____ binary digits.

2. Each hexadecimal number represents _____ binary digits.

3. EBCDIC stands for _____ .

4. ASCII stands for _____ .

5. The number −176 would be stored as _____ _____ in packed EBCDIC.

6. The number +176 would be stored as _____ _____ in unpacked EBCDIC.

7. The configuration of binary digits that represents a character is determined by _____ .

8. One reason that octal or hex is used to represent binary numbers is that

    _____ .

9. To convert octal to decimal you must

    _____    _____ .

10. To convert decimal to hex, you must

    _____    _____ .

# APPLICATIONS

1. Convert the following binary numbers to decimal.
   a. 10110.
   b. 1000001.
2. Convert the following octal numbers to decimal.
   a. 713.
   a. 6571.
3. Convert the following hexadecimal numbers to decimal.
   a. ACOD.
   b. 1C7B.
4. Convert the following decimal numbers to binary, octal, and then hexadecimal.
   a. 12,345.
   b. 1,007.
5. Convert the following octal numbers to binary. Check by converting both the original octal number and the converted binary number to decimal.
   a. 643.
   b. 71.
6. Convert the following hexadecimal numbers to binary.
   a. 2CF.
   b. B1C.
7. Convert the following binary numbers to hexadecimal.
   a. 10111.
   b. 111011.
8. Translate into English the following quotation displayed in the EBCDIC code:
   C8 C5 D3 D7
9. Translate into English the following quotation displayed in ASCII code:
   100 1101 100 0101 101 0100 100 1111 100 1111